T0269947

BAND
PEOPLE

BAND PEOPLE

Life and Work in Popular Music

Franz Nicolay

University of Texas Press

Austin

The lyrics to "I Want to Be a Sideman" by Dave Frishberg are reprinted by kind permission of Swiftwater Music. Portions of the chapter "The Family Business" appeared under the title "The 21st-Century Family Band" in Slate, February 1, 2018, https://slate.com/culture/2018/02/the-21st-century-family-bands-touring -with-their-kids.html.

Requests for permission to reproduce material from this work should be sent to permissions@utpress.utexas.edu.

♾ The paper used in this book meets the minimum requirements of ANSI/NISO Z39.48-1992 (R1997) (Permanence of Paper).

Library of Congress Cataloging-in-Publication Data

Names: Nicolay, Franz, author.
Title: Band people : life and work in popular music / Franz Nicolay.
Other titles: American music series (Austin, Tex.)
Description: First edition. | Austin : University of Texas Press, 2024. | Series: American music series | Includes bibliographical references and index.
Identifiers: LCCN 2023057879
    ISBN 978-1-4773-2353-3 (hardcover)
    ISBN 978-1-4773-3022-7 (pdf)
    ISBN 978-1-4773-3023-4 (epub)
Subjects: LCSH: Musicians—Employment. | Bands (Music)—Vocational guidance. | Popular music—Vocational guidance. | Bands (Music)—Social aspects. | Popular music—Social aspects. | Musicians—Interviews. | Musicians—Social conditions. | Musicians—Economic conditions. | Composition (Music)— Collaboration. | Popular music—Production and direction.
Classification: LCC ML3795 .N534 2024 | DDC 780.23—dc23/eng/20240322
LC record available at https://lccn.loc.gov/2023057879

doi:10.7560/323533

The publication of this book was supported by the Lowell H. Lebermann Jr. Endowment for UT Press.

CONTENTS

You start off in a band with your friends. You hang out with your friends, and you start goofing around and you play music; then you play a show at the youth center, then you play at the local bar. And you learn how to get along with people—because first of all, they're your friends, so it's fun to hang out with them; but once you start getting in a band and touring together and doing all that stuff, a lot of that goes out the window because it becomes a lot more intense. Because you're living together and it's like you're married. Then you start putting out records and it becomes a livelihood—if you're lucky—and then it puts all this other pressure on you.

SCOTT McCAUGHEY

BAND
PEOPLE

INTRODUCTION

Shahzad Ismaily has a treble voice that cracks slightly in its high register. He speaks in complete and gently enunciated sentences, with neither arrogance nor unwarranted humility. He is tall and hairless; gawky in a way which suggests a large insect—a praying mantis, perhaps—assembled from parts. He is likely to play under bright stage lights in a parka and fur hat, or in an air-conditioned studio in only shorts and bare feet. A deep dent cuts a trench across the dome of his skull from ear to ear.

His eccentricities make him memorable, but his musicality makes him meaningful. Shahzad—he is widely called by his first name—is the epitome of a "musician's musician": a multi-instrumentalist with a beatific enthusiasm for the art, who is apparently incapable of cliché and can whisper the magic into a recalcitrant recording session. Musicians like Shahzad Ismaily elide the boundaries between art and craft—a binary which some embrace and others reject. They are the musical middle class, laborers in the culture industry. They straddle the fuzzy boundary between collaborator and employee, family and co-worker, small business partner and idealistic volunteer. They are, to borrow musician Jason Narducy's term, band people.

Ismaily works at the convergence of jazz, indie rock, and the art world: playing or recording with Bob Dylan, Tom Waits, Lou Reed, and Laurie Anderson; with Bonnie "Prince" Billy and Sam Amidon; with John Zorn and Marc Ribot. His collaborators, unprompted, rave about his qualities as a musician and as a person. "It's all worth it to know people like him," says violinist Meredith Yayanos, "to be able to be on the same planet at the same time with Shahzad and make music with him . . . just thinking about him makes me remember, 'Okay, this is why I do this.' Because seriously, words fail. And where they fail is where the angels hang out, and that is music, and Shahzad is an angel to me. . . . He is absolutely one of the most luminous, wonderful, creative, joy-inducing collaborators I've ever had." Violinist Carla Kihlstedt echoes Yayanos: "He's one of the most beautiful humans and collaborators ever." She elaborates:

> My band 2 Foot Yard was a trio with him, so he spent many, many years on the road in the context of that trio, and he would never come out with his own music. We had to trick him into writing for the band. He would pick up his guitar during sound check and automatically, without even thinking about it, just play the most gorgeous music you'd ever heard. And you'd say, "What's that?" He's like, "I don't know, I'm making it up." So I started just recording sound checks. And as a collaborator, he has the ability to bring the most vulnerably beautiful things out of the people he plays with. I'm a different musician because of playing with him.
>
> He is a master at dragging it out of everyone else. Early on, when I first met him, he would always be pushing me to play instruments I'd never played before, or go walk in the woods and record myself playing accordion, and sneak into the Redwoods while no one was looking and stay there after hours. And he's always like, "How can we get the most vulnerable and powerful version of you?" And that's his mastery as a collaborator. For a while I was in an improvised band with him called Causing A Tiger, where for one record he just said, "Okay, you're not playing violin on this. You're too comfortable playing violin. You're just going to sing." At that point I hardly considered myself—I sang a lot, but I was uncomfortable with that moniker. I feel like if he could turn 5 percent of that skill on himself, the world would just ache to hear it.

He has played on almost five hundred records, but never released music under his own name. "Unfortunately," Ismaily says, what he has brought from his experience is "very high standards for myself of what is great music, or what is music that is really moving and compelling." He continues:

> The reason I say "unfortunately" is that that is prohibitive as well. In my case, because I've worked with so many outstanding people, I feel like if I was going to write my own music, it can't just be some sort of twelve-tone fusion-jazz bass player side project record. I would rather, if I was able to, that it be as compelling as a Patti Smith recording or a Laurie Anderson recording or some of the people that I have experienced directly. . . . I have an awareness of expectations at that level, [of] what the art should be or the music should be if I was to do it. . . . But a lot of the time [that awareness] tends to be a little inhibitive of me making my own work.[1]

The frustrated support musician is a pop music cliché—as is the overcompensating suggestion by their advocates that they are "the real stars." (The popularity of the trope in fiction and films, where the character of an ambitious sideman or backstabbing backup singer can serve a blunt dramatic purpose as antagonist, probably encourages overestimation of its real-life prevalence.) The difference is psychological as much as musical, suggests Bruce Springsteen in the Oscar-winning documentary *20 Feet from Stardom*: "It's a bit of a walk, from back by the drummer, or over here—that walk to the front is complicated. . . . I know tremendous backup singers who just aren't comfortable in that position. You gotta have that narcissism, you gotta have that ego."[2] And not everyone shares this ruthless sense of their career trajectory: "Twenty feet from my asshole! I'm a band person. A *band person!*" retorts singer Kelly Hogan. "There's no *All About Eve* bullshit in what I do. When I'm singing harmony, I'm not holding a dagger behind my back, waiting for my 'big break.' Hell no. I'm in the band, man. And that gives me great joy." Her frustration is that backup singers aren't always considered *band members* in the same way that other musicians are. "We are the noble sidemen," she says.

There is an honor to being in the band. But nobody looks at the guitar player or the drummer and imagines that, while they're playing their hearts out and kicking ass, they're really wishing they were center stage at the mic—with all the pressures, scrutiny and uncomfortable undergarments that go along with that job. . . . I wasn't a big fan of *The Commitments* movie [either], because at the end when they were onstage and the lead singer introduced the band, everyone was introduced with their full name, first and last—except the backup singers. They were just introduced with their first names. And maybe it seems crazy to you, but that bugged me then and still bugs me now. Those singers were in the band. Just like the guitar player. Just like the drummer.

For Ismaily, though, the thought of releasing music under his own name triggers a complicated mixture of perfectionist idealism, a very human desire for the influence that comes with being known, and a deep-rooted need to justify his life choices. His parents, immigrants from Pakistan, were skeptical of his musical ambitions, expecting him to become a doctor, and he dutifully earned a pre-med degree in biochemistry. He convinced them to reluctantly acquiesce to a time-limited attempt—"a few years"—to pursue music. He moved to New York at twenty-eight and supported himself teaching test prep for Kaplan, while assertively chasing creative opportunities.

I would go to lots of concerts in New York, and I would . . . walk right up to people after a show and ask if I could play with them, or if they needed a sub for anything, or if we could just get together to improvise. I was fairly forward, I'm afraid. Or at least, really enthusiastic. I was looking to play any gig, and I'm still that way. I feel for me that any gig that I play, I end up learning something about playing music, and getting better at it; and surprisingly the most weird, strange, maybe ineffective or badly set up gigs sometimes snowball into some other opportunity or experience that's really compelling. If I hang out with a young person and they ask advice about becoming a musician or working as a musician, my point of view is to say yes to everything and do as much as possible. There are other friends that are contemporaries, or older than I am . . . that have felt very radically opposed to that idea. They have said it is very important to curate your life, curate your career, be extremely mindful and careful of where your musical energy, your musical talent, your musical voice gets placed in the world. I don't happen to agree with that or feel that way.

For example, I played with this songwriter Anna Christie. I met her out in Joshua Tree, and played a little bit of music with her, and I liked her a lot as a person. She is completely unknown. And she said, "I'm playing in New York City. Would you be able to play with me?" I said, "Yeah, definitely, sounds great."

There are a lot of musicians my age, or who have done some of the things I have done, who would have immediately said, "Well, where is it, and is there a fee? What's the circumstances?" And they might have turned it down, because it ended up being for free and in this fairly crappy dive bar in South Park Slope called Freddy's. When I got there, there was just a super crappy-sounding drum set, and maybe three people, and it was a very depressing scene. I just walked in, and I was smiling and I was happy to see her, and we sat down and we played and we had a really great time, even though there was no good PA, no sound, just a completely ridiculous situation.

Then about nine months later, the guitar player that played that gig with her, who I didn't know before that night and hadn't seen since, sent me an email out of the blue and said, "I'm doing this recording with Steve Shelley, the drummer from Sonic Youth; and there's this very special songwriter, originally from Lebanon, now living in Paris, named Yasmine Hamdan; and I was wondering if I could request you to be on the recording session." I said, "Yeah, that sounds great." That came from that evening. So I still strongly feel like doing things that way is really important.

Ismaily's ambivalent sense of his value and how to quantify it, his pride as an artist and his sublimated ego, remain tied in complicated ways to his father's disapproval. "My father was not interested in me becoming a musician," he says, "and it was clear that one of the ways he valued work was getting paid for it. So I made a pretty uncomfortable hard equation, a permanent equation, between getting paid and being valued." At the same time, "you want to feel like you play music for the love of it, so if you get paid for it, it's psychologically tricky. . . . Are you there because it's a job and you are not that into it? Are you there because you enjoy it, and if you are there just because you enjoy it, should you do it for no money?" Meanwhile, of course, one needs money to live, and for a sense of personal dignity.

> I have started to say to people, when they ask me what would I like to get paid, I say, "Listen, I don't know your budget. You know your budget much better than I do. Here's what I would like from you: I would like for you to look at your budget quietly on your own and say, based on this budget, what is the best pay I could offer to give Shahzad for this recording. Then I want you to return to me and give me that number." Then I just want to say yes to that number, and [for] that be the end of the conversation.
>
> What I would like to do is have Damien Rice, whom I work with quite often, turn to me and say, "Hey man, I can pay you fifteen hundred bucks to be in the studio tomorrow." And I would like to have my friend Garrett—who is constantly struggling, mostly working as a janitor or tons of odd jobs—I'd like to have him turn to me and say, "I've thought about it a lot. I can pay you sixty-five dollars to work with me for ten hours tomorrow." And I'd like to say yes to both of those people.

Musicians who are trained through the professionalized programs in jazz and classical academia tend to be secure with their status as, well, trained professionals, and comfortable talking explicitly about the money they expect for those services.[3] Conversely, multi–winds player Stuart Bogie says musicians in the so-called indie rock sphere can be obtuse on financial matters for reasons of class background: "Their parents are likely professionals, they are not necessarily trained musicians themselves, but they are very gifted and they have great ideas and they are having a successful performing career—it's very difficult to talk money with these kinds of folks. The reason being is they never approach the music as a trade. They probably never sang a wedding." Guitarist Doug Gillard concurs: "It is the curse of this façade of indie rock—I do find that a lot of musicians are from backgrounds where their folks had some money, and they don't think in terms of music as a way to make a living. If you do that in a band situation, or in this so-called indie rock world or whatever this is, it's really not cool: 'Oh man, you had better look for someone else.'"[4]

Musicians who rise through the nominally amateur punk world, meanwhile, rarely have a plan for or expectation of a long-term career ("Artists usually define themselves in relation to art, its currents and schools, but rarely in relation to the very conditions under which art is produced," wrote the cultural theorist Bernard Miège).[5] "It's like well, yeah, there's no way I will still be doing this when I'm twenty," says drummer Bill Stevenson. "So when you turn twenty, 'Oh yeah, there's no way I'm still going to be doing this when I'm thirty.' Then you turn thirty. 'Ah, there's no way I'm going to be some forty-year-old playing punk rock,' and you turn forty. So I just keep pushing that date back." As a result, many never become comfortable talking explicitly about money—whether pay, royalties, or songwriting credits—and find themselves taken advantage of, or forced to have those conversations when real money is at stake instead of in advance. Complicity in one's own exploitation is one result of propaganda that appeals to core ideals.

Many musicians are, at heart, idealists: at a young age, they chose a difficult lifestyle out of a love of the art and craft. Their performative cynicism, while often well-earned, is that of the disappointed romantic rather than the born misanthrope. Many prefer to suppress and divert their resentments behind music-positive rhetoric. Ismaily prefers, for example, not to dispute songwriting credits. People who hoard them, he says, "maybe are doing that because they feel protective of their ideas. And maybe they feel protective of their ideas because they have just a limited set of ideas they can offer to people. So understandably, it's a limited resource; they're protective of it. They are protective of who they collaborate with, when they collaborate, whether they write with them—and if they do, they want writing credit.

> I feel like I want to just give. And, by giving intensely, that does two things: one, it feels like metaphysically it causes a good flow of ideas [in] the world. . . . The second thing is, I feel that way because I feel like every moment I pick up an instrument I have something new to say immediately; that's just a part of who I am, so I don't feel limited at all. I feel like if I play that guitar part and it's on your record, great. I could write even a better guitar part—not a better one, but I [could] write another guitar part five seconds later. To me, that little guitar thing, there are thousands of them right behind that one.

Still, Ismaily has had the painful experience of making significant contributions—collaborative improvisations, for example—which form the backbone of an acclaimed recording project, without sharing in the acclaim. He understands, of course: the artist of record "works on [their] record two years, obsessively, which I don't. I'm just there for four days. Then [they do] a beautiful job arranging, using all these ideas and making a compelling record. Then the record is written about in all these magazines; it's heralded as the most innovative new work that happened that year." But he can't help feeling some pique—not about the accolades themselves, but at the thought of the intangible symbolic currency that comes with them, and how he might use it:

> When the world respects you deeply or writes about you, it gives you more agency to do more things in the world. So if I was an extremely respected artist, I could—tomorrow—start to put together a charity concert for something I cared about and the press would write about it; people would come; I could call most bands I wanted to and they would say yes, and I do desire that agency. I desire the agency to be able to pick up the phone

and do things that come to my mind. And I do recognize that that agency is available to you when you are more respected and more known in the world. And that's the moment where I sometimes get bummed out about credit and writing.

Still, he hasn't made that record under his own name; has continued to play and produce and collaborate, to fill up his time as if subconsciously pre-empting the relaxed, unstructured time he says he needs to create. And perhaps those expectations are themselves unrealistic, self-erected barriers: to be "looking for the environment that gives [him] the room for total vulnerability and total presence" is a prerequisite for which it is hard to book studio time. Instead, Ismaily launched a label called 88 Records, dedicated to first solo records from "musicians who are heavily collaborative, heavily obfuscated, very talented hidden shadow-like people, who add a great deal of value and energy and beauty to the projects that they are involved with, but people don't really know their voice"—a description which sounds very much like a self-portrait. The productions are simple and unpressured, and Ismaily is proud of them. "I'm excited to be the person who lovingly pushes [their] friend off the . . . rocky ledge, to jump down into the beautiful clear lake below, [when] they are a little bit hesitant or scared to. Then once they do, it's like, this is so beautiful, [I'm] so glad you did that."

It's as if he is looking for a version of himself, to provide for himself what he offers others as a musician and producer—but to whisk away the pressure each passing year adds to his own expectations for himself. He admits as much: "Probably, in a roundabout way, I'm working out my own psychology. Because [a solo record is] something I want to do very much, but am terrified of, and maybe by helping other people do it over and over again, I might work my way around to doing it myself."

When he is despondent, he says, he critiques himself as "ultimately just a craftsman—and I'd like to be an artist. And when I bring up that duality, it's usually because I'm trying to critique myself quite harshly." But it is his unusual empathy and selflessness, his willingness to put his considerable gifts at the service of other artists' visions, which is perhaps the measure of his artistry. One often finds among musicians a humility striking in a trade which matches the practical skill of a craftsman with the ethereal ambition of the artist—perhaps the analogy is to the carpenter or the potter, who make art for use. And the distinction between art and craft is likely a false one: a carpenter has tools and wood and makes table after table. They may take as their goal featureless exactitude—each table the same as the last—or make many tables, each with an inherent, individual beauty and proportion. Ismaily suggests that the true antithesis to the artist is the simple technician. He brings up an interview in which Marlon Brando suggested that "he was no different than a plumber or a carpenter. He just had a craft and he did it, and he did it well, and he brought . . . his full self to bear on the experience, and did it to the highest level he could."

Exploring the nature of that craft in the service of art, and the ways craft and art inseparably overlap in collective creative work, is a core interest of this book. Ismaily is one representative musician whose career introduces themes taken up by a multiplicity of voices over the following pages: the contrast between the gushing appreciation of his peers and his low public profile; the challenge of assigning a monetary value to his creativity; his ambivalence about his work, and the tension between his professional pride and his acknowledgment of the social and cultural capital that would come with fame.

Band people are workplace colleagues in a musical labor market. Not all colleagues, though, are perceived as equal. Bassist Mike Watt refers to his "side mouse" work, which carries with it some of the implications of passivity, shrinking timidity, and simple diminishment. In his memoir *This Wheel's on Fire*, The Band's Levon Helm wrote that the group told their agent "when it came time to draw up the contracts we never wanted to see the word 'sideman' again. . . . We've had [to] tear up a whole lot of paperwork because it had that word in it."[6]

"I have never been called a sideman in my life," says Bill Stevenson. (The common term "sideman" also obviously includes an unproductive gendering.) As sociologist Howard Becker (whose *Art Worlds* is a crucial reference for this book) wrote, "These [occupational titles] carry a great deal of symbolic meaning."[7]

Rock-adjacent music, as a commercial product, is inextricable from its marketing, and marketing requires a limited number of faces to sell as "authors" of the product. According to Becker, he uses the term "'art world'. . . to denote the network of people whose cooperative activity, organized via their joint knowledge of conventional means of doing things, produces the kind of art works that [the] art world is noted for. . . . It seems obvious to say that if everyone whose work contributes to the finished art work does not do his part, the work will come out differently. But it is not obvious to pursue the implication that it then becomes a problem to decide which of all these people is *the* artist, while the others are only support personnel."[8] It was obvious to him (he credits his years playing jazz piano) that the star system of the art marketplace obscured the necessity of the "support personnel": the craftspeople without whom the work could not be executed. Persistent narratives of this music which reproduce tropes of lone, Byronic genius miss that it is, in fact, largely a product of careful craft practiced by groups of collaborators.

This book is not, however, the facile gripe session towards which "sideman" narratives are often nudged. Instead, it is a collective portrait of the kind of professional artists who have often thought deeply about their roles but are rarely asked to explicate them: "I'm not really good at the interview thing," says guitarist and keyboardist Jay Gonzalez. "I've only done a few." "This may be germane to the whole topic in general," says multi-winds player Peter Hess: "I don't think I've ever been interviewed before." "This is funny," says drummer Mike Sneeringer. "As someone who never gets interviewed, now I have a million things to say."

The Beatles documentary *Get Back* did me a tremendous favor in the process of writing this introduction, as it gave everyone who watched it—which, in my world, was almost everyone I knew—a template for theorizing the band relationship, an everyband Rorschach onto which they could project their theories of hierarchy and collaboration. Were you a diligent striver, the group-project overachiever who always showed up on time, nudging and cajoling your colleagues, desperately but futilely trying to avoid the resentful tag "control freak"? Paul was your guy. Did you believe in the ironic chaos-energy artist? John, of course. More fruitfully for my project, which of the two models for other-guy-in-the-band did you approve: the resentful, sarcastic third-wheel George, with his nose pressed against the window separating him from the creative core; or sweet, supportive Ringo, sometimes sleepy but always there to help and admire?[9]

I got stuck on this project, I think, as a way of making sense of my own career—my barely-bounded ambition to be a full band member *and* pro sideman *and* a legitimized composer/arranger *and* a cult figure *and* some kind of star and writer—and as way to acknowledge the demands of my ego while still identifying with the craftsmanlike self-respect of being a reliable, prideful, dignified session player— even, occasionally, a secret weapon. A circle probably impossible to square, but a significant part of maturing is (if one is lucky enough to have the opportunities) running up against the limits of one's abilities. I have been lucky enough, at least, to test those limits, and to confront, if not fully accept, that my strength may be supporting other artists, and elevating their visions.

In addition to personal interviews, I draw on academic studies of group dynamics and cohesiveness, hierarchies in "status communities," ethnographies of jazz and orchestral musicians, "sideman memoirs," theorizing of cultural work and collective creativity, and so on—as a way of contextualizing the band experience in a larger context of thought about (for lack of a more sophisticated framing) *how people deal with each other.*

Bands, for the purposes of this project, are considered primarily groups in the world of rock. To a large extent this is because I'm specifically interested in *the artistic and interpersonal dynamics of ensembles which mix long-term artistic collaboration, friendship, business, and the mentality that falls somewhere between family—siblings, cousins— and a gang: a self-organizing unit, reinvented from scratch (though often following certain commonly understood scripts) virtually each time.* This sidelines, then, certain other kinds of musical groups: jazz bands, which were the subject of several mid-century studies, tend (with some notable exceptions) to be modular and leader-focused, and hire sidemen whose employee relationship is explicit and under-stood, and who are (to a point) replaceable and interchangeable.[10] Hip-hop groups (again, with notable exceptions like the Roots) are archetypally a collective of multiple front people with shifting hierar-chies, and thus subject to a different dynamic—besides being frankly a world outside my expertise. The category of the non-touring profes-sional "session musician," who survives on a daily circuit of record-ing sessions, has—outside of pockets of film and TV professionals in Los Angeles, the jingle business in New York, and Nashville—largely withered, so to the extent I talk to "hired guns," they are a coterie of much less formalized (and unionized) touring professionals.[11]

These band people—in deference to the various ways in which my subjects identify in terms of gender and ethnicity, and acknowl-edging that no small number of musicians are driven out of the business by bigotry and harassment before they have the chance to become veterans—are overwhelmingly male and white. Studies by USC's Annenberg Inclusion Initiative indicate that the percentage of working musicians who identify as female hovers around the 20 to 25 percent mark (and supports the idea that this divide grows starker if one focuses, as this book does, on performers who are not primarily front people).[12] This is reflected in the interviewees for this book, of whom about one in five are women. That said, many of the musicians I interviewed preferred to focus on their identity as musicians (unless they felt that identity had been minimized respective to other catego-ries); and in deference to their privacy and to foreground that identity as *musicians*, I refrained from asking specific demographic questions. With that in mind, then, it is with some relief and hopefully not too much defensiveness that I leave further exploration of marginalized identities among band people to writers better equipped to speak on it.

The band people in this book are mostly over thirty. This may seem counterintuitive, given the historical focus on youth in rock. But the taboo around aging rockers has long since been overwhelmed by the sheer number of rock professionals enjoying multi-decade careers, and the nature of this project requires musicians with the perspective and ability to consider and speak about the arc of their careers—it requires a separation of lifers from short-termers, self-conscious professionals from semi-amateurs. "You get to a point," says key-boardist Paul Wallfisch, at which "most people quit or die. A few people figure it out really, really early, and have that total rock star thing whether they play for ten people or a thousand—and then there are the people who are in the middle: they haven't quit but they haven't died; they are not quite rock stars, maybe they do their own thing, but they are the band people."

This will never be a complete portrait. A snapshot is, by its nature, an artificially frozen image of a moving target: band people drop out of the life, and new ones—whose staying power is hard to assess—are minted every year. (I write in the ethnographic present, although individual or group circumstances may have changed since the time of the interviews.) The reader is immediately forgiven for asking whether I'm just writing about myself and people like me: to a certain extent, yes. Obviously, to those who know my CV, I have a personal interest in these questions. This is a snapshot taken in the mid-2010s by someone whose career flourished in the decade and a half prior to that, so my initial list included older musicians I knew by reputation and those I knew or admired as contemporaries. Still, as best I can, and given the practical demographics of the rock world, I've tried to speak to musicians across the spectrum of genre, training, and role (founding band members, session players, hired guns, and so on).

This brackets generations that came of age between mostly between the late 1980s and the 2010s: arguably, the prime period for small touring bands building organically, from the first wave of American DIY pioneers through the rise of independent internet promotion and distribution—from *Book Your Own Fucking Life* to Bandcamp. I conceived of this book as a collective portrait on the model of books like Studs Terkel's *Working* and Paul Berliner's *Thinking in Jazz*, mixing analysis, narration, oral history, and quotations from literature (academic and otherwise)—for long passages, an imaginary conversation between peers on common topics of interest, of the sort that too rarely happens in real life. I fear that it might, and hope that it doesn't, become a memorial to the evolution of an ideology shared by a certain kind of musician: from the conviction that one *shouldn't* make a living from music, through a brief period when one *could*, to the slow realization that no one *would*. A DIY ethos premised on the idea of independent control (whether individual or collective), of if not *seizing*, then *duplicating* the means of production and distribution, simultaneously reached an apotheosis with Internet-age distribution and connectivity, while being overwhelmed by corporate power and global emergency. The next generation of band people will be different: more representative of the larger society; forced into or open to monetizing everything but their artwork; perhaps once again abandoning the expectation of a self-supporting artistic life—regardless, the band people born near or in the new century are beyond the scope of this book.

These, then, are the *band people*: secret (and no-so-secret) weapons, side-of-the-stagers, hired guns, prolific joiners and members of bands, rhythm and horn sections, backup singers, consiglieres, accompanists, and composers—musicians not primarily known as front people or popularly understood as the authors of the works in which they participate, but without whom those works would not exist. What sociologist Jason Toynbee calls "social authorship," the "cumulative effect of small creative acts occurring across a social network of production,"[13] reveals itself both in musical effects like "swing" that require subtle, even unconscious, input from every band member, but also in the essential identifying traits of individual musicians—their *idiolect*, in the parlance of academic popular music studies—which combine to create distinctive, often irreducible, groups. Anecdotally, or in the conventional wisdom banks of music fandom, we can easily call up examples of bands whose *special something* disintegrated with the loss of one or more seemingly secondary members.[14]

What distinguishes band people from any other worker negotiating the contradictions, frustrations, and satisfactions of their job? In some ways, nothing. But there remains a fascination with the idea of a person who devotes their life to an ideal they adopted as a teenager, and have to adapt that vision to the mutating challenges of adulthood: what percentages of people playing music at sixteen or eighteen are still playing at twenty-six, or thirty-eight, or sixty-five? How do the skills of the music world translate on the street, if at all? We are comfortable with the mythos of creativity unbound, but what does creativity *bound* look like—creativity within parameters, and restraints (if one chooses to be creative within those bounds at all)? The narratives of band people are the statements of their worth, and their understanding of their labor.

You're interested in "all the fraught places," said violinist Jean Cook when I explained the kind of book I wanted to write. To talk about the role of a "band person" is to talk about art and craft. It is to talk about the value of fame, about a celebrity culture that requires the singling out of individuals from a collaborative enterprise, that privileges beauty or proximity or narrative. It is to talk about the politics of cultural labor, and the precarity that the working lives of musicians share with a growing segment of the larger economy. It is to talk about the myth of the genius working in isolation, and to uncover the wide pyramid of talent that supports that work—what Becker calls the "support personnel" of the culture industry. It is to once again challenge the myth of meritocracy: is it better to be the best player, or the best hang? It is to talk about political dynamics, and the ways in which social groups organize themselves: autocracy, aristocracy, democracy. It is to talk about individual psychology: everyone is the star of their own life, if not actually the star of their circumstances. It is to talk about freedom: the promiscuous freedom of relative anonymity versus the agency offered by fame. It is to taxonomize: specialists and stylists, generalists and chameleons, hired guns and band members, road dogs and punch-clock session players, the fan favorite and the quietly irreplaceable. Who are these band people—the character actors of popular music?

1

TRAINING AND EARLY GOALS

In the pre-rock decades of recorded popular music in America, the pre-eminent stereotype of a band person was the big-band "sideman"—the Willy Lomans of jazz, playing cards at the union office, sleeping upright in the band bus after a dance hall gig in Dubuque. In the peak years of the big band boom, *Down Beat* ran a column called "Sideman Switches," noting movements between bands. "These guys were like ball players," wrote Warren Leight in his play *Side Man*. "On the road, written up in the papers, endorsing trumpets in *Down Beat*. Bands passing each other in the night even traded sidemen: one first trumpet player and an alto for a second trumpet and a tenor to be named later."[1] The romantic vision of the workingman artist toiling in anonymity remains irresistible: the popularity of documentaries like *The Wrecking Crew*, *Muscle Shoals*, *Standing in the Shadows of Motown*, and *20 Feet from Stardom* underscore the vision expressed by the late songwriter Dave Frishberg in his "I Want to Be a Sideman":

I want to be a sideman
Just an ordinary sideman
A go along for the ride man
Responsibility free
. . .
I wanna be a sideman

Just a highly qualified man
A real professional pride man
Old indispensable me
Now I can cut whatever comes up
Fake and transpose
Won't make a fuss

. . .

I want to spend all my time
With music and musicians
I want to sleep in the afternoons
And let the leader call all the tunes

The academic literature, too, tends to focus on jobbing New York club date and Hollywood studio musicians, or a jazz world dominated by ad hoc jam sessions or by bands with an explicit leader and rotating casts of hired side musicians. It, too, emphasizes a pessimistic, even nihilistic pecking order, in which freelance musicians exist—as a 1988 study of theater pit orchestras put it—as a mass of replacement-level cogs: "These musicians, socialized to an ideal of artistic accomplishment, recognition, and personhood, instead are required to play an artistically subordinate supporting role"[2]—to the point that "free-lancers in Washington, DC, refer to the back door of the Kennedy Center stage where they enter and leave as the 'servant's entrance.'"[3] While their bleak view of thwarted artistry has little to do with the varieties of engagement and creative collaboration found in this book, they do offer a useful rubric for identifying the "indispensable" band person under consideration: "Is the individual: (1) unique or replaceable, (2) perceived as a creative member of the performance or not, hence, (3) a worthy focus of attention or not, (4) listened to or not listened to, (5) expressive or non-expressive?"[4]

Band people arrive at their identity—somewhere between a career and a calling—through a combination of luck and intention, ambition and ambivalence. Sociologist George H. Lewis wrote dryly but accurately in 1979 about what he called the "recruitment of pop music performers" into an industry whose marketing and self-image contain a contradiction: "At the same time as he or she is an integral member of this legitimate occupational structure, the popular musician projects the image of deviant. . . . The role of the popular music performer is both one embedded in the legitimate American organizational structure"—the corporate music industry—"and, at the same time, one labelled as deviant by the controlling ethos of that structure."[5] While the idea of the band person as necessarily "deviant" is no longer universal as rock-lineage music approaches its eighth decade, it is true that many band people are discouraged from thinking of their work as a career, and there remains no formal or institutional path to prepare them. For the most part, there is no "official" pedagogy of rock. While institutions like the Berklee College of Music do serve as technical, jazz-based pedagogy for pop performers, anecdotally, ambitious students tend to drop out when they feel they have the tools or opportunities they need. Ambition can be as suspect as ostentatious virtuosity in band circles. Early indoctrination into a particular set of assumptions about a musician's role in society has long-lasting consequences for their long-term creative and economic choices and sense of agency.

And ideology is as crucial as virtuosity in the mindset of a band person. The training of band people, after all, is hardly limited to technical ability. Lewis again: "The role is also one that requires a great deal of socialization and one that lacks the formal channels for such socialization."[6] That is, in a situation mostly premised on group generation and performance, one has to learn how to be a good hang, to generate (or acquire) a set of shared aesthetic values and references. H. Stith Bennett's *On Becoming a Rock Musician*, based on fieldwork in Colorado in the early 1970s, makes the point that the formation of bands, especially in the early stages of musicians' lives, is a process of repeated wheel reinvention—even when the shape and dimensions and requirements of "wheelness" are mutually understood, the details are very much up for negotiation:

> The career of *becoming a rock musician* is simply *being* in a local rock group. . . . While elite musicians are required to train and pass tests, the status passage to *rock musician* is easy— anyone who can manage to play in a rock group can claim the

identity. . . . Learning processes . . . take place *after* a person has initiated a self-definition by becoming a member of a rock group.

Even if there is no universally recognized "core knowledge" [to being a rock musician,] musicians do manage to move from group to group. This is possible because the formation of any rock enterprise is the initiation of a new and unique way of knowing how to make music together. That way of knowing is based on the amalgamated resources of its individual members, and that is why the category of personnel is critical. The group can make music together only if the "right" musicians are found.[7]

The charity event Rock Lottery—in which musicians are randomly assigned to ad-hoc bands and given twelve hours to write and rehearse before performing a handful of songs for a paying crowd—is premised on exactly this tension.

The sensitivity to monetizing one's art can be instinctive or conscious. Bassist Melissa Auf der Maur specifically avoided training as a musician after an intensely musical childhood, wanting to protect it as a space untainted by financial pressures: "I went to college and university as a photographer, because I knew that music was unrealistic and that music was like the love of my life, but there's no way I was going to make a living doing it." Photography would be the music-adjacent artistic career that protected the sanctity of her musical life: "I accidentally got invited to join the band Hole, [to] which my first answer was 'absolutely not, I'm busy.' . . . Music was going to be the love of my life that I never ever sacrificed to earning a living." Jean Cook was on a fast track as a competitive concert violinist, but turned her back on that high-pressure path "because I really liked doing music, and I never wanted to be in a situation where I was stressed or bored playing, so I choose what I play, I choose what I do; and I have other ways of supporting myself."

Drummer Ara Babajian has vacillated, but ultimately came to the opposite conclusion. "My goals were really just to be a rock star, you know? So I would even practice throwing sticks along with records, when I was at home, I practiced throwing sticks into the audience when the records ended." After playing in punk bands in his teens in Southern California, and spending his early twenties in "a very vibrant ska and punk and rock and pop scene in the early '90s in New York City," Babajian quit for a few years, daunted by the "uphill battle," before making "one last go. . . . I guess I was afraid of it turning into a career—not only was I afraid of paying my dues, but I was afraid of maybe not enjoying drumming or music as much if I monetized it."

Musicians who came of age before the twenty-first century could see a path to a career in rock bands as a plausible goal in a way that their younger counterparts can probably no longer realistically imagine. For guitarist Gerry Leonard, in late '70s Dublin, "Our goal was to get our band, get gigs, get signed, get a record deal, fame and fortune. There was a lot of blind faith."[8] (Eventually, Leonard came to New York with "a bag, a guitar, about $200, and the promise of a job.") Mountain Goats bassist Peter Hughes graduated with a degree in English and plunged into a familiar role as a college-town indie rocker supporting his music with transient jobs as a substitute teacher, graphic designer, and coffee-shop guy: "Sonic Youth was the model. . . . I saw the way they had grown as a band, slowly and organically and in a natural way, and when they went to a major label it wasn't like a huge sellout thing, it was just like continuing the trajectory [of] a band that [is] successful on its own terms, maybe never getting hugely successful but being able to have a career, able to play music and live a reasonably comfortable life"—the "perfect sweet spot," famous enough to support oneself but not so famous that it ruins your life.

Some stumble into a career as a band person. Murder by Death cellist Sarah Balliett "always thought it would be cool to be in a band, but . . . assumed if a band wanted a cello it would be [as] a novelty." Keyboardist Jenny Conlee had a degree in classical piano and some ambitions as a composer, but ended up in a touring band "just for a little bit, but then that became ten years." Bill Stevenson says, "I'm thinking there is no possible way I can still be playing when I'm sixty. But give me a call in seven years and I'll see." (Stevenson is now sixty, and has been a touring drummer for more than forty years.) Ethnomusicologist Bruce MacLeod, writing about New York club date musicians, quoted a fifty-something guitarist making a similar point: "Nobody ever became a musician to make money at it. We all did it because we loved it. You start to play, and all of a sudden you've got some gigs, you're getting paid, and you're a musician . . . you're in the music business. And you just wanted to play."[9]

For some, the choice of a non-traditional instrument was the turning point. Once Todd Beene picked up pedal steel, the novelty of the instrument and the scarcity of players overrode his inexperience: "[I] got some extra cash and I found a really old steel on eBay and started playing it really poorly . . . for a couple of years. I feel so bad that people had to endure me playing that thing live, because I just got one and started playing it. . . . [Then] a lot of doors opened for me." Fellow pedal steel player Bruce Bouton spent time in a "world-renowned madrigal and choir" and as a Byrds-influenced guitar player before "my buddy said, 'Hey man, there's a guy down the street, he's got a pedal steel for sale. You gotta get it. Nobody plays pedal steel.' So I got my mother to sign for a loan and I bought my first steel guitar." Sure enough, "somebody found out I had a pedal steel and he called me. . . . I got my first road gig with this traveling hillbilly band, and I was off to the races." Multi-instrumentalist Scott Brackett grew up in Redding, CA ("nothing to do out there except for get into meth and get pregnant") whose location between San Francisco and Portland made it an attractive stop for touring bands: "We couldn't pay the band . . . but we could maybe get you some gas money and put you up for the night and we'll throw a party and it will be a good time." The punk and ska bands in which Brackett played trumpet would open the shows, which paid off years later when one of those bands, Okkervil River, needed a trumpeter, and remembered him.

Some were professionalized early. Drummer Michael Bland started playing in church, where his father was also a musician, and where "a lot of [Black musicians] get our start, and as soon as we can [play] responsibly, they put you to work," and was a full-time professional by his mid-teens. Guitarist Oren Bloedow had paying gigs by the age of ten. Bruce Kaphan, a pedal steel player, was shaped by the regimen of working with high-end but relatively anonymous country musicians "at a honky-tonk palace in the San Francisco South Bay area called the Saddle Rack. It was like 3,000 people, two stages, five dance floors, just a crazy big nightclub/bar/honky-tonk. . . . We would constantly be learning new material, and the best studio players in the world were my teachers."

Many pass through academic music training. Joe Ginsberg received a degree in jazz from USC, signed to Warner Brothers with his band, and transitioned smoothly into hired-gun bass work and songwriting: a more or less frictionless touching of all the bases of a professionalized career. Nate Brenner grew up playing bass for his pianist father before attending the Oberlin jazz program, playing weekend jazz gigs in Cleveland and eventually trad jazz festivals and touring, en route to a future as an educator, before being sidetracked into Tune-Yards. Drummer Brian Chase, violinist Jenny Scheinman, and Peter Hess were also products of the Oberlin program.[10] Hess, in particular, saw himself as on track for a traditional career as a flexible working jazz and session winds player, "guys who could step into a Broadway pit or procure another big band gig or smoking in a jingle session, and do a wedding gig, just do it all, and that was the model I always imagined." His first touring gig after college was with the Tommy Dorsey "ghost" band (a group which continues after the death of its titular leader), "six and a half months on the bus . . . in only Florida, not a sleeper coach, just [sitting] in your seat of an endless awful Greyhound bus ride punctuated by three or four sets a night of mediocre swing for the blue-haired ladies in Fort Lauderdale. That was cool."

For others, university or conservatory music programs were a mixed experience. Drummer Jim Sclavunos "failed music. The professor memorably told me music is not for me, I should forget it." Keyboardist Jay Gonzalez studied classical guitar, performance, and composition at SUNY Fredonia, but after moving to Athens, GA, he says he spent a decade shedding academic baggage. "I'm not criticizing learning," says Gonzalez. "I learned a lot of good stuff, but at the same time . . . I wasn't built for it, and I knew I wasn't going to continue. . . . I went more caveman learning, studying rock 'n' roll, and learning more about recording in bands, and stuff I liked outside the classical side. Then I was basically trying to . . . erase all those lines"—to use his academic musical education as a toolkit, to be called upon as necessary. Drummer Brian Viglione "detested" his experience in the Berklee summer programs, "a bunch of disinterested students who couldn't play . . . and [a] lackadaisical atmosphere from the teachers." Carla Kihlstedt calls herself "a combination of over-schooled and under-schooled"; conservatory-trained (Oberlin, again) but "living a double-existence" and "elbowing it out at the sides" of a traditional classical training to the point where, when she moved to California after graduating, she didn't tell anyone she was a classical violinist. Still, her sense of how to live as a musician retained a sense of professionalism: "The models that were around me were all independent working musicians who did a combination of playing in other people's projects, getting hired for tours, being part of ensembles with their own trajectory. . . . Within a few years I had my fingers in a lot of different pots." Drummer Glenn Kotche says, "I identified myself as a drummer since I was three." He was "heavily into drum and bugle corps and marching percussion in high school," and earned a degree in classical percussion before expanding into Chicago's capacious free improv and indie rock scene. Keyboardist Eliza Hardy Jones also used a youthful ambition as a classical pianist and conservatory training (at—wait for it—Oberlin) to assemble the technical and improvisational skills for what became a more diverse career:

> I did not have the constitution to be a classical musician, especially a pianist. . . . There's room for like twenty great classical pianists . . . and I just didn't have it. . . . My brother was in a punk band and a series of very strange musical projects, and that was when I started to have the idea that I could be a musician, but not a classical musician. And my grandmother is a wild bohemian character, who had a big influence on me. I would go down to visit her and she'd say, "Okay, we're going to go into Richmond. You're going to teach a gypsy dance class at this public school." I would look at her and be like, "I don't know what gypsy dance even is." She said, "Oh, you'll be fine." [Then] she'd say, "I got to [play] jazz at a wine-cheese thing." I was like sixteen and I said, "I don't know jazz, Grandma." She says, "It's

fine, we'll work it out"; and we would go and fuck around at this wine-and-cheese thing. She would play violin, and she brought me a Casio keyboard which I had to fake jazz on. So I started to get some sense that you can just fake that shit; you can just make it up and people will pay you. . . . It was a fun and liberating experience from the classical world.

Drummer Josh Freese's father conducted the Disneyland Band.[11] He joined the musicians' union at twelve and has been "an upstanding tax-paying citizen since seventh grade." He planned, in the vague way of a middle-schooler, to attend Berklee after high school. But opportunities to tour and record led him to drop out of school at fifteen, "and then I never looked back. There was a time when I said, 'Maybe I should go to school,' in my twenties. And I thought, man, all the guys who are at that school want to do what I am in the middle of doing right now. So why stop?"

Some explicitly identified with the workaday pros. For bassist George Rush, "the people that I admired and wanted to emulate were the backup guys, were session musicians. [Maybe] that was because they were the ones that were guaranteed to get paid. . . . The guys that were legendary sidemen, but you knew exactly who they were from the first note they played." Viglione's father encouraged him to pay attention to "the culture of musicians, and rock musicians in particular . . . about the roles of studio engineers and producers and floor managers and all this affiliated crew." Drummer Peter Erskine's formative experience was when his parents took him to see a Broadway show in New York City:

And when I looked down in the orchestra pit and saw what the musicians were doing and heard the sound they were producing, I was pretty certain that that's what I wanted to do; and this was reinforced every time I spent time with an LP and stared at the photos that would be included of the session musicians. My initial fantasies all had to do with being a side person. I didn't sit around daydreaming about being a headliner, being a bandleader.

A traditional, even medieval, way to get into the business is to be born into it. Ethnomusicologist Paul Berliner's subjects "describe the process by which they acquired an initial base of knowledge as one of osmosis, [of] skills as much social as musical."[12] If a major element of "becoming" a musician requires "socialization" into a community (more on this in later chapters), the children of musicians have an obvious head start, inculcated early into the social norms and values of musicians. This can affect their sense of musical boundaries as well—it is not a stretch to assume that the in-home model of music professionalism also makes it easier to imagine themselves into music as not just a hobby, but a career. Keyboardist Rick Steff's father was "one of the 'Memphis Horns' . . . so Dad played on *Suspicious Minds*, *In the Ghetto*, and *Shaft*, and then he would come home and go play a circus gig or be a hired gun to do a Rod Stewart gig." (Perhaps Memphis was a particularly old-fashioned town in this sense.)

> When I got out of high school I was offered a few scholarships, and I just asked Dad, "What do you think I should do?"
> "Well, what do you want to do?"
> I said, "Well, I want to make records and I want to tour and see the world playing music."
> He said, "Well, for God's sake, don't go to college."

Bassist Matt Sharp had a destination in mind, if not a route: "By seventh or eighth grade, I completely identified as a musician, even though I didn't know what that meant, and didn't have any particular skill set to validate it. It wasn't like teachers were saying, 'Hey, you really got this talent.'" He pictured bands like "gangs . . . all sort of walking the street in some sort of *Repo Man* and *Road Warrior* existence . . . seeing each other in dark alleys. You don't even have any sort of realistic idea." Drummer Benny Horowitz says he now embodies "literally what [he wanted] to do: form and create a band from [the] ground up, something as a drummer—especially from the punk and hardcore scene, it never was *this person's thing*—it was a band thing. The idea of starting a band from scratch, writing all the material, getting that band to be a touring signed band, and then eventually being able to quit my full-time job and live off of music—that was literally all I wanted to do for all those years. And that's what I got to achieve, 100 percent and more—it got to a point where beyond just surviving off of music, I was able to, even for a bit, *thrive* off of music. I have a house and I have a wife and the family thing and all this stuff, and I don't know if or how I would have achieved that in another way."

The traditional route to being a band person remains the casual one, driven by passion more than training and happenstance as much as intention. Young musicians in jazz, wrote Berliner, "typically find points of entry into their local community within the intersecting domains of neighborhood and public school where they seek out knowledgeable peers who share their musical passion . . . [in] informal study sessions, a mixture of socializing, shoptalk, and demonstrations known as hanging out.[13] Berliner added:

Unencumbered by adult responsibilities . . . teenagers pursue [music] with a single-mindedness and unbounded energy that typify their impassioned involvement with other interests. . . . Unwavering devotion to music listening also characterizes [their] learning programs. . . . Students also treat recordings as formal educational tools. . . . Budding artists take control of their own music education with what must seem to them to be daring assertiveness.[14]

Joe Lally "started playing bass with somebody that [he] knew from high school after a show." He explains:

We were like, we need to start a band, and he said he would sing, so I said I'll play bass, literally went out and found a bass, found an amplifier and a cabinet. I had a job then that I could buy those things with, so I just literally went out and got them having no fucking clue, and I didn't necessarily purchase an amp and a cabinet that really complemented each other. It worked,

but it was just something you do. You just end up there. We just
started writing songs together. And that's how I learned how to
write music; or [that] to make music was to write with people.

It is this fatalism—not quite passive, but not quite willing to admit to
intention—that especially defines musicians who came up through
the punk lineage of the '80s and '90s (perhaps it simply confirms
stereotypes about Gen X). "I was definitely not considering a future
as a musician," says guitarist Scott McCaughey, who has been a full-
time musician for three decades. "It was definitely my greatest love
in life, music, rock and roll, but I never considered myself a candi-
date for making a living. I never pictured that. I never really strived to
become that. I just played music with my friends and had other jobs.
My whole life revolved around music, going to shows, hanging out
with my friends and listening to records, but I didn't really consider it
a viable option as a career. My whole life has just been sort of pretty
unplanned and unstructured. I just fumbled along until things fell
into place, and they're still falling into place as I'm fumbling along."
    It is this "group relationship as a source of skills" (as Bennett
put it), though, that operates in lieu of formal training for this other
tranche of players—a form of socialization by constant, informal
dialogue about aesthetics and values.[15] When drummer Janet Weiss
started playing music, she never thought it was going to be her job:
"That was not the climate in that era when I started playing. The climate was, you had a day job, then you played music. You did the thing
that you loved, which was music, in the hours that you were not doing
the day job. The mindset was not like it is now where people think of
it as a profession." "Music was something that was happening to me,"
Joe Lally says, "because of a refusal to do anything else—[because of]
all of the things that you're not doing, you come upon the thing that
you are doing."

2
"PLAYS WELL WITH OTHERS"
The Social Lives of Bands

We would be on stage and performing the duo songs, where I was playing acoustic guitar and singing "Mein Herr" or "Port of Amsterdam"—there were many times where Amanda [Palmer] would reach over and put her hand on my head, and sort of push my head down as I was playing, in a very coarse and blunt move, to push me back and down. And not in a way that was always necessarily linked to a lyric. . . . It was very much about: don't look at him, look at me.

BRIAN VIGLIONE

The Dresden Dolls present as close to the ideal of an equitable band as can be imagined: a mixed-gender drums and piano duo facing each other on the front of the stage in costumes and makeup, a performative conversation. Off-stage, as well, pianist Amanda Palmer and drummer Brian Viglione shared what Viglione calls "an intense work ethic," energetic and ambitious "teammates" exempt from the standard hierarchies of front person and accompanist: "I told her many times, 'Look, I'm not up there as your competitor. I'm not trying to steal your shine. I'm not [here] to [take] attention . . . away from you.' I said, 'We are in a two-piece band; both of us are stationary at our instruments, and I'm trying like hell, as you are, to put on the best show possible for the people that are sitting there so we won't just sit there like two clods, nearly emotionless except for our little arms waving around'—which she would agree with." But there are limits, and dominance, it seemed, had to be reasserted. "If Amanda was at the front of the stage, and I was in the back setting off fireworks and mooning people and just sort of clowning around to distract, that's one thing. And I can appreciate someone saying, 'Hey, this is my show, and I need you to have a certain level of seriousness and attentiveness as to what I'm doing as the performer who faces the audience.' However, that was not the situation with the Dresden Dolls. We were a closely related duo, both of us at the front, and [the] interplay was very direct and balanced between us musically and performatively. And to have my teammate feel that what I was doing was distracting from her personal glory and attention, to me, it spoke more about her own insecurity about her talent."

Viglione is, admittedly, an unusually demonstrative drummer. "I grew up watching Nick Cave and Jello Biafra and all the big arena rock bands. The point of that music was to really let yourself be free, if not completely unhinged, and [to] give something unique, expressive and cathartic to the audience. That's what I want; that's what I was inspired by. . . . I don't ever want to feel like I have to hold back on stage." Cave and Biafra, though, are the front people of their bands, and not every singer appreciates the competition. When Viglione later joined the Violent Femmes, "there were times that I was getting a little too into it. We were performing 'Gimme the Car' one night down in Australia, and I kicked my floor drum over, and my sticks were going flying everywhere, and [Femmes singer] Gordon [Gano] said to me, 'What's the matter, not getting enough attention over there?' And that stung."

Every band is a foreign country, with its peculiar customs and dialects, slang and standards. But every band is also (when it works) a small business, a romance, an employer/employee dynamic, a hierarchy, a creative collaboration, and something between a family— siblings or cousins, sometimes literally—and a gang. The rules governing those relationships and hierarchies are usually unspoken, unique to each collection of personalities, and have to be developed and negotiated from the ground up in each situation; often by young people whose priorities are driven more by idealism than by the practicality and the best practices of human resources management ("Pop music is not only cultural work," wrote cultural theorist Andrew Beck, "it is, apparently, very badly organized cultural work").[1]

The reality is that to form a band is necessarily to form a self-governing corporate entity that needs to exercise a single will. When we talk about band dynamics, then, what we're really talking about is political organization. The French lawyer Jean Bodin, writing in the sixteenth century, identified three possible forms of sovereignty: monarchy, aristocracy, and democracy. His near-contemporary Thomas Hobbes said that without concentrated sovereignty, there can be no coherent commonwealth—the body politic devolves into a roiling mass of competing interests. The frontispiece of his *Leviathan* features the image of a looming figure composed of many smaller people who are the source of its power: the leader represents the collective power of the state, just as the face or spokesperson of a band represents the group.

The traditional conception of the band hews to the monarchical or aristocratic mode of organization: a single leader, or pair of song-writers, who accept both credit and responsibility for the collective enterprise.[2] Beyond that arose a graduated economy of cool (soloists over rhythm sections, guitarists above all) which dictated standards of performance etiquette: a bassist, for example, should know their place, and not be too showy or talkative. (No doubt this has something to do with the cliché of the "girl bass player," that in an all-male band the obvious role for a woman was on the lowest-status instrument.) A flamboyant drummer like Viglione—or a different drummer, from an off-the-record story, who asked the singer if they could move a little off-center, so the crowd could see him better—violates one of the basic, unspoken expectations of rhythm section humility.[3]

The group that became The Band was one of the first to question this archetype, when the long-time backing group began playing sets without bandleader Ronnie Hawkins. "We were all singing and playing instruments," wrote drummer Levon Helm, "and to our minds that was the basis for a new kind of band—one without a front man. . . . This was a radical notion, like communism. But maybe, I thought, for the first time in our or anyone's imagination, the rhythm section could run the band!"[4]

With Marxian inexorability, the DIY bands of the 1980s revolted, favoring a democratic, even anarcho-collectivist, approach. Minutemen singer/guitarist D. Boon, says bassist Mike Watt, "thought what made the Minutemen political was the way we structured the band. He was influenced by the R&B [guitar players], and trebly and clipped playing, and he thought that left more room for the drums and bass. He thought there was hierarchy—we came from the seventies arena rock, [in which] the guitar players dominated. He wanted to make it more of an egalitarian way of doing a rock band, so that's where the politics actually was. He didn't really do power chords, he asked me to be up front. . . . What attracted us to the punk movement was getting to reevaluate all the fuckin' hierarchies and structures."[5]

But to what extent can the traditional hierarchies of bands be overturned? In his memoir, Bruce Springsteen wrote, "I knew I wanted something more than a solo act and less than a one-man-one-vote democratic band. I'd been there and it didn't fit me. Democracy in rock bands, with very few exceptions, is often a ticking time bomb."[6] He got what he wanted (though he found it harder to dispense with his employees than he had perhaps anticipated—fans have loyalties that constrain even an undisputed Boss), but his name had always appeared in front of the band.

"I've been in all manner of bands [with] all manner of political structures at the core," says Carla Kihlstedt. "The most successful ones are the leaders [who] are both strong and clear, but also incredibly generous, and [who] acknowledge the input and importance of the other people they chose to bring along." But even in Sleepytime Gorilla Museum, "as socialist a band as I could possibly imagine," she says, "if I really were to be honest, I could tell you that [there were] unspoken leaders of that band." The key is clarity: "I can function in any number of these political structures. And as long as I know the rules and know what's what, I'm fine."

While music as a capitalist product requires a star system, and the legal framework of copyright differentiates between "authors" and "performers," political and financial hierarchies will spontaneously arise in even the most collectivist groups. The following chapters grapple with one of the "fraught places" where democratic ideals meet the practical efficiencies of the political organization of bands: is democracy possible in a band, or even preferable? Do band people prefer a band that operates democratically, or a defined hierarchy? What makes a good or bad bandleader? How do support musicians and bandleaders manage the hierarchies that may be imposed on them from outside by press, fans, and management?

Then, there are the internal and very personal dynamics of a group (apart from creative work): To what extent should musicians prioritize being easy to get along with over purely musical concerns? Do gender politics come into play, and if so, how does the band—operating at that nexus between chosen family and small business—handle them?

In a classic study of leadership styles[7] (in this case, of adult leaders over groups of young boys)—demarcated into the categories of democratic, authoritarian, and laissez-faire—psychologists Ralph White and Ronald Lippett drew the following broad conclusions:

- —Laissez-faire was not the same as democracy. Laissez-faire was less organized, less efficient, and definitely less satisfying than democracy.
- —There was more group-mindedness and more friendliness in democracy.
- —Democracy can be efficient. . . . Boys in a democracy kept right on working while their leader was present or not, while in autocracy when the leader left, the boys stopped working as if glad to be relieved of a task which they "had" to do.
- —Work and play showed a higher level of originality or creative thinking in the democracies than under either of the other types of leadership. There was a larger amount of creative thinking about the work in progress than in autocracy, and it was more sustained and practical than in laissez-faire.
- —Autocracy can create much hostility and aggression, including

aggression against scapegoats. Autocracy can create dis-
content that does not appear on the surface.

The median reaction to the question of political organization in musical groups—democracy or autocracy—coalesces around a rueful
wish that democratic bands could work; but that unfortunately since
they can't (with consequences including lowest-common-denomi-
nator creativity, inefficiency, and inability to move quickly and deci-
sively), a clear leader is preferable to stagnation and conflict. Some
even propose that the egalitarian pose is a mirage; that a transparent
view behind the scenes would always show a hierarchy (or at least an
imbalanced division of labor).

The democratic idea, logically enough, seems more possible in
early bands, created from younger, more idealistic musicians engaged
in, as violinist Jenny Scheinman puts it, "the experience of finding
yourself with other people" and forming artistic sensibilities together,
around an experience of shared sacrifice—if it didn't happen for you
then, there seems little chance of experiencing it as you get older.
"You have to start at the very beginning and talk about it," says bassist
Andrew Seward. And "talk about it in the most idealistic terms—'Hey,
we have nothing right now. Nothing. Nobody even likes the band.
We haven't even put out anything, but I want this agreement.' I don't
even mean on paper." R.E.M. and U2 (and later Radiohead) occupy a
near-mythic place in the band imagination as world-straddling bands
who made—and stuck to—their early decision to split decision-
making (and, crucially, songwriting credits) equally, despite the
immense financial stakes that separate them from similarly minded
bands like Sonic Youth and Fugazi. It's no coincidence, many band
people conclude, that they had decades-long careers with minimal
(public) conflict. "I'm sure there were times where it probably wasn't
the most beneficial thing for R.E.M., for instance, to not have somebody really pushing forward and saying 'This is the right direction
we need to go to, and we need to finish this record now instead of
six months from now,'" says Scott McCaughey (who had first-hand
experience with the band's process), "but R.E.M. would have probably never lasted for thirty years if there was one person leading it, or

if one person was making more of the money, [so] they were really smart when they set it up. They did it in a really democratic style, so that everybody was equal in the group, everybody made the same amount of money, and that's probably the key to longevity."

"In democratic groups," wrote psychotherapist Saul Scheidlinger, "faith in the leader is supplemented to a large extent by a faith in the group's ideals and institutions."[8] In the more radically egalitarian groups, "the leader" is replaced by ideals: "Obviously it helps if you all look at it the same way, [and you] are all striving for the same thing together," says Joe Lally. The agon of democracy is the barrier which requires a critical mass of energy, idealism, and mutual trust to surmount: "If there was somebody in the band who just felt completely differently . . . I guess the democratic thing to do would be to feel like you'd have to hash it out with them to the point where eventually they probably just wouldn't enjoy being with the other three people." Drummer Jon Wurster concurs: "A huge thing about inter-band dynamics is to know when to step away, and when not to get into someone's face and know what not to say. [When] people don't know when to take that step back when someone is on edge, or someone feels really strongly about a decision or idea, that's when things can go very wrong." Democracy is inefficient, and takes time. Violinist Daniel Hart isn't convinced a fully democratic band is even achievable: "I've never seen it work, actually. . . . It takes forever to come to any decisions." Still, he prefers the messy attempt to "somebody telling everybody what to do." Stuart Bogie points to Arcade Fire as a band that had "the juice, the energy . . . they had to work together; then as success [arrived], they have experienced structuring and restructuring of how to run things based on what people want to do [and] what's realistic. When you're talking about millions of dollars, it's a simpler thing, there's more to go around." Bogie's own experience with Antibalas operates, for him, as both an example and a cautionary tale about the unpaid and uncredited administrative labor that accompanies leadership roles:

[Antibalas] reached their decisions through voting. Of course, there were people who had a stronger willpower; there were people that had a bigger mouth—I think I was one of the people with a bigger mouth. There were some people who would kind of bully things. There were people who would say, "No way, I veto that!"—though that's a presidential power; we don't have a president. Eventually we decided we did want somebody to be a president who decided, and that guy would be our ultimate quality control. We explored different ways of reaching decisions. Some people were more concerned with today. Some people were more concerned with tomorrow. I don't think that those two are mutually exclusive.

My dream for Antibalas was that they would elect a music director every year, and then that person would plan and work on things; and different roles for the band would have different directors, and people would serve respectively in each one, planning things. But the difficulty in that was that we didn't have the organizational backup. Orchestras and chamber groups that do that kind of thing, they will have grants that help them create and operate in that way. But we were lucky to get $200 each at a show. So when you are an adult and you are doing this, looking at it as your career, it becomes very difficult to rationalize spending hours of your day outside of the actual performances working on stuff administratively.

"I really like a hierarchy," says guitarist Nels Cline. "I played in democratic bands for most of my early years. . . . It's the vagueness that's difficult, and the inability to make fast decisions as a unit moving forward. You don't always have to make fast decisions, but you have to make unified decisions. If you can't make a unified decision, then you're never going to make a quick decision." He continues:

And sometimes you have to decide right at the moment "We need to do this, we have to take this gig," or "No, we can't do this song because it sounds like *blah blah blah,*" instead of endless discussion or unresolved energy that sometimes hangs over a democratic band, because one person has a strong voice and other people tend to recede. For example, I'm the person who won't take umbrage at what somebody says or does, until I've let it go so long that I become a monster. Then when I finally speak up, it's hideous; instead of being realistic and just saying "I don't like that and here's why" and just talking about it. Sometimes I let it go until it becomes this hideous energy; and when it finally comes out, people are really surprised and extremely upset about how hideously I suppressed myself. In a band like Wilco, it's extremely liberating that Jeff [Tweedy] knows where he wants us to go, and he knows what he wants, and we all really respect that and get along. And it's incredibly easy to be in Wilco, because everybody knows what his role is, and everybody is respectful to each other.

Since more experienced musicians enter a room with fully formed artistic concepts and personae, a musician who has arrived at a realization of who they are and what their goals are is more likely to settle easily into a subsidiary role or to take control, depending on their personality. A band, says Gerry Leonard, needs "to find [its] own internal dynamics, but also make peace with it and find out what you're good at." Certainly, Glenn Kotche says, a single leader increases efficiency: "It's much easier for business people, for lawyers and managers and booking agents, to focus in on one person." Groups assembled more purposefully will often sort into predictable hierarchies: "Veterans have more influence than newcomers; and composers, arrangers, or musical directors have greater power than do other players," wrote Paul Berliner. "Two common ideological positions represent opposite poles in this matter, the first focusing on the rights of the individual, the second on the welfare of the group."[9] A common progression is from the latter to the former, as musicians move from inexperienced to veteran, from amateur and collective to more recognizable professionalized divisions of labor and authority—and move toward an understanding of themselves as skilled independent contractors rather than limbs of a single body. "A democracy is great," says Leonard, "but sometimes you need a lot of time. . . . I'm often working in a situation where there's a job to be done and there's a time constraint, and there's a budgetary constraint; and if the artist employs me, my job is to get the work done in the best way possible and bring it in under budget and make it successful. If we have democracy, [and] we're five hours into the session and people are still trying to decide whether they should do this song or that song, then I don't think that's a creative place. I think that's a frustrating place." Both bassist Nate Brenner and violinist Meredith Yayanos reach for a similar metaphor: "I've seen it go either way," says Yayanos, "just the same way I have seen polyamorous relationships go both ways. Being really devoted to a band, it's your chosen family and it can be just as intimate—if not more so." "It's like being in a relationship with four different people at the same time," says Brenner. "It's easy for feelings to get hurt and for people to feel left out."

One of the reasons aspirations to democratic governance are so associated with younger bands, posits Benny Horowitz, is a reverse correlation with longevity: "The bands that are really democratic are sometimes the bands that fucking don't get anywhere. No one in the band was grabbing the horns. No one in the band was [saying], 'Come on guys, this is what we need to do,' and that person actually got something done."

> The number of creative decisions that bands confront is endless . . . each is a possible bone of contention. . . . Bands that survive either develop an authority structure that violates romantic mythology, creating a gulf between the way the band presents itself to the outside world and how it actually operates, or members reach an accord on a division of labor that all can live with, acknowledging the value of one another's contributions.
> DEENA WEINSTEIN, "CREATIVITY AND BAND DYNAMICS"[10]

There are staunch skeptics. "Democratic bands, I don't know," says multi-instrumentalist Larry Mullins, known professionally as Toby Dammit. "Do you know of any? The moment $100,000 comes down the pike, everything gets really strange." "There is always a musical hierarchy," says keyboardist Paul Wallfisch, "so there is always a leader musically, and in terms of work done and everything. I have never heard of a democratic band, really, no, fuckin' bullshit." Saxophonist Ralph Carney adds, "There is always going to be somebody that tries to take charge. It's just how people's personalities are." Democracy, says keyboardist Marc Capelle, is "misunderstood hierarchy."

A critique familiar from politics, but unexpected in aesthetics, is that egalitarianism tends toward a lowest common aesthetic denominator: "The concept of majority rule is basically anti-creative," wrote composer Gunther Schuller.[11] "Maybe cohesiveness is overrated," says Jim Sclavunos. "Maybe bands and artists are so often told they need to be [unified], that [they] are less experimental as a result." Shahzad Ismaily concurs: "Group music making . . . pushes music toward a common denominator that is sophomoric and lame in its intentions. And that's a shame to say, because I want it to be much more compelling." He goes on:

It could be a matter of mismatched process. For example, let's say you want to be part of a collaborative group music-making endeavor. Then I would say, if you have the room in your life to meet up with those people three times a week, three hours at a stretch, for two years straight, then you have a chance to make amazing collaborative music. And if, outside those hours [when] you are meeting, all of you are reading books about art, about life, about architecture, and living amazing experiences; and then you bring that back into the writing moment you have together, and you are critiquing one another's ideas, and pushing them to other places or suggesting flipping them over or trying them backwards or trying them in different contexts— [then] you might have the potential to collaboratively write in a way that's even more compelling than the dictatorial oligarchic one-person bandleader approach. But without that, if you are just a band that's going to be [together] for three days in a row for five hours a day, and you are going to try to write all your material together, you are going to be dumbed down to straight quarter notes and an A-minor chord. The time pressure is so intense that you can't even rehearse the material, so you just go with something simple.

"Artistically," says Jenny Scheinman, "it is so hard to find four people who can create one sound, like the Beatles or something, [to] come together in a unified way. It is just very hard to have relationships with four people on that level, and often one person ends up doing too much of something and gets cranky about it, and everything falls apart, that classic scenario." Emergent bandleaders receive their power, Bennett wrote, in exchange for "a willingness to handle the logistical hassles . . . by these actions the organizer is demonstrating his or her abilities as a leader/decision-maker, and that the outcome of this organization will be, in some sense, 'his' or 'her' group."[12] "There's got to be a head chief," says Josh Freese. "I have [a] friend [whose] band are largely successful, and they sell out arenas around the world, and they pride themselves on being a democratic band; they pride themselves on [saying] 'We're splitting everything four ways, no matter what'—and they are constantly fighting, because no one has official control. I'm about to quote someone who I can't stand—but Gene Simmons once said, 'A family owns a car, right? It's the family's car, but someone has to drive it. There is always two people in the front and two people in the back.'" The Drive-By Truckers were asked in an interview about their longevity, and Mike Cooley said (paraphrasing the Melvins), "The secret is to kick somebody out every now and then."[13] Freese emphatically agrees:

> Yes! You do, just like any business. We're not just jammin' in the garage with our friends, but on a large scale doing it professionally. Yeah, people get fired. People fuck up. People hold other people back, people make bad decisions. People like to think that it's all soul and just about the art and all. But once you're doing it for a job, and you are making a living doing it, it's also a business, whether you like it or not. It doesn't mean you don't like music. It doesn't mean you don't care about your craft. But

if it was just about the art, then go work in the fuckin' restaurant down the street and do your art at night.

Leonard identifies a middle way: "Even if I come on board as a musical director, if there's somebody in the band who's better at something than I am, I'm going to get them to do it . . . I'm going ask people to do what they're good at. I'm not going to go to Catherine Russell, who's a masterful background singer, and tell her what to sing. I'm going to ask her what she thinks, and she's going to tell me, because I have that relationship with her, and she wants to know what needs to be done. If that's a form of democracy—maybe it's a form of diplomacy."

Broadly speaking, veteran musicians are realists. "Usually, even in a democracy, one person pushes his or her ideas," says Janet Weiss. "Watering down ideas is not a good idea, so you pick your battles." While the Dresden Dolls were, says Brian Viglione, "very democratic," at the end of the day, "somebody has to be the end of the line and make the final call . . . so Amanda would be that person, but I had faith in her business savvy. . . . If you feel confident in the leadership of a particular band, then that's great." Jenny Conlee refers to bandleader Colin Meloy, approvingly, as a "benevolent dictator." When Peter Hughes joined the Mountain Goats, he was joining an entity in the awkward epistemological position of being a solo project whose leader emphatically insisted on its presentation as a band:

However much we are a band, the Mountain Goats is always going to be John. We will go back and forth about a lot of different things, but at the end of the day John has veto power, and we all respect that; and over the years I have learned to trust that he is right. There have been times where he wanted to veto stuff and caved to pressure; then you look back on it later and it's like, yeah, John was right about that. A lot of John's approach to music and to being a band is pretty counterintuitive, and there would be things where I would just want to tear my hair out—but we have both gotten a little bit easier on each other, and among each other collectively. He [has less of a] stranglehold on certain ideas; but [I] have also learned that if John feels really strongly about something, then that's probably what we should do.

In general, most musicians simply welcome clarity about their roles. "I like the freedom to contribute, and I like the certainty of delivering in a certain way," says Peter Hess. "It's good to have someone who has a vision and someone who has a direction they want to go," says multi-instrumentalist Scott Spillane, "because it usually ends up being that way anyway." Drummer Michael Bland says that "having structure . . . tells me the space that I have available to me to create."

It may be the sheer uncertainty around roles in bands that aspire to or profess egalitarianism that is the root of their instability. So too the very definition of "bandleader": a familiar but usually informal appointment which can be defined (in various divisions of labor and relative importance) as front person, primary composer, spokesperson, ideological commissar, logistics and finance coordinator, etc. The consensus position is in favor of what multi–winds player Doug Wieselman describes as "someone who's got a vision that is driving things, but [also] that everyone has a voice that can be at least acknowledged . . . democratic in the sense that everybody has potential input." "If the leader in charge listens to the masses," says drummer Michael McDermott, "that leader can only be a better leader." "It really helps," says Dammit, "if there's someone to be the be-all and end-all of arguments . . . hopefully that person has good, fair scruples and is qualified to lead."[14]

"LIKE A FAMILY"

The basic strain that predisposes rock groups to crash and burn comes from the difference between a close-knit circle and a specialized impersonal organization. In a close-knit circle, members are valued simply because they belong to the group.

In an organization, members are valued only for their contribution to the achievement of the group's goal. . . . Each band must
resolve the tension in its own way or break apart.
DEENA WEINSTEIN, "CREATIVITY AND BAND DYNAMICS"[15]

Some [leaders] confine their interaction with band members
to the settings in which they rehearse and perform together.
Others hold the ideal that a band should function much like an
extended family. Curtis Fuller represents this view: "With the
Messengers, we hung out together. It's like the group that hangs
together, plays together." . . . Such close relationships can work
only among players who have tolerance for each other's differences and mutual admiration for one another's musicianship.
PAUL BERLINER, *THINKING IN JAZZ*[16]

For all their realism about the political organization of bands, band
people still overwhelmingly prefer the *emotional* life of their band(s)
to aspire toward that of a (chosen, temporary) family or gang—as
opposed to a site of workplace professionalism, a handful of co-workers who nod politely and see each other on stage—even as they
acknowledge that the metaphor also involves the kinds of squabbles
and long-simmering resentments that are also a feature of familial
relationships. (Significantly, Weinstein wrote, bands that feature
actual siblings rarely say that their band is "like a family.")[17] "I like
family vibes," says Jenny Conlee. "We always play a board game
before we go on stage . . . and when we're not on tour, we still do stuff
together—kids' birthday party, we're all there."[18]

Musicians instinctively reach for familial metaphors—especially
marriage and sibling relationships—which include not just close-
ness, but conflict. (Presumably the age differentials in bands preclude parental metaphors, maxing out at "elder siblings"; "mom" and
"dad" are generally reserved for tour managers and other enforcers of
schedule and discipline.) "There [are] people who I would never do a
tour with again," says keyboardist Eliza Hardy Jones, "but if you were
to ask me about this person, I feel like, 'Oh man, I love that guy.' It's
very familial, [where] even if you struggle with a sibling, where you're

like 'We just didn't get along,' you have no choice but to love them."
"You don't spend that much time with those people without becoming family," says Andrew Seward, "where you just fucking hate them
and you want to strangle them sometimes, but you also love and you
care for their well-being." In a predominantly male milieu, the sense
of brotherhood can blur the line between the genetic and the gang.
Guitarist Oren Bloedow "was very attracted by the idea of a band of
brothers," adding:

> I was infatuated with the Beach Boys and [the] Doobie Brothers,
> and I just wanted a lot of brothers. What I was hoping was that
> I would be able to face life with multiplied powers—I would be
> stronger . . . a gang of guys that shared in-jokes and camara-
> derie. What they didn't tell you in the movies was that we were
> incredibly fractious and were always having really dramatic and
> incredibly petty disagreements.

The image of a band as a fraught (or polyamorous) marriage is
equally powerful. "The word 'band' means a 'union,'" says drummer
Lori Barbero, "and if there's not really a union amongst the people in
the band, I just think it's fraudulent. Find someone who you're compatible with; and even if they don't play the greatest, they'll learn,
because you'll rehearse, and people can change and get better. It's a
lot harder to change peoples' personalities and compatibility than it is
to change their style of music. You can't change people, really, it's too
hard. It's like being married to somebody." Like a marriage, connection can sour: "I watched friends of mine who have been in the same
band and worked with people for years and years and years and end
up turning into some weird marriage—where as adults, you harbor
resentments, and you love each other deep down, but you can't really
stand each other anymore, and you don't want to hang out with that
person at all when you get off the road," says Josh Freese. "And it goes
from 'We're a gang' to an old grouchy married couple-slash-business
partners." Trombonist and trumpeter Gary Church wrote that "leaving the Merle Haggard band was a little like getting a divorce."[19] On the
other hand, an apparently successful long-term relationship inspires

respect: "I really tried to take a lot from Sonic Youth," says Barbero. "The people that have played together for decades—that's family, and you have to admire that.[20] Even if you don't like their music, you have to admire that they've stuck to it for so long, and they still have passion, and they still are together. It's like, you see old people on the street and they're holding hands and you think 'Oh my god, they've probably been together fifty years,' and your eyes well up a little bit."

The "family-feeling" is not merely a matter of touchy-feely good humor. Psychologists who work on group cohesiveness identify it as an important component of the group's effectiveness and longevity: "The more cohesive the group, the more effectively it can influence its members."[21] "A band offered an active social life," wrote anthropologist Sara Cohen in her study of rock bands in Liverpool:

> In this way it provided its members with both a context and a focus for their relationships and thereby a measure of security. . . . One man described being in a band as "a bit like being in a family." . . . It could also be likened to membership of a gang, club, or sports team (as the words 'band' and 'group' imply), all of which can arouse strong feelings of unity and solidarity, loyalty and identity, a sense of belonging. . . . Band members charted the history of their band, describing in detail the movements of members from one band to another as if relating the genealogy of their own family.[22]

What several of the researchers refer to as "we-feeling" could be experienced as a double-edged sword. On the one hand, wrote psychologists Dorwin Cartwright and Alvin Zander, in "a group that has a strong feeling of 'we-ness' . . . the members are more likely to talk in terms of 'we' than 'I.'"[23] Bassist John DeDomenici echoes this: "I like the family thing, because even though it's not your name on the band, I feel like when things are going well, it's more like a 'we did this' thing, like 'we accomplished this.'" Higher levels of cohesiveness, of "we-ness," encourage the development of shared norms, shared language and inside jokes, and a streamlined sense of purpose. On the other hand, in the words of sociologists Stephen Groce and

John Dowell, cohesiveness can be experienced (like in certain family dynamics) as coercion or obligation, "as the forces exerted on members to remain in the group."[24] Cohen again:

> Members . . . were aware that the functioning of their band and the quality of its creativity depended on the continuation of good relations and communication within the band. . . . The manager of [one band], realizing that members of her band had little in common and barely knew each other, organized regular "band outings."[25]
>
> Some musicians, because of that pressure to get on well with fellow band members, preferred to work alone. . . . Several comment[ed] that one should not get friends involved in the same band because friendships "got in the way" of band membership.[26]

"I am a social person," says Mike Sneeringer, "but I don't necessarily rely on the band for all my social interaction. I know some people like that. I like being part of the family and being part of the group. But there are times when I would be okay in a gig where it was a little more, 'Hey, see you at the office.' . . . As I have gotten older, I'm fine with alone time, and I don't require as much constant input that I used to." Michael McDermott endorses the balance: "I like family professionalism. . . . I love when there is a family vibe, but I like it dialed in."

HIERARCHIES

Sociologically, we know that groups display four properties of characteristics that distinguish them from their individual members (Hare 1976). First, social groups have goals which are supra-individual—they transcend the individual goals of group members but are compatible with them (Cartwright and Zander 1968, 104). Second, groups evolve sets of norms which establish the boundaries within which interactions occur. Third,

groups develop varying degrees of differentiation, usually in terms of a power/influence hierarchy and members' roles within the group. Finally, groups display greater or lesser degrees of cohesiveness, of bondedness among group members.
GROCE AND DOWELL, "A COMPARISON OF GROUP STRUCTURES AND PROCESSES IN TWO LOCAL LEVEL ROCK 'N' ROLL BANDS"[27]

This utopian capitalist model of work is saturated with politics: participants at all levels are slotted into hierarchical systems of property allocation and power relations.
MATT STAHL, *UNFREE MASTERS*[28]

Bands are an unstable mix of formal structures, in that they are a business, and informal, in that they rarely have a *stated* hierarchy. The hierarchies that exist within bands, especially those which appear over time, are among the most sensitive topics any long-running band has to negotiate: members who thought they were in a democratic band realize they aren't; one-time bandleaders find that the group has a new center of gravity; musicians whose ambitions placed themselves as the stars of their dreams find themselves not the star of their circumstance. Famous examples abound: Levon Helm quitting the first Bob Dylan backing tour, telling Robbie Robertson, "It ain't my ambition to be anybody's drummer" ("Levon also probably remembered that the Hawks had been his band, and he just didn't feel comfortable not being the leader anymore," added road manager Bill Avis);[29] Charlie Watts punching Mick Jagger after the latter called him "my drummer" ("You're *my* singer," Watts reportedly retorted);[30] Duke Ellington's gradual assumption of control over what had begun as a collaborative group.[31] "When all of the players and drummers get together, the conversations they have about the front people are very funny," says Melissa Auf der Maur. "Like, 'I know what you're going through. . . . You know what it is to work in that structure where the bass player and the drummer don't have publishing or say, even though they just devoted themselves to this band for five years.'"

In his *Discourse on the Origin of Inequality*, Rousseau spec-
ulates that inequality emerged at a point when individuals
became capable of accumulating an embryonic wealth or capital he called "public esteem." The first cultural medium of the
dawning process of social ranking is not wisdom or learning
. . . but music. For Rousseau, it seems, the linkage between
music-making and social hierarchization is so self-evident that
at this pivotal point in the *Discourse* he imagines and proposes
musical performance as both the preeminent site of distinction and the first act of social mobility. . . . "Whoever sang or
danced best, whoever was the handsomest, the strongest, the
most dexterous, or the most eloquent, came to be of the most
consideration; and this was the first step towards inequality,
and at the same time towards vice. From these first distinctions arose on the one side vanity and contempt and on the
other shame and envy." . . . Music is the matrix of inequality;
being handsome, strong, dexterous and eloquent all have value
in this account, but not one comes before singing.

MATT STAHL, *UNFREE MASTERS*[32]

Most groups . . . arrive at one distribution which is more or less
explicitly recognized by all members. Certain functions are
assigned to certain individuals, and the other members are forbidden to perform them. . . . Many formal organizations make it
plain in a multitude of ways that individuals located in the lower
ranks are not expected to contribute to the planning activities of
the organization. Similarly, decision-making is often restricted
to a few "key" people.

. . . From the point of view of the individual member, his
location in the structure of the group is of decisive importance.
. . . The degree of satisfaction that a person derives from his
location in a position, and the degree of frustration of his
desire to change positions, will obviously influence his morale,
productivity, and mental health.

CARTWRIGHT AND ZANDER, *GROUP DYNAMICS: RESEARCH
AND THEORY*[33]

"I would say that we are partners," says Peter Hughes about his role in the Mountain Goats, "but it's kind of both." He elaborates:

John is the Mountain Goats legally. . . . If I go play a show by myself, it is not the Mountain Goats. If John goes to play a show, he is the Mountain Goats by default. But in the way that we plan things out, and we talk about stuff—whether creatively or career-wise, tactically—we make those decisions as a group. We make them together; we talk about them; we hash them over.

There is a lot of stuff that goes through John that I don't see or hear about or have to even think about. He will pretty frequently call me up and say, "Hey, what do you think about this?" So I guess my role is like an advisory one, but I definitely feel like I have a stake in this. It's not like I'm just playing in some dude's band. So it's a weird hybrid of being a sideman and being in a fully democratic band (like that Sonic Youth model of everybody having an equal say in songwriting and everything else). Obviously in the songwriting respect, it is John; but in a lot of the other respects, it is still very much a co-op.

To a great extent, the stratification of a band—its relative clarity, and the level of contentment among the personnel—emanates from the leader. In groups where the leader is also the band's namesake, the power structure is obvious: the leader's name is on the record covers and T-shirts. "I didn't talk about Glenn [Miller] as a member of the band," wrote trombonist Paul Tanner. "He *was* the band."[34] As bassist Jason Narducy puts it, "If I have a great show and Bob [Mould] has a bad show, it's a bad show. If I have a bad show and he has a great show, it's a great show." A sensitive bandleader (more on this in the next chapter) is responsive to this dynamic: "Our opinions are asked from time to time, but it's usually known that if the person at the top doesn't like the idea, it's not gonna happen," says John DeDomenici. "But that's always done in a very, very polite way. And when that does happen, I can tell that they don't necessarily like saying it. And we all understand that if we all like it, but the one person who's in charge doesn't, it's not going to happen. And that makes sense—it's their band."[35] Michael McDermott and Joan Jett had "been friends, [but] to go from [being] friends to her being my boss was seamless, because I get that she's my boss, and she very much knows what she wants and what she doesn't want. At the same time, she's been so generous with 'How are you doing? How do you feel? How did you think the show was? What are your thoughts?' It's very much equal; and it's refreshing to know that some Rock and Roll Hall of Famer is going to be that cool and that down to earth. . . . I'll speak to Joan about how the show went; and Kenny [Laguna], who's the manager— he's just another head of state." Many nominal bands exist, as Glenn Kotche says of Wilco, "as a vehicle for [a songwriter's] lyrics.[36] [Jeff Tweedy]'s writing the songs. And [the way] people perceive music, the song writing or the lyrical content in most rock music tends to be the focus. It's rare when you have the sideman, the person who's not seen, being the focal point of a band. Who would that be? The Roots; I guess Flea to a degree, or sometimes guitar players."

In bands less organized around an obvious leader, hierarchies can take some time to develop. "The Rolling Stones didn't start out as Jagger/Richards," says Jim Sclavunos. "They started out as a much more balanced group; and over time the Jagger/Richards mythology evolved to the point where all the other members seemed to become somewhat marginal."

Many writers have looked for the origin of group structure in the characteristics of the individuals composing the group. . . . Some people like to assume responsibility while others prefer to be told what to do. Some gain satisfaction from fame and exhibitionism while others are shy and retiring.

CARTWRIGHT AND ZANDER, "STRUCTURAL PROPERTIES
OF GROUPS"[37]

Even when there was an accepted leader, the band's own development could lead to changes. One or two people had often taken the original initiative and for a time retained the leading role, but as the band began to perform more widely different people sometimes came to the fore; or a band was founded by mutual agreement but one player gradually emerged as dominant.

RUTH FINNEGAN, *THE HIDDEN MUSICIANS: MUSIC-MAKING IN AN ENGLISH TOWN*[38]

All communities have systems of stratification based on the differential access to wealth, esteem, and power.

ROBERT A. STEBBINS, "CLASS, STATUS, AND POWER AMONG JAZZ AND COMMERCIAL MUSICIANS"[39]

Drive-By Truckers "did a brief thing opening for Tom Petty," says Jay Gonzalez. "He sometimes gets a bad rap [as a bandleader], but you can tell the focal point on the horizon was always keeping the band together, and the good of the band, even if it was a bad or tough or cold-hearted decision. . . . You see bands, and you don't know the dynamic; and then if you are lucky enough to get a glimpse into it— like, I never realized what an alpha dog personality [Heartbreakers keyboardist] Benmont [Tench] is—not in a bad way. He's such a strong smart dude, and I remember reading recently that it was his band, and Petty kind of took it over. So he really is almost a band-leader personality—and then the struggle between Petty being the leader and Campbell being the concierge; it's just fascinating to me. It's almost like an iconic version of a band situation."[40]

When bass player Howie Epstein joined the Heartbreakers, wrote Petty biographer Warren Zanes, "there were now categories of membership, and his was entry level"—and bass players, to grossly generalize, seem more comfortable with their place in the band pecking order than any other category.[41] "Because drummers are really loud, [like], 'Hey, look at me,'" says bassist Joe Ginsberg. "In the bass community, you realize you're never going to be the focus." As any labor theorist could tell you though, even the lowest-status member of a community has power they can exercise. "No matter what, government is always through consent," says Oren Bloedow. "Even Ringo—who was not a shot-calling guy in the Beatles—during the *White Album* sessions, when things got really dark, he did leave and they had to cajole him back, and fill the studio with roses and stuff like that. And Ringo was definitely the easy guy in the Beatles. But he's still capable of making his displeasure felt. So there's always a collaboration—it has a lot to do with appreciation and respect, just understanding that people have interlocking skill sets, and having some awareness of 'John does seem to be awfully good with words,' or whatever."

> Leadership cannot emerge unless the members of the group assume different responsibilities. . . . The [leader] cannot perform all the duties of all the members. His own accomplishment is therefore dependent upon the performance of others. Each member must work within the organizational framework which defines the limits of his participation. . . . This organizational structuring is not viewed alike by all persons. To some it appears as a barrier to participation or recognition. To others it appears as a prod and stimulus to greater effort and participation. For still others it provides a secure and comfortable sphere of activities and working relationships.
>
> RALPH M. STOGDILL, "LEADERSHIP, MEMBERSHIP AND
> ORGANIZATION"[42]

Emerging strata within a band can quickly be exacerbated by external influence (beyond the normal fan fascination with lyricists). On a business level, it's simply easier for managers, label representatives, and the like to have one or two contacts within the group. From a media point of view, a star system is a familiar and convenient paradigm: "It is easier to put one single person on the cover of a magazine or in an interview situation on TV or on radio than it is to put a band—easier in the sense of it takes less effort on their side, not easier because a camera can't take a picture of four people," says Sclavunos. "It's just easier for them to decide on a single picture of a single person rather than a single picture of four people." He adds:

> Another aspect of it is that it has become an accustomed format. In rock bands the singer/guitarist configuration has become the given, so nobody in the media will question it. You

don't find people going, "Yeah, but what about the bass player?" Or "How about that keyboard player over there?"

Still, he admits, "It's better to be involved in a band with a front person that they are interested in than a band with a boring front person. There's the conundrum." Even a famously democratic band like Fugazi attracted a mythos around a single member, Ian MacKaye: the satirical site *The Hard Times* ran the headline "Season 3 Of *Serial* To Identify The Three Other Members of Fugazi." That's "an inevitable result of Ian having done interviews since like 1981, and run a record label," says Joe Lally, and "an enormous amount of documentaries about the eighties and nineties [in which] people talk to Ian." The band would "disregard [that] as the outsider's view of what's going on. We would be sure to not let it have an effect on the inside of the band, in the songwriting; and everybody was going to have their say. . . . If you're a solid enough unit, nothing is going to affect you that's going on outside, 'cause the four of you are . . . going to make the decisions that keep you as strong an entity as you possibly can be; which then deflects all the nonsense."[43] Still, the external pressures can affect internal dynamics within the band, says Benny Horowitz. "You need socially conscious adults to make it work." He explains:

When I say "socially," I mean someone who can walk into a situation and know to pull back a little, see where somebody else is at, read the room a little bit. Things like that become so crucial in a band dynamic. And that would rely on the fact that your main person who's getting more attention is doing it in a way that doesn't put other people off. Great bandleaders learn how to be diplomats. . . . Then on the other page, the people in the band need to have a certain level of contentment, a certain level of humility in what they do, and they need to know where to sit sometimes.

These subcategories and classifications of membership, organization, affiliation, and hierarchy are not purely in the service of regulating ambition, ego, and efficiency. Well-organized bands tend to have a legal existence and financial arrangements: corporations, salaries, retainers, even health plans. For all that, individual musicians may not be clear on their status—are they band members? Employees? Are they session players who just happen to get called for a particular band's every project? Are they full band members, but not part of the corporation? Do they have future claims to the master recordings? Many band people don't have the vocabulary to ask those questions until well after the questions have been settled. Prolific joiners and collaborators have the luxury of occupying different roles in different projects, even drifting closer to and farther from the heart of a project as it engages and then loses their interest.

"It's that grey area between member and employee," says Scott Brackett, "[which] happens when nobody talks about money before money starts coming into an operation." He goes on:

> With Okkervil, Travis [Nelson] the drummer was sort of the business manager, and Will [Sheff] was the songwriter—it was his group. . . . Trav's view was that we were sort of all members. But I think all along, [Will] viewed it as we were hired guns. As time went on, those perspectives became more obvious. Then we had a manager come on and he—rightly so—was trying to get us to firm up some of this stuff, and try to get a handle on what people's roles actually were. But most of us were drunk all the time, and I was twenty-three or twenty-four at this time, so it was a lot more of an emotional conversation about . . . I don't think we ever had a really good conversation about any of it, until after I left the band.
>
> That was part of the reason I moved over [to Murder by Death]. For one thing, it was an opportunity to do more stuff, because they needed a Swiss Army knife, and that's my thing. But with Okkervil, [because] at that point we had the resources to get whoever we needed to do whatever, there was less chance for me to be as involved; I had less opportunity to play, get the cooler parts and stuff like that. And Murder by Death did pay cell phone plans; I had health insurance with those guys;

they took care of their people. So at that point I was like, shit, employee or not, it feels really good to be taken care of like that.

Financially, drummer Nigel Powell says, backing band the Sleeping Souls operate as employees of Frank Turner. But because of the circumstances of their partnership—they joined him as a pre-existing band, under a different name—"we're in a limbo area between being a session band and being a *band* band. We're definitely not a *band* band, because the thing is he writes all the songs and he has all the say—but we're not a session band to the extent that we're not, I don't think, replaceable, and we've been with him for a long time. . . ."[44] [And] because it was our ethos in life, we started off doing it for free, just helping him out. It was like, yeah, we're all in this together; we'll figure out how it works in terms of money later on. Which muddies the waters very slightly. If it had been 'I'm hiring you for this much for the first tour,' then we would be automatically employees right from the start, but we started off in this strange area where we were gung-ho and involved in a non-mercenary way." For John DeDomenici, "there are times when you feel just like an employee, and it's not the best. I'd rather feel like a band member—but at the same time, there's different kinds of band members. I like being *the band*, I like being a member; but you know where your place is." Having a clearly defined role is key, says Todd Beene:

If I'm going into a thing where some folks say, "We want you to do this tour with us, for this amount of time, and we are going to pay you this much money," I'm like, yeah—I like the music; I like the people, and I know what my role is. I don't have to be there all the time; I don't have to be emotionally invested in it or creatively invested in it to still have fun and feel like I'm contributing. It's more about those gray areas, which is the hardest part.

I felt like I was a member of Lucero most of the time, but I don't think I really was. I'm trying to think about how to explain the differences. I had some issues over a recording that we did with a producer. I would say only two [songs] made it on the record with my part intact. I went into it feeling like I was a member of the band, and from then on I felt, "Yeah, you are not really a member of this band." I think understanding my role in it led to me ultimately leaving the band. It's not because I wasn't solely a part of that record. It's more like . . . I would have never been anything but the pedal steel player.

Considering oneself a "band member" is, to a large extent, that confidence in one's stake in the aesthetic ownership of the project. "When you are in a band, you're a team; and that becomes your identity in a way," says Jon Wurster. "You do want your personal stamp to show through more in a band."

In fairness to bandleaders, these arrangements are often formed in evolving situations, in which bandleaders are not necessarily any more clear about what they want than anyone else. "I didn't start out being like 'I want to be in six bands,'" says Jean Cook. "It was, 'People are asking me to do something; I'll do that.' Then after fifteen years, 'I've been doing everything that these people have been doing the last fifteen years; I guess I'm in the band.'" Cook outlines various shadings of relationship: "With [songwriter] Jon Langford, I'm very much a collaborator. At the end of the day, he writes the words and he drives the project and the pace, but we think that we're considered collaborators. And that's happened over fourteen years of working together, where at this point he knows that I'm reliable enough that he can count on me as a partner." With other groups, she's an employee; but in one, the bandleader "would never get another string player for his stuff," while another bandleader has an alternate violinist.

Contractual relationships or other internal distinctions may exist within a band while remaining invisible to the public. Jay Gonzalez is "on salary [with Drive-By Truckers]; and the band is basically Patterson, Cooley, and Brad as far as the core, as far as business-making decisions. Essentially, Matt Patton and I are musically part of the band, [but] we are more or less hired." Melissa Auf der Maur was on a contract with Hole and the Smashing Pumpkins: "That's why, in my mind, when I left [Hole], I was like, 'You guys were the ones who made me sign a contract, so I'm going to leave when it's done.' [With the] Smashing Pumpkins, it was also a year contract [for] a certain amount. In both cases, I was a hired, contracted person, but considered a member of the band." Cook adds that a disadvantage of membership is that "as soon as you are a member [or corporate owner] of the band, you have to assume costs." George Rush uses the band Hem as an example: "Every time they tour, there's a four-person partnership which I'm not a part of, so when the big checks come rolling in, I am not one of the recipients of those checks. But I have become the fifth guy that gets consistently called whenever they perform, and [I] have been scolded by them numerous times for saying 'you' instead of 'we.' But at the same time, I am an employee—there have been times when they have taken a loss touring, and I for sure am not going to take a loss touring."

Comfort with this blue-collar view of musical work—as Mike Watt puts it, "in real life, the non-musical things, the guy during the daytime at the job, he's got to take orders from the floor boss"—can be a matter of personality. Some musicians are simply never going to be satisfied without some level of buy-in. When Janet Weiss has toured as a hired gun, she "enjoy[ed it] in a way, but I'm a little high-powered for that. . . . I'm not laid back when it comes to the music being good or the show being good. I push, push, push, always."

Another benefit—besides not having to shoulder the responsibilities of budgeting, planning, and writing—is flexibility. "Life is about taking turns," says Mike Watt. "You can't learn everything always being the boss." Drummer Mike Yannich "definitely liked feeling like a band member," but prioritized being replaceable for the sake of variety: "I wanted to play as much music as possible, a week with this band and then a couple weeks with another band." John DeDomenici values the freedom to pursue other projects: "A lot of times, [band-leader] Jeff [Rosenstock] will be stuck home for a while. He has to write, and I can still go out and play with other people. I don't have any responsibilities. I don't have to focus on the creating, so it gives me the freedom to just go out and perform more."

A band is a state of mind. "From the very beginning of the Mountain Goats," says Peter Hughes, "it was very obvious the Mountain Goats was John [Darnielle], but even then he had this idea that he didn't want to be [a solo project]—that's why he called it the Mountain Goats instead of John's Ordeal. He didn't want to be just doodling on acoustic guitar, he wanted to be a band; so that concept was already part of the conceit from the beginning." With Joan Jett, says McDermott, "I'll refer to 'You guys,' and Joan will go, 'No! We, us.' Maybe I've just gotten really fortunate and lucky with who I played with, but nobody's ever made me feel like I'm just this hired gun or this employee."

ON BANDLEADERS

Most history deals with winners. The history of art deals with innovators and innovations that won organizational victories, succeeding in creating around themselves the apparatus of an art world, mobilizing enough people to cooperate in regular ways that sustained and furthered their idea.

HOWARD BECKER, *ART WORLDS*[45]

Leadership may be considered as the process (act) of influencing the activities of an organized group in its efforts toward goal setting and goal achievement.

RALPH M. STOGDILL, "LEADERSHIP, MEMBERSHIP
AND ORGANIZATION"[46]

Most band people are happy to be led. Leadership skills, in worlds like business and the military, have been the subject of extensive study and thought. In band worlds, "the person who does a lot of the writing winds up doing a lot of the leading, and that isn't necessarily the same skill set," says Stuart Bogie. Consider this a virtual roundtable, convened on the question "What makes an effective bandleader?"

On one point, there is near-unanimity:

Michael Bland: The more direct the better. I have a very healthy ego; but I don't mind being told what to do. It's your ship. You know where you want to go. Let's get there. You drive.

Robert Faulkner (in "Orchestra Interaction: Some Features of Communication and Authority in an Artistic Organization"): The probability that an authority will be given obedience is dependent in part upon the extent to which his communications are viewed as authoritative. . . . The crucial test of charisma and expertise can be found not only in communicative strength and persuasiveness, but also in the responses of organizational subordinates. Conductors call for new ways of thinking and playing; that performers are receptive to this is recognized in the recurring phrase, "He has to show us what he wants, he has to have that personality, then we'll follow him."[47]

Doug Gillard: I prefer where someone owns being the leader— "This is how we do things. This is what I expect from you; this is how the pay works out. This is what we get for live appearances. We will be making this merch money. You don't get any, or you get some, blah blah blah."

Ralph Carney: It's good to have the vision. I think a good bandleader is in fact a band*leader*, where you're following their lead.

Marc Capelle: If you are a bandleader, you cannot be gormless. You have to say, "No, the bridge goes here, and that's the right note."

John DeDomenici: I definitely respect people that know what they want, and can explain it in a concise and clear way. I don't like it when people [are] like, "Change that," and they don't know how. I like direction, a lot; and the more direction the better.

DJ Bonebrake: If [bandleaders] know what they want and can explain it, that's the best thing in the world. If they know how to explain it, and if they're organized. . . . And if the bandleader is like, "Oh, I don't know, do something," everything falls apart.

Mike Sneeringer: If you want help getting somewhere, I want you to know where you want to go. Like, "Hey, drive me somewhere." "Where do you want to go?" "Oh, let's try over there. . . . No, I didn't like that. Let's try over there. . . . No, take me here."

I don't like to be a part of the experimentation process . . . when it's like, "Try this," then a month later it's like, "Oh, I don't like that anymore. Now try this"—then you just sort of feel like a volume knob.

Peter Hughes: John [Darnielle] had always had this very specific idea about what Mountain Goats is and is not. It was very Catholic, lots of rules for the Mountain Goats; and that's part of what kept the Mountain Goats really pure for a long time—and still does.

At the same time, a clear and articulated vision doesn't mean authoritarianism. "The system of authority in the orchestra," wrote sociologist Robert Faulkner, "is more than a pattern of static roles and statuses. It is a network of interacting human beings."[48] Band people, for reasons of artisan pride and simple humanity, don't want to be seen as robotic cogs in someone else's vision. Keyboardist Joe McGinty praises Jesse Malin, for example, as a bandleader who "could be specific without being limiting. He could be creative, but he also had a vision that you had to work with."

Brian Viglione: I admire . . . knowing how to delegate work to your team members, and then putting the trust in those team members and in their skill to execute it without having to go in and micromanage, second guessing the work of people they have hired to do those jobs.

Glenn Kotche: The quality is to give some license—trust the musicians that they're going to make good decisions. I do know people who are in bands [where] they can't stretch out really, even to the point of a drummer [being] expected to play the same fill every night. I'm glad I'm not in those situations, and haven't been. I like bandleaders who realize the talents of the people that they've assembled.

Mike Watt: If you are going to call shots in some places, you have to let go in other places. . . . There has to be a dynamic that is elastic enough to survive stresses.

Gerry Leonard: It is good to have the framework in which to create; and as a bandleader, that's my job—to create the framework, and to make sure that everybody understands the frame and the boundaries and what's supposed to go in the picture. Then the sandbox can start to happen.

I know there are certain styles of bandleaders [who] will come in and they've got it all structured and they want it their way. They'll even go to the guitar player and put their fingers down on the fretboard. That, to me, makes me go, "I don't want to even be in that room." That's not making it easier to me. That's some kind of extended ego trip.

Todd Sickafoose: It's instantly recognizable when somebody is uncomfortable with letting people have a chance to learn the music enough to get inside of it, and be comfortable with it, and have their way with it. When a bandleader has either very strict ideas about what they want to happen or is uncomfortable being patient with that process, that's probably the worst thing in a bandleader, because a lot of things get shut down in that situation.

But conversely, someone who is comfortable with that process and does have patience—letting people have an entry way to your music, then . . . people can get inside of it and have discovery.

Fred Hersch: At times, I have to fight not to tell anyone else how to play. It might not be what I had in mind, but that's the whole point . . . to be open enough to accept what someone else has to say.[49]

I've written in other contexts about the parallels between a touring band and a military unit. But artists require a care and feeding that is not stereotypically prioritized in the military. "Many bandleaders feel it necessary to flex their muscles, and constantly remind you of their authority," wrote Gary Church, "but the good ones always make you feel like you are working with them instead of for them"[50]—bandleaders, in George Rush's formulation, "who themselves are trying to feel like, and then trying to create, an atmosphere that they are 'of the band' themselves." Church's bandleader Merle Haggard "always made the band feel like a part of his successes. It was never 'I've got a number one record,' it was always 'We've got a number one record, boys.'"[51] Bruce Bouton appreciates Garth Brooks's attention and loyalty: "Garth takes care of everything out there. I don't know where he gets the energy, but he micromanages everything. He's totally aware of what's going on. He's the biggest artist in the world, and he shows up every single day for sound check. If he wants an arrangement changed, he sits there and works with the band. Policies on the road, everything like that. It's just, 'Hey, you got some issues? Come talk to me.'"

Eliza Hardy Jones's introduction to the Grace Potter band set a similar tone: "The first show I played with [Potter], I got hired about four days before the first show, flew to LA, didn't know anybody, had to learn [new] faces—a private gig at a casino in Las Vegas. I really didn't know her or know anything about her. Before we went on stage, she had this huddle where she said something really kind and thoughtful about each one of us, and thanked each one of us for being there, and gave us this pep talk, like 'What we're going to do is going to be so great, and I'm so happy that you're here with me.' And that has set the tone, where everybody is incredibly kind and supportive and really trying to be helpful and healthy; and just in terms of the longevity of a tour, you need that."

For Hardy Jones, "One of the most important things about a bandleader is to set a vibe that we are a team . . . that they care about you as a person, that they care about your artistic voice, and—especially with touring—that they care about your health, about your mental health, about your physical health, about what it means to essentially be living with people in a box on wheels for months and months at a time. As a bandleader, there is something important about taking care of your band, not just musically but interpersonally." If something had happened to a member of Marc Ribot's band, says Shahzad Ismaily, "he would have done everything he could to figure out what happened, how he could help, and what's the kindest, most ethical choice he could make about your circumstance going forward as he could."

Guitarist Jon Rauhouse extends that to the larger team of a band, the crew and management: "If you are lucky enough to have a crew, then treat them like you do the band. . . . And we have had to let go of some crew members that have been snippy to other crew members. [Good] bandleaders care about how everybody who represents them in the world [treats] other people. . . . Conversely, if a bandleader doesn't realize their management or their agents or whatever are being very shitty, and they get it pointed out to them, they should do something—and a lot of them don't."

Profoundly appreciated is humility ("I appreciate a bandleader who understands that he is in control mostly because someone has to be, not because he is divine or infallible," says Sarah Balliett) and, especially, tact: that crucial ability to tell musicians, says Jon Wurster, when "you have an idea that you really like and it's not working for them . . . there's ways for bandleaders to make their wishes known that can be really helpful or really hurtful." This sort of leader, says Stuart Bogie, "give[s] you notes that don't feel personal, that appeal to your intelligence as opposed to demeaning you." For Joe Ginsberg, the skill is about reframing a personal aesthetic preference as a group endeavor: "that ability to not just say, 'Hey man, you're the problem in this song,' but instead say 'What's causing that to happen? How can we *as a group* address it so that someone's not getting called out?'"

Small gestures toward awareness of the physical and logistical needs of band people go a long way: "You've got to feed a band," says Marc Capelle. "Buying everybody coffee after rehearsal is huge," adds Paul Wallfisch. "Or you are on the road, the promoter fucked up and the breakfast wasn't included in the hotel; you should buy everybody breakfast." Bassist Caitlin Gray appreciates "a bandleader or band members who have a healthy lifestyle. I don't really like to go on tour with bands that eat takeout or fast food and party every night." Several request a sensitivity to time—for example, says Peter Hess, the "eight hours in between sound check and the gig"; others mention having travel logistics lined up in advance. Part of this can be setting accurate expectations, says Todd Beene: to be able to say, "We are going to go do this thing; if you want to go, it's going to be like this. Either we are going to stay in a hotel every night, or I've decided we're camping at KLA the whole way to save money. I want everybody to know upfront before they ever get involved, so they know what they are planning on doing."

Toby Dammit acknowledges that this is "an enormous weight" to put on a bandleader (in the absence of a manager and/or tour manager) "to have all those logistical responsibilities, on top of artistic responsibilities, on top of just trying to perform in front of people at night and be natural and relaxed. That's really hard." Multi-instrumentalist Joey Burns adds that you can't keep everyone comfortable and well-rested all the time: "There's times when you have to decide, 'We're going to wake up really early the next morning to do a radio show, because it's really important. But we're going to factor in some time where you have the opportunity to take a nap, or just be alone or have a hotel room where you can just chill out.' It's not always likely that you will find the optimum [balance]. But if people know that you're trying to do your best to make it comfortable and enjoyable, they'll appreciate that." He adds:

> At the end of the day, there's always going to be grumblings. And they've got to get those feelings out too, and that's part of being a bandleader. You can't always be doing things perfectly. I think just acknowledging it; or saying, "Hey, let's take a walk, or let's talk, or let's party until four in the morning and get everything out and move forward." That honesty and openness and admitting that, "Oh, I fucked up. I'm sorry. I'll try not to do that next time."

Conversely, there are some traits in bandleaders that are widely disliked. One is open and/or public criticism: "'The look of death,' as we call it, I have never appreciated," says Mike Sneeringer. "If I fuck up, I know I fucked up." One singer Joe McGinty "worked with early on was always criticizing the band, losing his temper, always berating everybody, and nobody wanted to be in that band."

When Scott Brackett was touring with Okkervil River, bandleader Will Sheff "was reading a lot of biographies [of] people like Mick Jagger and Sam Cooke and Lou Reed and James Brown, [who] don't treat their band very well. . . . When I read that stuff, I was like, 'Ugh, God, I never want to be like that.' [But another] way you can interpret that stuff is, 'In order to be a prolific master of my own destiny, I have to do some of these things; I have to make some of these hard decisions; push people harder than they want to be pushed,' and stuff like that. There's a lot of that mythos, and cultural habits within the industry." Big band sideman Drew Page wrote that "tyrannical leaders never seem to understand that, while they can get precision, they can't get warmth or loyalty and dedication from musicians who despise them. Tyranny seems, instead, to breed negligence."[52]

The natural flip side of the enthusiasm for clarity expressed in the previous section is distaste for, as George Rush says, "a control freak that doesn't know what [they] want. It's the worst possible combination for a bandleader, somebody who is just bound and determined to micromanage every aspect of what their sidemen are doing, and yet doesn't know what the fuck they're doing."[53] Especially if they then lean on their band to fill in the gaps, says Peter Erskine; "if someone is functioning in a position of being the big decision maker, the composer, and then they sit back and let everyone else do all the heavy lifting creatively"—when, in Josh Freese's words, "you are just sitting there, reaching and grasping in the dark for stuff—that's no fun, when they don't know how to explain what they want, or they passive-aggressively sulk, and you're not sure what you are or aren't doing correctly."

While "some ego is necessary to do what they do," says Sneeringer of singer/bandleaders, "no one wants to deal with someone who is completely self-important." Reputations precede them: When Sneeringer was asked to audition for one band, he "mentioned [the band] to a couple of other people, and they were like, 'Oh my God, that guy is a fuckin' nightmare; how can you work with a fuck like that?'" Those reputations extend to the way bandleaders deal with club and production staff: "It's funny how the game of telephone works in this industry," says Sneeringer. "It is actually pretty small. [People] probably don't think, 'I'm making this lasting impression that's going to make it back to the player side,' but in reality it is extremely back and forth, how someone deals with club staff—it is very telling [about] how they are as a person." This extends to a respect for the skills of the musicians you've employed, says Stuart Bogie:

> Any time anybody in the band—even jokingly—[says], "Hey, don't fuck this up," I do get a little upset. I sat in with an awesome band, and they made some crack about, "Don't fuck this up, guys." And I was [thinking], you know what, I didn't want to say anything, but they were fucking up the whole part the whole time. They wanted us to play this awesome '80s song

that will remain nameless, but has a very elaborate horn part, and they made jokes about that. They weren't paying very well. We were doing it to have a presence with them—which didn't lead to recording, which didn't lead to further work, so we were kind of being used. And they told us not to fuck it up as a joke, because they think that's funny; but the irony is that they were playing the part wrong the whole time and that they didn't take it seriously. I do get sensitive about that kind of thing.

Don't even joke about things that are demeaning to the employees. That's not your freedom. Make a self-effacing joke, but don't make a status joke to people who are working for you. It's not cute, especially when those people are very well-educated and very well prepared in what you are hiring them to do. Educated is the wrong word. Educated implies a whole other thing. What I mean is someone that is a very skilled laborer, treat them with respect.[54]

Finally, a musician wants to trust that a bandleader matches their level of commitment—"the ability to trust that the leader is going to at least be there," says Brian Viglione, "and not drop off the face of the map. One of the most damaging people that I have worked with had the tendency, when there was a certain amount of momentum going, to all of a sudden drop off the communication map and not take phone calls, and act [like] if they ignore the problem everything will go away, when there's a lot of other people working to make things happen for their benefit as well as for their own." Melissa Auf der Maur remembers when "we were on the cover of *Rolling Stone* and it said, 'Courtney Love is a soap opera; Hole is a band.' But you know that 'Courtney Love is a soap opera' was like ten times the size of 'Hole is a band,' and that's what the story of that band was; the music was quite secondary. . . . We were fucking frustrated all the time; or like, this is unbelievably annoying. Sometimes [Love] would talk for half the set, not play music. Then we would be ready to sit and write songs, and she'd be late." Lori Barbero had, by default, taken over much of the running of Babes in Toyland: "It always happens—after we tour, Kat [Bjelland] just goes AWOL. That's what she does; it's just the way it's always been. Her voicemail is always full, intentionally; and she doesn't look at email because she doesn't have a computer— or she says she doesn't, I don't know." She continues:

> We've really had a wonderful time traveling and playing and going to new places, and when she's on tour and she's in her element, it's the greatest thing in the world. But when she comes back—she just ducks out. She didn't used to be that way, but as she's gotten older she just kinda . . . disappears.
>
> She used to operate as the bandleader . . . but right now I'm the manager, I'm the publicist, I do interviews, I do the money stuff, I take care of paying the rent. She doesn't drive, I pick her up for rehearsal, I drive her home. Every email and every text that we get, I'm the one who deals with it. I work with our booking agent.

At the end of the day, the difference between good and bad bandleaders may be more instrumental than emotional. "I can't really think of anything more effective than giving people money," says Jim Sclavunos. "That usually solves a lot of problems. People seem to have an incredible tolerance for all sorts of things when there is money involved. That's my advice. Pay people."

It can be cathartic for band people to criticize bandleaders: "Interview a sideman," said an anonymous bandleader quoted by Bruce MacLeod, and "you'll find out that they think all leaders are shitheads. We're corny or idiots or whatnot."[55] I asked musicians what lessons from the leaders they'd worked with they brought back to their own work as leaders. Did becoming a leader give them a new perspective on past experiences?

For DJ Bonebrake, the epiphany was about the difficulty of the public-facing part of the role: "I understood what a burden it is for a lead singer to be the front man, to be the voice of a band. If you say the wrong thing, you can alienate the audience; or you can bring them with you just by talking to them, just by being a personality. I don't have that kind of personality; I'm not the lead singer type. I really am the guy you don't see. So I learned what a burden it is for someone like that. The lead singer—sometimes they want that, they need it. We all know that pain-in-the-ass lead singer who's just so talented; they drive you crazy, but they have *that thing*. And then you appreciate that." Jay Gonzalez has taken the lessons not from his sideman work to his leader work, but vice versa: "I have learned that it takes a special certain personality trait to be a natural bandleader, and I don't think I necessarily have that. [It] makes me appreciate what it takes to run a band, and try not to be a pain in the ass about band decisions and stuff like that, understanding that basically it is a constant stream of decision-making, and not everyone is going to be happy all the time."

Several people spoke about the importance of "casting" or "curating"—who you call for a project. Many support musicians will have only had the experience of getting the call, not making the call(s). Paul Berliner wrote that "the initial selection of personnel is itself a compositional act, requiring a special kind of sensitivity . . . [which can] profoundly affect the group's chances for success as an artistic enterprise."[56] It's a question, says Marc Capelle, of "creating a supportive environment for the music to happen, and then casting it like a Robert Altman movie, like Robert Altman meets James Brown. You want this great weird cast of characters that doesn't have a choke collar on, that goes for it, without taking it off topic."

The aspect of leadership which can be the hardest to inhabit is that of discipline. "It's hard, when you're playing with your friends, to criticize each other," says Joe Ginsberg, "but if you let [something] slide for one or two shows, then it becomes habit. So part of that job that's really important, and maybe the most difficult, is saying 'Hey, we need to tighten this up.'" Ralph Carney has struggled with letting people go gently; but, he says, "[John] Coltrane was probably the nicest guy, and he had to do that. It's just one of those things: 'Sorry man, this sound ain't happening. I'm sorry Pete Best, we're getting Ringo.'" Guitarist East Bay Ray—the rare non-frontperson bandleader who is in the position to hire and fire singers—is, he says, a stickler: "I've seen a lot of bands from our era, they get lazy and they get sloppy and they start sounding like crap, and that's going to be noticed. . . . If somebody does something, a jam, showing off, one night, that's fine, that's humor. But if they do it two nights in a row, and it's designed to put the spotlight on them and not the song, and screw up the parts for the other people, then I have to say something. . . . You're not the star. The songs are."

Matt Sharp put himself through a period of conscious exploration of his abilities as a collaborator and a leader:

> In 2005 to 2006, I had decided that I was going to put together another incarnation of The Rentals that was going to be that "all for one, one for all" [group] where everybody has a say in the creative experience. And before I decided to do that, I went back to all of the people that I've ever worked with before, one by one, and from the time when I was not very good at it. I knew people's recollections of the experiences were probably not very favorable, and I wanted to know about it; I wanted to hear what their feelings were, even if there was nothing I could do about it. And if necessary apologize to them, if they had a very negative experience . . . and see if any of that can be informative for how you go forward. I tried. I'm not saying I was successful. But it certainly started me off from a place of treating people with respect, listening to people, not directing people without concern for their own feelings, and that kind of stuff. It's really those experiences which are the school of it all: going back and listening to those people who said, "You know what, you were a real asshole back then."
>
> So many musicians are in some way introverted, and that moment on stage [is] their moment to be extroverted. So those people aren't usually the best communicators. . . . When you're a band that's starting to do well, there's nobody that really took us aside and said, "Hey, we need to sit down with everybody and let's get some communication skills going." My early experience was that everything just stays incredibly passive, and nobody wants to face any of those conversations. So everything gets consistently swept up under the rug, until you get to the point where it can't be ignored anymore, and usually that's where it gets ugly.

Tegan and Sara were a group that I was very inspired by. They had been basically on the road since they were sixteen years old. And they handled themselves in a way that was so inspiring, in the way that they dealt with all the people within their world, from their managers, to the people in their band, to the person selling T-shirts, to the person doing lights or doing sound or whatever. [It] was truly a revelatory experience: "Oh my God, communication is a possibility." There is a conflict with the guitar player in the band, and they sit down and talk it out. . . . That was such the polar opposite of my experience with Weezer—in Weezer, we had no ability to communicate with each other. Maybe it's just because of how the arc of our success happened, but we just did not have those skills; and to watch Tegan and Sara just fascinated me.

FACE OF THE BAND

The bandleader [is] the intermediator between his band and the public, providing, in a sense, the "personality" of the band, the focal point through which the public reacts to the entire band, whether favorably or otherwise. . . . The member of the band takes his identity from the band itself—he is part of the band, and, while he is working in the band, gives up a certain portion of his individuality . . . whereas the leader gives the band its identity, even when he is not the musical head of the band.

ARTIE SHAW, *THE TROUBLE WITH CINDERELLA*[57]

Bandleaders are called upon to act as, or automatically treated as, spokespeople for the band.[58] Bands, though, are not necessarily unified entities. I asked band people whether they've found themselves in a position of listening to the bandleader talking on mic, on stage or to the press, and thinking, "Actually, that doesn't represent my opinion."

"The majority of people don't understand the distinction" between a front person's opinion and that of the band, says Mike Sneeringer. "There are definitely situations in the past where people have said something, maybe front of stage on the mic, where I cringe and I'm like, 'Man, what do I do? I don't want to look like I endorsed that, but here I am sitting right behind that person.' I'm lucky I haven't been put in a major situation where I have to be like, 'If you ever fuckin' say that again, I'm going to quit.'" Jon Rauhouse has: "The one time it did happen—I don't want to say names, [but] this ain't [Neko] Case—I had to tell them if they did it again, I was going to leave, and they stopped. It is hard for people in this industry because everybody feels threatened every moment for their job. . . . A lot of younger musicians, they will put up with a lot of crap, because there are guys that it instantly goes to, 'Well, you know, we can always get somebody else to do that.' So a lot of people let a lot of shit slide."

Drummer Ara Babajian did go so far as to quit a band over on-stage banter. "There were many times that happened with [Leftover Crack singer Scott] Sturgeon," says Babajian, "when we'd be playing a song like 'Life Is Pain,' and he'd be talking about how we shouldn't reproduce, there shouldn't be any more children in the world. Meanwhile I had two kids at home, and I'm thinking to myself, 'That's one of the stupidest things I've ever heard.' Or we should kill cops, which is just a ridiculous slogan to me, it's propaganda and sloganeering and advertising—that stuff used to bother me. But I stopped taking it so seriously. I started laughing about it. [But then,] I had worked at the World Trade Center up until the Friday before 9/11, knew a lot of people in the building who died, and just couldn't square that with being in Leftover Crack as they were celebrating this [with] anti-American rants each night on tour. I stopped playing with them, and took a year off from playing altogether."

Several musicians felt that audiences are discerning enough to understand that one person—especially one with extreme or provocative opinions—doesn't speak for the group. World/Inferno Friendship Society singer Jack Terricloth, says Peter Hess, "was always such a confident nihilist that I never really felt that any extreme opinion he might utter would be construed as anything but his." He adds:

But then on the other hand, I worked with Balkan Beat Box for a long time, and they're all Israeli—I was the only American—and we would occasionally do JCC things where they'd be asked really pointed questions about Israel and Palestine and the occupation. And I knew how anti-occupation they were, and in certain circles with American Jews the three primary guys in the band wouldn't go as far in public as they would in private as far as being outspoken. When pressed, they never failed to really put up, but sometimes it was only when really pressed. And there was one member of that band who I'm sure was very frustrated by that, because he was much more outspoken, and would in fact say, let's not do a gig for the IDF. There were times where I wished they'd speak up even more strongly than they already were. Although their situation was so much more complicated than mine, and I was really just a fly on the wall. I had far more questions than answers.

Janet Weiss presents it as part of the choice of the kind of person you work with: "I try to play with people that I am not going to get in that kind of jam with." John DeDomenici agrees: "When you're in the band, [it gives] the person the ability to speak to a large amount of people, and you don't want to be associated with someone that's a bad person. . . . I know specifically in Jeff [Rosenstock]'s band he tries to not say anything that's too polarizing, because he knows that the band is made up of a lot of different kinds of people, with a lot of different opinions—of course, as any band is. For instance, if he got up on stage—he's a vegetarian—and said, 'I don't think anyone should eat meat': he told me that he doesn't do that because our drummer Kevin eats meat, and that's shitty to him. Like, he shouldn't tell Kevin how to live."

For Weiss in Stephen Malkmus and the Jicks and Eliza Hardy Jones in Grace Potter, the fact that the bandleader's name is the headline provides some distance: Malkmus "says a lot of crazy stuff in interviews," says Weiss, "[but] nobody thought that was the band, the four of us, speaking through the singer." Hardy Jones "know[s] when Grace is getting interviewed, and she's saying these wild sort of sexual things that I'm not gonna—we disagree about feminist issues all the time. I know [what she's saying] in no way has anything to do with me. She's Grace Potter representing Grace Potter."

In addition, says Hardy Jones, a bandleader may not be exactly expressing *their own* views on stage: "You can have . . . that character on stage that you play. And that character on stage can be different from who you are in real life. And when people are talking to you, you're often forced to choose who they're talking to. Like, are you talking to Eliza Jones, the human who's just living her life, or are you talking to the Eliza Jones that was on stage? For me, those are often different people. So that's the other thing to keep in mind when a bandleader is being asked questions, that sometimes they're still playing that character, they're playing that role, and you just gotta roll with that." Jean Cook "work[s] with a lot of people who write songs, and they tell stories, so they'll tell stories from what I'll call their point of view. Like, Jon [Langford] has this story about how we met, which is not how I remember how we met, but I also don't care. And he also doesn't remember most of what he says on stage afterwards. You're entertaining people, you're telling stories. . . . In most cases, how you tell the story of the work that you do, I just leave that to the storytellers."

VESTIGIAL LIMBS

A consequence of the star system is situations in which people—press, label, business associates, fans—focus on the singer/leader to the extent of acting as if the band is a slightly vestigial background entity. In bassist Stuart David's memoir, he tells a brutal story of an early Belle and Sebastian show in which the band was having technical difficulties: "[Singer] Stuart [Murdoch] kept strumming quietly, and then Vanessa from [label] Jeepster—who none of us had properly been introduced to yet—shouted 'Do it acoustically, Stuart. The band doesn't matter.' And then she started to dance."[59]

"That should be a whole YouTube video" compilation, says Marc Capelle, "of the uncomfortable couch interviews on MTV, where there's the one or two guys talking, and then the squirmy hungover guy. Or the not-hungover-enough guy." Bill Stevenson is confident enough to not be bothered: "One of my buddies said, it's not that I care about the Grammy—fuck the Grammy—but when you get a Grammy, you all stand next to each other side by side. So if people love [singer] Milo, good, that's good. I want them to. But that is old news. Nobody ever puts me in the backseat. If anything, it's the other way." For DJ Bonebrake, "it only bothers me when it's uncomfortable—when I'm sitting there not talking, when they don't want to talk to me." He continues:

> They were doing some documentary a few years ago, backstage, filming. And the interviewer didn't even know I was in the band. There was a small couch and I was standing there, hovering; then they finally realized I was in the band and asked me that one perfunctory question, and by that time I was almost mad. I didn't want to be there at all. By that time, I'm falling asleep, it's tough; it's embarrassing. So I've learned when to engage in these interviews. Sometimes they'll be like, 'We need the whole band.' Now it's gotten to the point where [I realize] they don't want to talk to me, so I'm going to go to the bookstore. I'm going to take a walk.

"I have always felt bad for [bandleaders] going to do nine interviews in a row somewhere," says Jon Rauhouse, "and me and [bassist] Tom Ray, we get to go to the zoo and pet kangaroos in Australia. That just happened in Boston—I got to go play the organ in Fenway, and Neko [Case] had to do some phoner. I'm totally fine with being that guy." Paul Wallfisch concurs: "While [Michael Gira] is doing fifteen interviews in London, we can just go to the Tate."

In general, band people experience this as a freedom from an emotionally demanding chore. "It happens all the time," says Sarah Balliett, "and I am eternally grateful. I would rather not talk to anyone. Ever." "I love it," says Ara Babajian, "because I just get to be the drummer. There's no pressure on me to be the spokesperson for the band. The people who do come up to me after a show are usually very respectful.[60] I get a lot of readers; I get a lot of guys who stand in the back of the hall come up to me and say, 'I don't ordinarily do this, but I just want to say, I really appreciate your work,' so it's easy for me. I see some of the bombardment that [Scott] Sturgeon [of Leftover Crack] and Vic [Ruggiero of the Slackers] have to go through at times, and I think 'God, that must be tough.'" "Sometimes when I would get bored with Lucero," says Todd Beene, "I [would leave] the venue and I would just come in front and wait in line, just to hang out and see what people were talking about, and talk to people, because nobody knows who I am, which is totally fine with me. . . . It's the perfect thing—if you can be in a really successful band and still be able to maintain anonymity when you are hanging out, and still get to play for all these people and get people excited and have fun—that's a pretty good spot." Peter Hughes sees it as a consequence of a division of labor that suits him:

> The onus is on [John Darnielle] for so many more things. He's the one who cannot go out in the room and use the bathroom, if there is not a backstage bathroom. I can go out to the bar and get a drink or use the bathroom. There might be one or two people who go, "Oh look, it's the dude"—but I'm not going to be mobbed by people wanting me to tell them my life story. It still does happen occasionally . . . and because it doesn't happen as often, I'm completely happy to do it.
>
> John really has to put himself out there. Usually he will do a signing line after the show. He started doing it as a way to have a sanctioned interaction with people. And it's a huge emotional drain for him, because people who come to Mountain Goats connect with the music and John's songwriting in a really, really intense way, because of the nature of abuse survivors. You have a lot of people coming with really heavy things that they share with John, and he has to bear witness; and God bless him. He sees that as part of the work, even though it's a huge commitment; and it doubles the amount of work both in

a physical way and an emotional way that he is taking on every night, but he has realized that it is better to do that than to not do that. So that's part of being the front man.

And while he is doing that, me and [drummer Jon] Wurster are tearing down drums and packing stuff up, and then we get to go and sit on the couch. The work that we do is a little more grunt work, but that's totally fine. I have a huge amount of respect and appreciation for the work that John is doing in that regard, so I'm definitely happy to give him some leeway—I'm not going to be like, "Dude, you are going to load out your amp tonight."

"I feel bad for Colin [Meloy] sometimes," says Jenny Conlee, "because he has to get up there and do the frontman thing, and he's actually not a very frontman kind of guy. He has to pull it out of his soul or stomach every night; I get to go up there and just play—it's really great; it's low pressure. I feel bad for him because he's the least social of all us, but he's the one that gets marauded. He tries to go to the bus and people are, like, yelling after him. They want us to sign their posters too or whatever, but it's more sweet. It doesn't look like fun. I think he likes the attention, and also doesn't like the attention."

Others are more vulnerable.[61] "It does [bother me]," says John DeDomenici. "Everyone has feelings—but that's just part of the territory. I learned how to shake it off after a while. . . . It's not the greatest, but at the end of the day, I just learned that you got to just deal with it, because of the other things that I do enjoy that I get to do, because I'm not the leader." The anxiety often correlates with less clarity about one's status in a band, or a band which is transitioning from a democratic to a more stratified organization. In the Loved Ones, Mike Sneeringer "was an equal member. I felt not like a sideman, really, in that band. So if interviews happened that I didn't know about, I was, I would say at this point, overly sensitive about it, every photo shoot—to me, the identity was *the band*. I was hypersensitive about that slowly being taken away from me—which I perceived at a couple points, and was not happy about it."

In Sleater-Kinney, Janet Weiss was protective not of her own status, but of the egalitarian nature of a band with two singers: "Since Carrie [Brownstein] is so famous—sometimes it bothers me at shows when all the photographers and people are looking at Carrie and not looking at Corin [Tucker]. . . . That band is very much, like, the three of us are important. But the two singers, their thing is *the thing*, their connection, and their history, and the way they write together— you can't pull one person away and have it be as good. When people are focusing too much on Carrie—I can see why people do, she's an incredible performer, she's got a lot of moves, she's really fun to watch—I like it to be equal between those two, because I think they're both good and they're both important."[62]

At least as far as press goes, support musicians can shoulder some of the burden. In Against Me!, Andrew Seward "would be the VP. I would be able to do stuff that Laura [Jane Grace] didn't want to do . . . with Laura, or just by myself if she didn't feel like doing it. She'd say, 'Hey, will you take this?' Yeah, I don't care, I don't mind talking to people." Semisonic drummer Jacob Schlichter wrote that "while Dan [Wilson] was talking to *Rolling Stone*, the *Los Angeles Times*, and the *New York Post*, John and I spoke to less-experienced reporters . . . I was the rock equivalent of a client at a barber's college. . . . I rambled across the pages of the *Lincoln Journal Star*, the *Topeka Capital-Journal*, and the *Pointer*, the student publication of the University of Wisconsin at Stevens Point."[63]

For those bothered by being nudged into the background, the issue is less about ego than perceptions about who is responsible for the successful art work. "It seems obvious to say that if everyone whose work contributes to the finished art work does not do his part, the work will come out differently," wrote Howard Becker. "But it is not obvious to pursue the implication that it then becomes a problem to decide which of all these people is the artist, while the others are only support personnel. . . . The problem of reputation is central to the analysis."[64] Nigel Powell says that "it does bother us . . . when people talk about the albums [as if] Frank [Turner] did everything. Whereas we know the depth of involvement we've had—which is very significant—and when that is distinctly not recognized by people, reviewers and such, sometimes it just annoys you."

Doug Gillard is careful to say that "it never makes me resentful of the front person of the band. It is not their fault at all." For Scott Brackett, on the other hand, "the front person really has to continually correct that. It's up to them in a lot of ways to change that. There's a lot of stuff that's out of their power, because they print whatever they want to print about your band. But there is definitely this idea that you can just swap out band members for whatever, and I really don't think that that is true. Obviously my opinion is somewhat biased. But even as a listener, there are configurations of bands that I consider to be *the* band, that particular band. And if you take out this person or that person, it's not the same band. But the same thing happens to other businesses too, there's the CEO who's out in front, and they're the visionary, the genius, the one who makes it all possible. I feel like most of the time, it's just the [front] person that says, 'We're going to go over there.' Then it's up to the crew to make it all happen."

Though drummer Thor Harris was bothered "in the past," he's embraced a subtly different freedom than the one articulated earlier in this section. Harris now values the "freedom to move around with lots of different people and do lots of different things." A front person in a popular act is more tied to the particular sound on which they've built their public appeal. "The power of the artistic person in the band is that they typically are calling the shots, and creatively and financially they are being rewarded more," says Sneeringer. "They are doing more work; they are writing songs; they are doing press." But that makes them less nimble: "That is their identity, so if that starts going down, it is not as easy for them to just say, 'This isn't working out so much, let me find something else.'"

A critical distinction [is] between the artist and the support personnel. The artist performs the core activity of making interpretive choices which are unique and indispensable to the work, whereas support personnel carry out all other tasks necessary to the production of a work of art.

[Support] musicians receive constant reminders of their non-personhood. Nevertheless, their self-concept includes the characteristics of serious musicians who are dedicated to artistic performance and a desire to be recognized as such by audiences.

JON FREDERICKSON AND JAMES F. ROONEY, "THE FREE-LANCE MUSICIAN AS A TYPE OF NON-PERSON: AN EXTENSION OF THE CONCEPT OF NON-PERSONHOOD"[65]

"Being a drummer for so long, I get it," says Benny Horowitz. "I completely understand why people connect with singers more than drummers. They write words. They write stories. They're the ones letting people on the inside, and people would naturally feel a more natural . . . connection to those people. You're in the back, whaling away; if you're someone like me, you don't really draw a whole lot of attention to yourself." He goes on:

I always think about the level of attention that a singer gets, and the fact that I probably wouldn't want that. There's all this stuff that goes along with their job that is scary—if you're going to make a great record and get the bulk of the validation; if you're going to make a bad record, you're going to get the bulk of the negativity. I go through this with [Gaslight Anthem singer] Brian [Fallon] all the time—we'll get a review and I'm often in the mind-set of "Ehh, fuck it, man, you know one person, blah blah blah."

I do sometimes feel frustrated with the fact that you don't receive as much acclaim and attention. I think it's natural. I wish it didn't exist in me, and I wish I was a pure enough creative that it didn't bother me one way or the other. But it does. Then by the same token . . . I have the liberty to go out and talk to people every night after shows, but it's easier for me. These kids act natural, and I just go out and I sign some shit, and I'll talk baseball, or I'll mess around with people. And then I watch Bri come out and it's like it goes from, "Oh, let's talk to this cool dude" to like—[long intake of breath]—people just don't know how to act natural, because they look up to him. They feel this weird connection, they've been listening to him sing and listening to his songs, and the relationship is different. I do enjoy being the one who can be like, "Yeah, I'll go get a drink with you guys," and I'll wind up at some bar. And he doesn't really have the liberty to do that anymore.

AC/DC is always my reference for this, because I have this conversation with a lot of people, my wife included, and they often think I'm being self-deprecating, and think I'm just looking at the negative side. Which is probably the case. But I'm always like, what's the drummer from AC/DC's name? And no one ever fucking knows, you know? And that's literally the machine behind the most powerful rock band, one of the highest selling rock bands in the history of music, and that guy is such a key integral part to what that band does. And no one knows his name. And that guy's gonna come and go and probably not get the credit he deserves for what he did.

Maybe we're just more replaceable. People just look at bands, and when they see someone like me, who's a big personality and loud and obnoxious and puts his two cents into every decision the band makes and is pretty good at drums, but not fucking the next coming of John Bonham or anything, I can see where someone would look at me and they'd be like, "This would be way easier for me if this was some dude I paid a thousand dollars a week, who has fucking six pack abs, who went to Berklee, who can play this shit in his fucking sleep." I understand that aspect of it. But I like to think that I bring some flavor that that dude couldn't bring, a little extra spice.

"GOOD HANG"

All genuine communities have institutionalized behavior in . . . education of newcomers in the appropriate values, attitudes, and behavior. . . . The young jazz musician typically comes to the jazz community as a late teenager, already socialized by the wider community. As a jazz musician he is re-socialized; this involves a partial defection from his earliest set of values and an acquisition of a partially new set from a new set of significant others.

ROBERT A. STEBBINS, "A THEORY OF THE JAZZ COMMUNITY"[66]

Talented performers belong to the industry long before it displays them; otherwise they would not be so eager to fit in.

THEODOR ADORNO AND MAX HORKHEIMER, "THE CULTURE
INDUSTRY: ENLIGHTENMENT AS MASS DECEPTION"[67]

Bands, it's fair to say, don't hire based on orchestra-style blind auditions. There is no aspiration to unfiltered meritocracy. In fact, a truism of the business is that employability and longevity are to a great extent social—is the musician a "good hang"? (As critical theorists Theodor Adorno and Max Horkheimer wrote, the latter is often subsumed into the former: "In every career, and especially in the liberal professions, expert knowledge is linked with prescribed standards of conduct; this can easily lead to the illusion that expert knowledge is the only thing that counts.")[68] After all, a touring band spends twenty-four hours together but only an hour or two on stage; so personalities matter a lot more than technical chops in band hierarchies—to quote Scott Spillane, "If you're an asshole, no one is going to [want] you to be in their band." Obviously, it's a sliding scale: a front person has more leeway to be difficult than a support musician ("Some members of a band [can be] viewed as difficult, but never the bass player," says Andrew Seward). In some cases, socially fluent members of the crew—or tour managers, by virtue of their logistical authority and access to off-road management—can exercise more influence than lower-status band members. It is worth marking that hiring based on this nebulous affinity ("I just like having X around, they're cool") is one of the factors that buttress the biases and homogeneity for which the rock world has been criticized: people tend to like being around people who share their cultural and social outlook, and anyone expending energy questioning or confronting the norms of their touring party is unlikely to last long.

Those norms and expectations of behavior are rarely explicitly taught or stated. This can act as a sorting mechanism: those more gifted at picking up cues, and malleable enough to adapt to them, are more likely to thrive in the business.[69] Older mentors play a large role, both modelling and correcting, by methods ranging from a quiet word to outright hazing.[70] Musicians whose parents (usually fathers) are also musicians are clearly at an advantage; and it is perhaps worth observing that these unspoken norms are often driven by traditionally masculine values.

Band people have a variety of opinions on the general rule succinctly expressed by guitarist and producer Josh Leo: "Being a good sideman is a lot like being a good kindergartener: plays well with others."[71] They tend to come down very strongly on one side or the other of the question, as if either answer were self-evident: some agree wholeheartedly ("If you practice enough, you can get the music together, but it's hard to change people's personalities," says Mike Watt; ditto keyboardist [and Fenway Park organist] Josh Kantor: "I would rather play tunes that I'm not into with people that I am into, than the other way around"); some find this attitude harder to maintain than others. Others agree up to a point, but when push comes to shove they prioritize musical results—if there's a difference of opinion in the studio, they say, you can smooth over an argument post-facto, but you can't change a record after it's made ("I'll get into fights with people for something I think better serves the song or the band, probably ten times out of ten," says Benny Horowitz). Some find that their relationship to the question changes over time, with youthful arrogance giving way to an understanding that it's better to be easy to deal with; for others, as they age (or grow more secure in their reputation), it matters less what people think of them.

Band people, appropriately, often learn this lesson by example. When Tune-Yards opened for Arcade Fire, the former's Nate Brenner identified the latter's Stuart Bogie as a model: "Immediately I realized—this guy, the reason he has such a good career is his attitude. I'd totally hire him for anything, and want to keep working with him just to keep hanging out with him. That's the best example of someone that has a career playing the saxophone based on his networking and his talent, but [also] you want him around because he's such a fun person." Bogie, for his part, says that it's "incredibly important" to him to be perceived as easy to work with, and doesn't find that attitude difficult to maintain: "At the end of the day, I'm no hassle for the artist. I don't object to their ideas; I don't make faces . . . I also don't kiss up, because I want them to trust my opinion. So basically I shut up, smile and try and play my ass off. I spent eleven years in bands and orchestras learning how to be attentive and obedient as a player. . . . You have to learn to make this as smooth for the artist as you can."

Josh Kantor is similarly inspired by Jon Wurster and Kelly Hogan: "Obviously [Wurster] brings so much to the table as a drummer, but I sense that he brings a lot to the table as a traveling [and] recording bandmate interpersonally, and being somebody who people want to work with because they just want to be in the same room with him. The same with Kelly Hogan. She also is a fantastic musician and fantastic person, and bands want to be around her, and bands want her to be in their bands. So I want to be like Kelly and Jon."[72] Wurster, too, learned by (negative) example: "I see so many—not just drummers, but instrumentalists or singers who are way better at what they do than I am at what I do, they are at a genius level, but they don't have those personal relationship skills that are just as important as the musical ability. . . . Nobody wanted to work with them after a while, and they were trouble; or they became involved in substance abuse, and they fell by the wayside."

Many musicians self-deprecatingly give their accommodating personalities more credit for their careers than their musicianship. "I think being a good hang gets me probably more jobs than my musicianship, and I preach about that," says Thor Harris. Jay Gonzalez thinks "honestly that was a big part of me getting the [Drive-By Truckers] gig. I don't think it was necessarily all a musical thing. I think they knew I was easygoing, and they probably needed that at the time, chemistry-wise." Shahzad Ismaily feels "sometimes, in my darkest moments, that's the only reason I have work. It's not because I can play well at all." Scott McCaughey doesn't think "people come to me and ask me to play on their records or tour with them because of my musicianship necessarily; [it's] for my personality. I think that people think I'm easy to get along with, and I'm somewhat capable on a number of different instruments." A not-insignificant aspect of Peter Hughes's admission into the Mountain Goats was his affability: "Back in the day, John [Darnielle] was an intense dude. He was very high-octane, and in a way that was a little bit off-putting to some people. And for whatever reason, I just had a lot of patience for that." Josh Freese even became sensitive to the implication that "'Yeah, Josh Freese gets all those gigs because he's a nice guy. He's got good stories.' I'm like, 'Well, fuck, I can play.' Shit, man, I started getting real tight and defensive about it."

For certain instruments and roles, an accommodating personality is a competitive advantage in a business in which (quoting MacLeod) "the freelance sideperson's livelihood depends in large part on maintaining good relations—on the surface at least—with leaders and contractors."[73] Guitarist Matt Kinsey lives in Austin, where "everybody's a guitar player, too many guitar players. . . . I do like to be pleasant, but . . . it's important, 'cause there's a lot of people that could do what I do." George Rush knows "guys that have got gigs with their personalities. The guy that replaced me in the Losers Lounge has a real bass player personality—easy to get along with, 'This is what I'll do, and I'm not gonna play too many crazy notes.' I ended up adapting my personality to fit my perception of what the role of the instrument is—I became a little less cantankerous. I became a little less precious. There are a lot of really good bass players in New York City, and guys would have lined up waiting to take your gig. So maybe I better figure out how to be a little more easygoing."

Jim Sclavunos emphasizes the trade-off a support musician must make between being accommodating and being taken seriously as an artistic collaborator:

> It's too easy to fall into the clown role as a drummer. I think there were too many good-natured, fun-loving drummers in the '60s that set a bad precedent—Keith Moon in particular. Yes, I think it is good to get along and have an enjoyable atmosphere. But sometimes work gets pretty intense, and if you feel strongly about something you have to take a stand on it. . . . Sometimes

people get pretty hot under the collar about their opinions about certain minute things that other people can't even hear, but to fellow musicians it might be of the upmost importance at that particular moment. In those circumstances I don't think it pays to be obnoxious or antagonistic, but I do think sometimes you have to take a strong position, and that may not make for the most pleasant interaction.

Joe Lally came into Fugazi determined to enhance the collective nature of the band—not because he was a bass player, but because of strong convictions about what makes bands work:

I joined [Fugazi] knowing that all the previous bands all the three other guys had been involved in had broken up, to me, prematurely; and there was always a member [for whom] it [didn't] work for them for whatever reason. And the band ends, or they go away to school, or they don't want to [continue]. But I really set out to try and be a band member that was also going to make the band work. I was going to do everything I could to make it a continuous project, and I wasn't going to say no to somebody else's face: "Oh no, you wrote that; I'm not going to play that." There was a conscious decision from the very beginning, because Ian had ideas that other people had rejected and I thought they were good, and I could add to [them]. I was going to be part of a band, and I was gonna make this thing work. I always felt that your role is more than just being a giant personality.

The social aspects of band life are, of course, exacerbated on the road (especially on the kind of tour Nels Cline calls "failure runs"). "If you have to live together—six people in a van for six weeks at a time," says Scott Brackett, "in those conditions it's advantageous to be well-liked. People will look after your gear better, if you leave something on the stage. If you've been off flirting with girls instead of packing up your gear every night, and you've been a drunk asshole to everybody, people are definitely not going to look after your shit for you. . . .

Or when you get drunk and do something stupid, you might not get fired if you're pleasant to be around. Whereas, if you're an asshole—I've seen guys get canned who I don't think would have, if they had a different disposition." Glenn Kotche has realized "seeing other players who just blow my mind, but maybe don't get asked to play a lot—and I understand, oh yeah, I've seen this person be pretty difficult, or this person's always late, or this person is always borrowing gear, or is missing some piece of their gear."

> In a free-lance system, people get jobs on the basis of their reputations. . . . Support work can in principle be done by any competent technician. . . . You need ability, then, for free-lance success, but it is not enough. . . . Reputation helps.
> HOWARD BECKER, *ART WORLDS*[74]

Since most band work is acquired by word-of-mouth, says Todd Beene, "When you start talking about—whether it's crew or another musician—'Do you guys know anybody who could do this, for this amount of time?,' the first thing you are thinking about is people you really like and get along with on the road. If somebody is an exceptional player, but just doesn't 'get it,' and is a pain to be around, that person is not going to get very much work." When you are "living in a tube with wheels one hundred fifty days a year, with everybody's butt and elbow right in your nose," says Rick Steff, "you can be the best player in the world, but if nobody wants to sit next to you on the bus, you've got a problem." Mike Watt says, "Especially the way I tour, with no days off, and you just keep going: these guys who can feel the pea under twenty-five mattresses—I used to put a tiara on the dash of the boat. I just have to point at it."

It's not simply a matter of musicianship versus clubbability, says Carla Kihlstedt. A level of resilience and adaptability says something about how a player will perform in a collaborative relationship:

> If you were to look at a core sample of my life and take a look at a slide show of one night a month, one night would be sleeping

in a bus with a bunch of stinky sweaty men . . . then the next month, I'd be staying in a four-star hotel in Mallorca on tour with Tin Hat; or I'd be sleeping on someone's couch. So I think being a collaborative musician teaches you flexibility in every aspect of your life. It teaches you a non-judgmental flexibility: "Okay, here's the story tonight." And it might be that the venue that you're playing, and sleeping on someone's couch afterwards, is one of the most fabulous local, heartfelt, open-hearted experiences you'll have all year. Very quickly, you learn not to judge things or experiences by their outward appearance. And not everyone is set up to do that.

It's worth mentioning the effort it can take for some musicians to meet the social expectations of band and touring life. "Just hanging can be tough," says Jay Gonzalez. "As much as I do place a big premium on being a guy people want to hang out with, and enjoy socializing, I can also be pretty private. I remember that especially having eleven roommates [on tour] was taking a toll on me. I [had been] living with just my wife and kid for so long, [that] it had been a long time since I had constantly been around folks. I'm social enough, but that constant meeting folks is sort of overwhelming. Basically, when I go home, I shut in for a week and don't talk to anybody." Daniel Hart is "not a hanger, honestly, especially on the road. It's a job to me, and I love seeing friends in cities, people I wouldn't get to see if I wasn't going on tour. I don't drink and I don't do any drugs either. . . . Usually, if there is something happening after the show, I would never go. I would just go back to the hotel. Especially if I had to sing, I just wanted to make sure that I could get as much sleep as possible, so my voice would be rested." Ara Babajian "find[s] that a hard thing to maintain, because I prefer to go straight back to the hotel and read once the show is done. . . . I've always been like that, but it's not the best way to promote yourself, to promote inter-band relations, [and] to give yourself a reputation as someone who's good to have around. I have to sort of force myself out of my shell in order to improve my reputation. Some days I have the energy for it, and some days I don't.

I can turn it on and off, but it gets harder and harder as I get older to do that." Mike Yannich says, "A lot of times I'm a chameleon; I tend to follow by example how other people are acting. If you're on tour for a long time, you end up being irritable, feeling that the other people were hard to deal with, so then I became hard to deal with too." Personalities inevitably show, says Kotche. "If you're an asshole and you pretend to be all friendly around people, the asshole side is going to show its head at some point."

While many musicians describe their relationship to likability as a progression, that evolution goes both ways.[75] When woodwind player Doug Wieselman was starting out, he was more self-conscious and harder to get along with: "I was scared of everybody," he says, "just a lot more fear." Mike Sneeringer feels that he has "become much more docile and much more giving as a drummer," and feels he has "been positively rewarded for that." Benny Horowitz "used to be this guy who was like, everything requires brutal honesty all the time, and life is too short and there's no bullshit. You get older, and I started to feel like, all right, [I'm] a little much to be around sometimes." A band grows together, as well—the longer the catalog, the less life-or-death importance attaches to each aesthetic decision. The Mountain Goats, Hughes says, "have been playing music together for so long that you can tell when somebody feels really strongly about it—[if] that's the thing that's really important to you, you can have it."

Others move away from prioritizing pliability. "I'd rather people thought that I was good at playing," says guitarist Katie Harkin. "I've gotten less concerned with [pleasing] as I've gotten older." To hire someone solely because they're affable, she says, is "like hiring a therapist rather than hiring a guitar player." Lori Barbero says that when she was younger, "I used to think about [being liked] and it used to worry me, and I used to make sure that I was a people pleaser. Now that I'm older, I don't give a fuck what anyone thinks." Meredith Yayanos says that she cares "less and less as I age. . . . I really value a bit of bluntness and a bit of ruffled feathers over seething quiet."

Paul Wallfisch would "much rather have an ornery talented guy. Ornery is one thing—prickly and hard and edgy can be great and fantastic. You can be all those things without being an asshole. And there are a lot of very passive-aggressive people out there who think they are sweet, but they're assholes." The personal and the aesthetic are related, he says: "Ugly people tend to express themselves in ugly ways." Janet Weiss wants to be a good hang, but admits, "I can't say I'm necessarily easy: I'm very forward. I don't like to keep things in. If something is bothering me, I want to talk about it. I get riled up; I'm emotional." She adds:

> But also, [as a drummer,] you are *banging* on something. I'm so primal when I'm playing and it's very emotional, and I expect *myself* to have it be real, and to have it be about something that's personal. And sometimes it's hard to just turn that off and be mellow about touring, or things you're uncomfortable with, or how you want the band, what direction you want the band to go in. It's an easy thing to get emotional about.

GENDER POLITICS

The music business has a (deserved) reputation for sexism, but the women I spoke to for this book pushed back on the idea that it was monolithic, pervasive, or particularly resistant. "I don't understand, honestly, when I hear women talk about 'a sexist industry' and all that," says Melissa Auf der Maur. "Everywhere is sexist. What isn't? Music business is a little bit better than others—you think of a CEO of a bank; I mean, I feel like I'd be more likely to have a decent experience in music as a woman. . . . I had the best tour of my entire touring life on my first album. Robert Smith from the Cure curated his own traveling Lollapalooza called Curiosa, and I was the only girl in the entire tour. That was 2004, and I had already spent the '90s in a rock band where we were generally the only women on a bill," and it was "not at all, never" a challenge. "Not an issue," says Jean Cook.

It's worth proposing two caveats: first, that the majority of these interviews were conducted before the renewed attention to sexual harassment in 2017 and beyond, which caused many people to re-evaluate their experiences. Second, the sample here is almost certainly self-selecting: anecdotal evidence suggests that many women who found their experiences in music intolerable simply left the community: "I have certainly been in a position where I have felt like I was not treated as an equal because I was a woman," says Eliza Hardy Jones, "and it drove me insane, and I did not stay." Nels Cline has "seen that again and again with female artists, that the guys tend to throw a lot more shade and a lot more attitude on women than they do on other guys. . . . I'm sitting there working for a female artist—let's say it's [Geraldine Fibbers singer] Carla [Bozulich], let's say it's my wife Yuka [Honda]—and the recording engineer, when I'm tracking, will start asking me all the questions instead of her. She's the artist, ask her, she's sitting right next to you in the fucking control room. But they keep asking the guy! That shit's unbelievable that it still happens, but it happens all the time. Guys can be not in reality sometimes about who the boss is, and they want to be the boss, so they just start acting out in all kinds of weird ways. Some of that happened in the Geraldine Fibbers; and then Carla, she used to say, would have to become 'mean mommy.' And she hated becoming 'mean mommy.'"

Still, the band people in this book paint a picture of a generally considerate environment, especially among fellow musicians. Jenny Conlee has "never been bothered by being the only woman in the band. Most of the time there are other women on tour either as crew or extra musicians. In my working environment, everyone is pretty respectful. I feel like one of the guys, I guess; I want to be treated as an equal. I do equal work, carrying gear, setting up the PA, driving, and no one treats me any different. When I was younger, I was very proud and wanted to do everything myself; as I get older it feels OK to let people help me with the heavy lifting. There have been a few incidents at venues where security did not believe that I was in the band, telling me that 'girlfriends' were not allowed backstage. I have no problem setting them straight on that." For Caitlin Gray, "the challenge definitely, for the most part, hasn't been among other musicians. The bigger challenge is to show up at a festival and realize that there's no other women to hang out with, or that we don't really come across to sound engineers or lighting directors or anything. So it's less issues interpersonally within the band, and more a general sense of feeling like you're in the minority." Auf der Maur used her presence as a message in itself: "In the case of Hole, we were the only women on the bill usually, and we were making a larger statement than just the band Hole. For me, a very big part of my presence there was just representing any old girl playing bass, just representing women. [Also,] I was completely behind the idea that the wild, demonized witch woman [Love] needed to have a platform to speak. As much as she was difficult, I do believe that Courtney's story to the world is important." In both of the bands (Sleepytime Gorilla Museum and Tin Hat) with which Carla Kihlstedt did the bulk of her touring, she was the only woman, and "always relished it when another woman would come on tour with Sleepytime; it was always really a welcome change. I honestly never did spend a whole lot of time thinking about it. It felt like those relationships were as much family as anything, and it honestly didn't faze me one way or another." She goes on:

> Recently I've done a bunch of other projects that involve more women, and I've totally enjoyed that. I do think women are inherently more complicated—myself included, in many ways. And I know that might be a—I don't mean to throw the gauntlet down by that statement, but I can tell you as a mother [with] a boy and a girl, that's true in my experience, both in my own life and in my life as a parent. It wasn't on purpose that I was the only woman in those two groups. It was really by happenstance.

"In most bands that I have been in, I have been the only woman in the band," says Hardy Jones. "And there are things about that that are challenging; and there are things about that that I think people assume would be challenging, that are not. I am a very old-school feminist. I am very loud about my ideas, about being treated like an equal." She adds:

> I think people assume that my delicate woman sensibilities would be offended by rude messed-up men, which is just silliness. I grew up with boys, and I got friends that are guys. I like dudes. I'm very dude-ish. I've never been on a tour and been

like, "All these dudes with their foul mouths." People will say that to me, "How do you deal with all these guys, they're so smelly"—and I'm like, that's not a thing I've ever even thought about. The thought that, as a woman, it's been harder for me to be on tour because somebody's armpits smell—that's not something that I've struggled with.

Still, "if you look at my career and my tours and all that stuff, about 99.9 percent of the time, I'm the only woman," says Jenny Scheinman. "And it is tedious. It is something that has become more unappealing as I have gotten older." She continues:

It was something that I was totally blind to, definitely through my twenties. And I think blind to it because I was so obsessed with learning, and was a little bit oblivious to the personal dynamics of everything, just trying to learn and trying to get my next gig. I just put up with a lot, but after a while I . . . looked around and realized that I was surrounded by men, and wanted to hang with some of my peeps as well.

It actually pushed me into doing more singing gigs and work with singers, because the audience for that genre tends to have more women. It wasn't really conscious, but I think part of what I really got off on when I started singing was that I was looking out into an audience that was not just men over sixty and eighteen-year-old guitar players—not to diss the jazz audience, but when you tour as a jazz musician that is a lot of what you see. I just did a long tour opening for Ani DiFranco and playing in her band. It is a totally different experience. And it was long waited-for, and totally enjoyed.

3

THE WORK OF BAND PEOPLE

Music fans, but also musicians themselves, are often uncomfortable defining playing in a band as "work" in the traditional sense. There is a feeling that the platitude "do what you love and you'll never work a day in your life" should apply, that gratefulness should trump complaint, that as artists, they should be above the petty concerns of commerce. As one musician told Matt Stahl "about indie rock band life, ironically reversing the US Navy's recruiting slogan. . . . It's not just an adventure, it's a job."[1]

The oft-cited metaphor of band as "family" misses something crucial about bands, wrote Deena Weinstein. "You'd think that bands were held together with nothing more than emotion. The metaphor . . . erases the sense of a rock band as a small corporation with objectively evaluated workers." She quotes guitarist Mike Campbell: "Groups are a very complicated thing. . . . It's like a family, it's like a business relationship, it's a very emotional thing."[2] Even more, this profoundly fraught and complicated relationship must be renegotiated, even reinvented, each time; usually by young people who have no sense that they are setting up the creative and financial parameters by which—if they are successful—they'll have to live for decades: "Rock bands start from scratch. Most groups with which we involve ourselves—at work, at home, in recreation, religion, politics, and other pursuits—have a model for roles and authority that precedes any specific set of people. This structure serves as a blueprint that newly formed groups can more or less follow. Bands have no such models, except for genre requirements. . . . The media's inattention to the working life of bands and, worse, their promulgation of the nearly impossible all-are-creative model, leaves each set of young musicians to reinvent the wheel themselves."[3]

But the question of work is not simply one of money: it's a narrative of one's life, and a statement of one's worth. If music is work—more specifically, to quote sociologist Mike Jones, it is "simultaneously work and pleasure; more accurately, it is work masquerading as leisure"[4]—we can discuss "the music industry as workplace," with hierarchies of power relations, instabilities in status that manifest in tangible ways, shifting ratios of art and craft, and, especially, the status of the musician as a worker relative to the products of their labor. As sociologist Mark Banks put it, "Creative cultural worker[s] exist at the very axis point of political struggle between the forces of art and commerce."[5]

Cultural work is work. It may be poorly or irregularly compensated; it may be characterized by failure; it may be—as Matt Stahl wrote in his analysis of recording artists and the politics of labor—hard to think of culture workers as laborers (or for the workers themselves to self-conceive), since "the stars of popular music often appear to be so free and to be doing such enjoyable, expressive, and fulfilling work that it almost seems strange to think of them as working people."[6] But by any definition, popular musicians—band people—are engaged in the creation of commodities (whether reproduced material or ephemeral performance) for exchange and do it in professionalized workplaces: "They write, perform, and produce in highly organized teams that demand coordination," wrote Robert Faulkner; "they face routine work pressures, try to handle mistakes at work, control the activities of colleagues, and cope with the risks of personal failure."[7]

The worlds of culture work and wage labor are converging. Unfortunately, wage labor is coming to resemble cultural work, in all its precarity disguised as agency, rather than the other way around. The glib comparison is via a facile pun on the so-called "gig economy," which, in its purest imaginary, turns every worker into a free-lance contractor. It's marketed as a worker's dream—flexibility and agency—but any musician has a specific and relevant story to tell about how that fantasy functions in an American political economy still very much built on the assumption of the "company man," on W2s, regular paychecks, and employer-furnished health plans. (Record labels have also found it convenient to treat musicians as contractors rather than employees, and health benefits enjoyed by label employees are not traditionally included in musicians' deals, at any level.)[8] Musicians were the canaries in the coal mine of the precariat, accomplices in their own swindle ("Thanks @spotify for adding my song to their #BBQParty #playlist!!"); and the musician can sound very much like social theorist Götz Brief's definition of the efficiently alienated worker: "From the standpoint of efficient management, the ideal production material is described as follows: It is obtained at the lowest possible cost but is nevertheless 100 percent effective; it is highly adaptable, is economical to use, and is readily moveable from place to place; it is a calculable quantity, can be used without unwelcome side effects, and can be replaced at a moment's notice."[9] For all musicians' stereotypically leftist sympathies, "the rock profession is based on a highly individualistic, competitive approach to music, an approach rooted in ambition and free enterprise," wrote critic Simon Frith. "The ideology of rock, in its uneasy combination of professionalism and nonconformity, remains essentially petit bourgeois" in its values, especially those quintessentially American values like striving and bootstrapping.[10] Because there's so much pressure in pop music from people willing to work for basically nothing, an oversupply of amateur or semi-pro wannabes much greater than the ranks of career professionals—what Taylor refers to as "the reserve army of labor for the capitalist music industry"[11]—a hypothetical union to control, say, fees at a rock club paying five bands a night, is hardly imaginable.[12]

The work of band people, then, is inseparable from the work of "normal" people going to their job, dealing with its daily frustrations, balancing the demands of career and family, organizing their lives to fulfill what they perceive as financial, creative, or personal necessities. (Albeit in a workplace with looser than usual standards around on-the-job intoxication, and one which has outsourced its HR responsibilities to social media.) Scott McCaughey joined R.E.M. at the peak of their stadium-filling stardom just as he became a father: "We really needed money, you know . . . at the same time, you know, when you're gone nine months out of the year, it puts a heavy strain on everything. My daughter still looks back on it and kind of hates the whole music biz, because I was gone all the time."

Seen from afar, playing guitar in what was then one of the world's biggest rock bands has a glamour that dissolves such concerns in the glare: the portrayal of art as work strips it of a mystique which is valued by both those who consume and those who make it. But workaday rockers, even at the highest levels, share the same frequent-flyer lounges as traveling business people, buy the same stowable rolling suitcases, and spend the same hours on FaceTime with their families. The young lawyer who realizes she won't make partner and leaves to hang up her own shingle shares an experience with the third songwriter in a band who goes solo. The architect who prefers quotidian home-remodeling jobs to star-making office buildings has something in common with the bass player happy to play a supporting role—"I love being the fat guy on the side doing his thing," says Jon Rauhouse. And many people have had the experience of accommodating the sky-high ambitions of their youth to the more modest, circumscribed reality of their middle age: one realizes their limitations, or rejects the pressures of putting oneself forward, or prioritizes the comfort of a supporting role ("I needed to take a break from being the guy who wrote the songs. . . . I get to travel, I get to play, but I don't have the pressure of being the creative guy," says songwriter-turned-support musician Mike Yannich). These are the realities of working adults, whatever their career.

This is all a rather bloodless and unromantic way of thinking about rock and roll, one might say, an art form that reveres its Dionysian roots. But the figure of the rocker has sobered significantly since its Byronic peak in the 1970s and '80s: for one thing, the apparent prudishness of younger musicians is the natural decency, or discretion, of a generation raised on new language about sexual propriety and fearful of online public shaming for off-the-clock behavior. More to the point though, without the giant sloshing pools of industry money that once accompanied rock success, would-be carousers have to take more responsibility for their own logistics, behavior, and consequences. In the decadent era, bands might not engage in extensive touring until they were at a financial level that involved a staff of enablers; the DIY movement of the '80s and beyond means that any band who reaches a level you've heard of has spent years with a baseline level of trustworthiness and collegiality: someone has to be sober enough to drive after the show; someone has to order the merch, book the hotel rooms, and rent or pay the insurance on the van. My interlocutors for this book repeatedly emphasized that they prioritize being a "good hang"—both in choosing collaborators, and in defining how they would like to project their own personality—over pure musicianship. A refrain: band people are workplace colleagues.

CREATIVE COLLABORATION

But the premise of their workplace is collective artistry. Novelist Anthony Trollope credited the man who brought him his 5:30 a.m. coffee as a central contributor to his creative output. Howard Becker cites this as an example of the large and sometimes nebulous network of collaborators who make art works possible, a reality which is often at odds with the multifarious emotional and financial incentives to assign credit to single creators: "Art worlds routinely create and use reputations, because they have an interest in individuals."[13] Still, Becker says, it is clear that "all artistic work, like all human activity, involves the joint activity of a number, often a large number of people. Through their cooperation, the art work we eventually see or hear comes to be and continues to be. The work always shows signs of that cooperation."[14] The review of a theatrical production singles out directors and star performers, but is enabled by the set designers, dramaturgs, stage managers, and gofers. A book is credited to an author, but requires the input of copy editors, book designers, and printers. "A musical idea in the form of a written score has to be performed," wrote Becker, "and musical performance requires training, skill, and judgment. Once a play is written, it must be acted. . . . Imagine . . .

a situation in which one person did everything: made everything, invented everything, had all the ideas, performed or executed the work, experienced and appreciated it, all without the assistance or help of anyone else. We can hardly imagine such a thing. . . . The list of credits which ends the typical Hollywood feature film gives explicit recognition to such a finely divided set of activities."[15]

The post-1960s mythology of the rock world combined a conflicting valuation of the band as collective unit with the romantic ideology of individual creativity: "It is here that the major ideological tension present in the creative process of rock bands entered the mix," wrote Deena Weinstein.[16] This tension—between the standard narrative of the individual "genius" and the reality of collective creativity—had already presented itself in American music in the new institution of the jazz combo. Per musicologist Christopher Small:

> In jazz a soloist appears at his or her best (which is not the same as "most virtuosic") when collaborating with equals, the composer realizes his or her compositions most fully when they are taken up and developed by fellow musicians, the individual realizes his or her gifts best in the company of a committed group. Thus the notion found in many histories and other studies of jazz, of the great individual artist-hero—Charlie Parker, John Coltrane, Miles Davis for instance—creating out of his own nature and genius, has to be treated with great caution.
>
> Of course, there have been many outstanding artists over the history of jazz, but we should beware of treating them as great isolated originators, as the classical tradition treats Beethoven, Mozart, and J. S. Bach . . . or indeed as the world of commercial entertainment—showbiz—treats its stars.
>
> . . . The Basie band consisted of individuals each of whom was in his or her own right a musician of superb skill and musical intelligence, who realized those qualities to their fullest by placing them at the service of the common enterprise. It was a remarkable social, no less than musical, achievement, not the least of which lay in the realization that the problems can never

be solved once and for all but must be solved again and again every day and require constant vigilance and diplomacy.[17]

Even more than what Ruth Finnegan calls the "composition-in-performance" model of the jazz band, the rock band typically exemplifies a model of "collective composition . . . the 'prior composition-through-practice mode.'"[18] That is, regardless of which member(s) bring in the building blocks of a song, the compositional process is to a large extent collective: "This system of 'prior composition' is different from that of the classical model not just in being non-written but also because a piece is not by just one individual or fully worked out before being given to the players. Rather, it is developed through a series of practices by a whole group who then themselves perform it as their own joint composition. One member of the group usually starts it off by 'coming up with an original idea'—a snatch of tune, riff, theme, set of rhythms or chords, or (less often) a verbal phrase or verse. This is played or sung to the group and gradually worked up into a complete piece."[19] Finnegan described a writing rehearsal she witnessed, whose protracted wrangling and vague language will be familiar to anyone who's ever been in a band practice:

The keyboard player had brought along one of his songs which he played to the others, and provided skeleton chord charts. They played it through roughly then stopped to discuss how to change and develop it—should the intro be repeated twice? How could the chorus, verse and break be combined best? What should be the chord sequences just there? How about trying them this way (partial demonstration by one player) or those that way? How about trying this bit again with different percussion combinations? Was it all "too E-minorish"? Then came another play-through, with the drummer trying out new developments, breaking off to discuss yet again and readjusting the electrical equipment. The rhythm guitarist was encouraged to "do something special if he felt inspired," with the others giving him a cushion to take off from. Later they went on to other pieces with similar stops and starts: was it too "jolly," needing "sharpening up"? Would the bass be more effective playing a simple leisurely downwards scale rather than cluttering it up with chords? Would the words sound better changed round? Was B-minor or D-minor more effective on the keyboard? Should the drummer play less forcefully just there or was it brilliant the way it was? Similar try-outs and discussions went on with all the pieces, for hours in all over a series of weekly rehearsals, resulting finally in a public performance at a local booking. The two main composers mostly took the leading roles in the discussion, but it was not a case of individuals directing a group but of creative participation by all four players, working out the piece collectively for joint performance.

This was not an isolated case, for almost all the bands stressed the collective and protracted process of developing their own material, at the same time attributing responsibility for particular elements to named individual players.[20]

This "oral and active group learning mode" is the core, and even distinctive, experience of creative collaboration in a band context. Additionally, because of this method of group composition and arrangement, individual members are less easily replaceable than jazz musicians operating from a knowledge bank of shared repertoire and ad hoc arrangements: individual idiolects become, in many cases, indivisible from the distinctive "sound" of a group. In some sense, this individual autonomy within a group identity is what's offered to a band person in lieu of a regular salary or defined working hierarchy: "Not only was each player a principal (the only player for his or her particular part)," wrote Finnegan, "but the balance, interaction, even the musical content was worked out by individual players. . . . The players worked in an atmosphere of autonomy and self-fulfillment." She added:

That this did not necessarily prevent dissension was obvious from the short life of many bands; indeed, the personal intensity of this mode of musical expression perhaps rendered such break-ups particularly emotive. Nevertheless the creative experience inherent in this musical co-operation was one element pulling the members together in a highly personal commitment to the band and its joint achievements.[21]

It is this phenomenon of not just collective composition, but a composite voice, that is the beating heart of both the creative excitement and crediting conflict that animates many band narratives. The post-1960s emphasis on bands which generated their own material was a less obvious fit with the existing legal and financial framework of songwriting and publishing oriented around professionalized songwriting teams; and the romantic ideology of the artist/genius that accompanied it made the psychological stakes of individual versus collective credit more charged. East Bay Ray joined his other Dead Kennedys bandmates in a lawsuit against former lead singer Jello Biafra over issues that included songwriting credits:

Jello Biafra, the lead singer, he wrote most of the words, not all; and I wrote a lot of the music. Some songs were collaborations with all the musicians. We had different processes; Klaus Flouride, our bass player, he'd bring in a complete song. I brought in complete songs. Biafra would bring in lyrics—somebody described it [as] he'd have, like, a crayon drawing [of a song], and Klaus and I would put it in musical forms. Then other songs, like "Holiday in Cambodia," they came from jam sessions in the rehearsal studio and the parts were put together to make the song. I think our best songs were more collaborative.

One of the things that made it work is that we all listen to slightly different music. Klaus has a huge 78 collection and is into '30s and '40s jazz, and I was born into '60s music and probably I like melody more than the others, more pop music; and Biafra was into garage bands. So everybody brought something a little bit different to the table, and then two and two equals five.

[It's] not democratic. You don't vote on art. But—like a good stew—you can put in different ingredients, some vegetables and some broth and some spices, and that's what a group collaborative band is. Lennon and McCartney together wrote better songs than Lennon did by himself or McCartney did by himself.

But more on the dirty nuts and bolts of credit and money later. The core work of a band person is in the creative collaboration which involves a balance between individual voice and "serving the song," the translation of often vague directions into concrete musical ideas, integrating into pre-existing musical relationships, negotiating the difference between live and recorded performance, and all the extra-musical skills that make one musician invaluable where another of equal technical skill may be replaceable. The most crucial of those skills is, no doubt, the ability to exercise the diplomacy that makes creative collaboration both possible and a goal musicians find valuable enough to subsume their individual voices. "You always hear people saying, 'You guys made this better than I could have imagined,'" says Todd Sickafoose. "That is a real thing, and the whole goal ... the beauty of collaboration [is] the Ouija board thing: no one spells the sentence you are making, but all together it somehow happens."

Gerry Leonard has concluded that making music "is a very social event, and it can be a political event. You have to be very careful not to tip the balance in the wrong way, because if you make somebody insecure, you're not going to get anything good from them; or if you make the artist insecure, you're going to start developing a wall between you and the artist." The balance, for bandleaders working with musicians, is between treating those musicians as tools with which to manifest one's vision, and treating them as independent artistic agents. "You have to intuit or consciously decide how to constructively relate to your band members so that they are as expressive as they can be and feel totally free, and like they are contributing a lot," says Jenny Scheinman, "but also that you are able to see your composition blossom and find the voice within your head [from] when you wrote them." Leonard is "always interested in what the musicians in the room have to say. If nobody has an opinion, then I have an opinion. But if somebody says something, I'm always like, 'Why did they say that?' I'm curious about it, even if it is upstream against the way [I] want to work, or [my] idea. Very often I find, if you remain open to that stuff, that you can actually work those ideas in, in some way. Maybe not in that moment—maybe it comes later, or maybe it comes in the fourth version of the song or something. You go back to, 'What was that idea you had about taking those two bars and putting them here' or whatever. When you create a situation like that, then people feel invested, and they feel like they're being represented, and they feel like they can play as a musician, and that you want them to play and do what they do—and that's when you're going to get the best out of them." Conversely, he says, there's a security for a musician in working for a leader who is able to precisely articulate what they want: "It's always difficult to go to somebody and say, 'Can you play less?' or "Don't play here.' [But when] I'm in on a session and somebody else is producing, and goes 'Gerry, I want you to play in the chorus; I don't want you to play on the verse,' I'm like, 'That's great. Now I know what to focus on.' When you're working with experienced musicians, they're happy to take those kinds of directions, because they know that you're not trying to steal the limelight or shut them up."

"Something I have been puzzling over for years," says Scheinman, "is that in different genres of music there is completely different etiquette about how bandleaders instruct their side people and how bands talk to each other about the music. Long-time string quartets famously argue so much, in such a personal way, that they have their own therapists. They will get into long disputes over up-bows and down-bows, the finest details of the articulation of a piece." She continues:

> This isn't true of all jazz musicians, but in general, there is this tremendous respect for what the players are bringing in terms of their interpretation of the piece. And because they are not used to really directing each other—you wouldn't sing a drummer a beat, or tell them to use a specific kind of hit on the snare—jazz musicians get completely thrown off when you do direct them. They are totally not used to it, and can become extremely self-conscious and clam up and leave all

that intuitive momentum that usually gets them into a badass solo or a super-expressive moment.

Peter Erskine has an anecdote about playing on an album Barry Manilow was producing:

> He seemed like a pleasant enough guy, but he started micro-managing the jazz group, which is just not an effective way to get the best out of the players. Then this guy came over and started to say to me, "And yeah, Peter, don't play that part on that cymbal; play it on the other." And I held my hands up and I started to shoo him away, like "Shoo, get, go away," like to a fly. I said, "Don't even think of starting to go there with me."
>
> Looking back, was that defensive? Yeah, but it was also more establishing a boundary line: "This is who I am. This is what I do. I'm not going to tell you how to voice something for two of the flutes, and thank you for not suggesting what cymbal I should play." So oftentimes there's a little bit of a pissing contest that goes on in terms of who can say what, and you feel that out on every project.

One of the loveliest, deepest, and most fraught relationships in the band world is that between young musicians who develop their aesthetic together, as part of a collaborative learning process. "That's the reason that Rivers [Cuomo] and my relationship worked very well together at the beginning of [Weezer]," says Matt Sharp. "How incredibly curious the both of us were, and both being very analytical people." He elaborates:

> I was out almost every single night trying to get some sense of, "Okay, who are we? What are we trying to be and what are we trying to do? What about this band that I'm seeing don't I like, and [what] in any of these bands can I find out that we like, from a melody that comes up at the very end of a song to what kind of shoes do they wear? Why is that off-putting that they're wearing new kinds of clothes, or that their guitar tone sounds

the way it does?" . . . From that you can figure out where you want to be.

You're learning together. We were always asking those questions [about] "Why is this thing that we're listening [to] good or not? Why is this group something we should be striving towards, or something we should be running from, or what is it we could take from them?" Those endless conversations about those things informed the direction that we were going to go, the sound that we're going to create together, the feeling that we were trying to bring together. Those things were profoundly influential on me, as I would imagine I was on him, because we were discovering all those things together.

As bands work, like with us being each other's confidants, [the process] was supporting the directions within his writing that I thought were positive, and steering us away from the places that you don't want to find yourself in. At the time, he was really writing some things that were eye-opening—oh yes, that actually sounds like things that I want to listen to. Which, your entire life up to that point, was probably not the case. In junior high school when you're trying to write songs, [they] aren't the things that you really would listen to.

When Rivers and I were at our best together, I felt like we were profoundly influential on each other, and able to call each other out, and able to say, "Yeah, I'm very proud of where we're going," or "No, we shouldn't be going in this direction." . . . I was very aware of our relationship, where we were both in harmony together, and we were going towards something with the same goal in mind, and discovering everything together, and learning all those things together, and forming what it is that we ultimately would become.

COMMUNICATION AND TRANSLATION OF IDEAS

Support personnel have difficulty [performing adequately] when the employer does not use technical language sufficiently

precise enough to describe what he wants the technician to do;
he will know if the result is not what he wants, but cannot give
positive directions.

HOWARD BECKER, *ART WORLDS*[22]

Even among [musicians] there is no proper vocabulary. There is
only technical jargon plus gesture. The layman knows neither
convention. . . . If he knows a little of these, communication
merely becomes more difficult, because both jargon and sign
language have one meaning for the outside world, a dictionary
meaning if you like, and five hundred meanings for the insider,
hardly one of which is ever the supposed meaning. The musician
and his employer are like an Englishman and an American, or
a Spaniard and an Argentine. They think they are differing over
principles and disliking each other intensely, when they are
really not communicating at all.

VIRGIL THOMSON[23]

One of the chief challenges for a trained musician is interpreting the
directions of collaborators—archetypally, singers; but also producers—
who either have a) strong ideas which they are unable to articulate (at
least in technical vocabulary), or b) no clear idea what they want, but
strong opinions on what they don't want. The musician can audition
a series of ideas, but this can lead to frustration if they don't produce a
solution. Often, the conversation takes place on the level of metaphor
("If the communication is good," says Doug Wieselman, "sometimes
it's more like a look, or even body language"). In a group situation,
one musician may take the lead as chief translator between an artist
or producer and the group at large—whether a de jure music director or simply someone "on the same wavelength"—and who understands, as Stuart Bogie puts it, "the emotional arc of presenting ideas
to people."

Especially in rock contexts, familiarity with a basic catalogue of
shared references is crucial: "Colin [Meloy]'s very musical, and very
smart," says Jenny Conlee, "so he's like, 'I want some piano on this,
pretend like you're in Elvis Costello's band,' or whatever." Too much

of this can become overwhelming, says DJ Bonebrake: "They go, 'Play it like Keith Moon.' You play it, and they go, 'With a little bit of Mitch Mitchell on the left hand.' And pretty soon they give you some other drummer, and they're like, 'Play the right hand part like this.' And you're like, 'How do I do this?' Some sort of reference is good, but it can stiffen you up and make you afraid to play anything . . . that's when you have to go, 'Forget it, I'm just going to play the way I play.'"

Rock artists may also have an individualized glossary of half-understood terminology, which trained musicians must come to understand: using "bar" or "measure" to refer to phrase lengths; or, as Glenn Kotche says, "I know a 'drum roll,' to a rock person, what they mean is 'a fill down the drums.' You know, where drum roll to an orchestral musician means a press roll. Little things like that."

The most effective technique is giving options—best, a series of yes/no decisions. "When someone's like, 'I don't know, that's too dark,' or something," says Kotche, "I go, 'What if I use these sticks or these rods instead; and what if I put this on the cymbal and do *this* to start to brighten things up, how's this?' . . . and also parts—'What if I move the high hat to this beat instead? Does that go with your strumming pattern? Does that make it feel a little more grounded for you, or should I just scrap this idea altogether?'" An extended string of ideas can become a frustration for both parties, what Josh Kantor calls "successive failure: 'No, try it different this time. No, I don't like that either. Okay. Now do it this way. No, I don't like that either.'"[24] Nate Brenner recalls early working sessions with Tune-Yards vocalist Merrill Garbus: "I couldn't tell if she actually knew what she wanted, and she was being passive-aggressive; like, 'Let me hear all of your ideas first, but I already know what I want.'" The onus falls on an empathetic artist to keep the session from falling under a cloud of negativity: "When I sense that they know what they want, but they don't know how to articulate it," says Josh Kantor, "sometimes they're the first ones to say that—'I recognize that I don't know how to articulate it and I hope that's not frustrating, but I do know what I want. I want to search for it and try to bring it out of you.' You can work with that." Jim Sclavunos sees the impasse as an opportunity: "It can, paradoxically, be a quite open situation. They are looking for something from you because they don't know what they want, but the message might be delivered in a very negative way; like, 'No, that's all wrong.' So the language might be critical and negative, but the actual situation—despite appearances—is quite open, because they are open to *anything other than what you are doing.* So the trick is to find out what that thing is." If Jean Cook helps an artist to walk through the slow process of discovering what they want, "that's where the hourly rate comes in."

Players of non-canonical rock instruments are often called upon to perform skills which traffic in the stereotypes that have accrued to their instrument. For those players, self-awareness saves time. For Cook, a violinist, this tends to be string pads: "'Classing it up,' I guess would be one way of putting it. It's not dissonant. It's not challenging. It's just adding a little sheen to things. Nine times out of ten, if it's somebody that I don't know, that's what they're looking for." For musicians who have pride in their instrument and a distinctive personal vocabulary, this can be a challenge. "If I get hired to improvise on people's music and they have a clear idea of what they want," says Peter Hess, "maybe it's rock and roll tenor, or maybe it's a total freak out—what I really want to do is make that sound like me, my harmonic language, my rhythmic language, my total timbre language. And more often than not, that's not what somebody is after on their bar-rock tunes, or their ambient dub thing, or their post-minimalist thing. . . . Those are some of the situations where I've got to tuck in my shirt and tighten my tie. Other times, after the fact, I thought, 'I could have really loosened up and put something on that, but I didn't know I had that freedom.'" Hess goes on:

> I was doing a record in 1999 for a Hong Kong pop star, and my friend Dave Rickenberg was playing tenor next to me. It was kind of a jump blues tune, and there was a producer from Hong Kong who was spending a fortune on this record, and we were doing it in a fancy studio in New York. Dave played a pretty straight-up tenor solo on this jump blues. He might have been expressing it, or he might have played some substituted harmony, or he might have colored outside the lines a little bit—but for a jazz record in New York City, it was by no means wacky.

The producer gets on the talkback and says—with a Chinese accent that won't translate into print—he said, "We do again. I think you are 'outside man.' We do again, and you play for common people." Dave leaned over to me, and in his Texas drawl he said, "Is he saying what I think he's saying?" And I went, "Yep." Dave did it again, and colored a little more inside the lines and played a couple of blues licks, and he got the job done.

That challenge, and the limited nature of people's reference points for certain instruments, can easily slide into insult. Stuart Bogie will "try to reference iconic saxophone audio imagery. I will say, 'This is a Clarence Clemons direction. Are you into that?' Some people will say, 'No, I don't want that sort of jovial raging saxophone,' and other people want something mellow like Stan Getz." But Bogie has "had people describe things I love in almost offensive ways, because they don't like it as an approach," elaborating:

When I was in the *Fela!* musical, there was a scene where they wanted Fela to seduce his American lover Sandra Izsadore with a saxophone solo, so I had eight to sixteen bars to work this out. The era was '68–'69, so I thought the most beautiful thing that I could do would be something sort of modal, like the softer parts of a Wayne Shorter thing, and that was way too subtle a concept. I started doing it that way; and after I played the solo, Oren Bloedow came over and said, "Stuart, that's one of the most beautiful solos I've ever heard you play." I said, "Thanks man, I never get to do that; this is really cool."

Over the next few rehearsals, the producer kept walking up to me and [saying], "It sounds like smooth jazz, what you're doing there." And I'm thinking, *smooth jazz*? I'm not even playing with that sort of articulation [or] phrasing at all. I'm going straight for some cool jazz, a modal thing. And he says, "Ah, it sounds namby-pamby." And I'm like, "Okay." Then the director said, "Stuart, you've got to do something else for this. I need you to 'squeeze the lemon.' I need you to really seduce this woman with your saxophone." And—not that I make a habit of this sort of behavior—

but I think there is only one person in this room who has had a romantic encounter through playing the saxophone, and it's me! I think I'm the expert! Not that the saxophone has been the aphrodisiac that the world may imagine, but what it does have, I feel like I have at least been exposed to. So I was like, "Fine, fine, fine." And I did an impersonation of what I thought was old burlesque saxophone, you know like "*va do va vu va ve va vu vuh.*" I'm like, this is ridiculous. And after, everyone was saying, "Yeah!" And I'm like, "What? You like that?" And they say, "Yeah, yeah, that's perfect."

Afterward I was getting a drink of water and one of the dancers came up to me and [said], "Stuart, I don't know what you were doing with your saxophone in that last run-through, but that was fantastic." I'm like, "Are you kidding me? This is what impressed you?" Okay, all right, I get it. I've just got to get out of my own silly head and remember that I'm painting in primary colors; I have things to communicate, and too subtle of a tonal area isn't going to work. I was dead wrong, and they were right. It's a different thing, what translates on Broadway. If you go to a Broadway show, I think the actors probably experience a similar thing—if you go up there like a film actor, you are not going to communicate anything. It's not going to reach the edge of the stage. You need more concrete gestures.

Long-term collaborators can develop, as Nigel Powell says, "the short-hand that bands have, where you started describing things in certain ways, and then you have a slang for bits or the way things should go . . . a communal intelligence now that we can draw upon"—or, even better, an unspoken understanding of what the bandleader favors.

Metaphors end up shouldering a good deal of the semantic burden. "Since music and sound and groove and ambience and texture and all that is all so subjective," says Peter Hess, "maybe metaphors are all we have." When Nels Cline worked with Mike Watt, making his "vision manifest was him saying—or yelling—'bicycle wheels, propellers' . . . and you're trying to come up with sounds that will reflect his imagery." Jenny Conlee does "a lot of commercial work, and they're like, 'Make it sound like moss dripping,' and I need to figure that out." It can even be a relief, says Brian Chase: "Sometimes it's nice to hear somebody describe a passage like they're describing a movie, instead of 'Keep that syncopated pattern, that dotted eighth note thing.'"[25] Victoria Williams, says Joey Burns, "would describe things like a story: 'This song is a cloud in the shape of an elephant, and it's trying to squeeze through a keyhole to get into this room.'"[26] This technique, says Brian Viglione, is particularly effective with song-writers, "because they tend to be very feeling-based. If they don't have the terminology at their disposal, they can say, 'Well, this is where I'm coming from emotionally.' And I work very well with that, because a lot of my playing is based on emotion too. When I try to listen to the lyrics of a song, that can help guide my drum performance, because I can play off the lyric. There's that symbiotic relationship between the story being told, and how I can help support that."

Sometimes, ironically, the metaphorical approach can lead to a literal solution: Toby Dammit "had a guy one time who was really try-ing to describe this crazy sound he wanted, a special effect in this part, but he had no idea what the instruments would be, or what would make that sound." He tells the story:

> I said, "What does it sound like to you in your imagination?" And he goes, "It sounds like if someone picked up a large pile of garbage full of wood and metal, and just dropped it on the ground. I said "Well, all right, give me five minutes." So I went and I accumulated a bunch of garbage and wood and metal in the studio. I found a sidewalk area, something with a hard sur-face, and I picked it all up and I dropped it on the ground. I said, "Like that?" He said, "Yes, exactly." And that's what we used.[27]

Still, says Bogie, "I can talk about colors and principles and feelings, but how that translates into sounds is always totally different. It's like looking at a shirt and trying it on—there's no substitute for hearing it." Eliza Hardy Jones says, "Dave [Hartley] . . . will say, 'I want this to be like you're dragging to the hoop at the end of the fourth quarter.' I'm like, okay, that's basketball. That has nothing to do with what you want me to do musically." Ralph Carney "tell[s] people, don't have too many complicated flowery notes. There was a singer—I won't say who[28]—they just loved to say, 'It's like dirt. You're walking through the dirt, and there's Chinese food all around and there's a floor.' What? Please, just say it."

CHAMELEONS VS. INDIVIDUALISTS

I've used the analogy "character actor" to refer to band people—but that category can include both those who remain essentially recognizably themselves regardless of part, whose personal quirks and tics are the core of their appeal; as well as the discreet craftspeople who "disappear" into a role—the Jeff Goldblums versus the Mark Rylances. Sometimes, as Toynbee wrote, a bandleader like Duke Ellington or Charles Mingus will "construct a soundscape out of the characteristic dialects of his instrumentalists. Perhaps the major compositional method of both the jazz auteurs was the organization of a dialogic environment in which the musicians were obliged to speak as 'themselves.'"[29] Jazz here represents a different case, since individual autonomy and improvisational contribution are more valued than in rock or pop, where sidemen are sometimes viewed as more interchangeable. Still, the rock equivalent might be a bandleader like Wilco's Jeff Tweedy, who places his harmonically simple songs at the disposal of highly distinctive support musicians. Whether a band person is a unique flavor leaders and producers deploy for a particular effect or a chameleon with a broad toolkit can become a question of self-awareness— I may consider myself broadly capable, but if I'm called on for either faux–Tom Waits accordion schtick or florid Roy Bittan–style rock piano, have I been unfairly pigeonholed, or do other people have a more objective sense of what I'm actually good at?

Here, musicians self-assess: do you think of yourself as a player with an identifiable individual voice, or do you pride yourself on being a chameleon? Or is a personal style something that can only be determined from outside?[30]

"Horace Silver would say that there are personality players and there [are] technical players," says Marc Capelle. "[I'm not] somebody who can go in and just say, 'I am Pat Metheny. No, I'm Link Wray. No, I'm Charlie Christian,' or whatever." Nashville multi-instrumentalist Jim Hoke labels the binary as specialist—"the guy who does one thing really well, and he's known for it. . . . There's a guy who plays great high notes on the sax, say"—vs. generalist; and says that the latter is typified not by their technical chops but by their ability to quickly identify a niche in the song that can be filled by their particular, if limited, skills: "I'm a bad enough accordion player that I'm good in the studio, because I'm not gonna overplay."[31]

Pedal steel players Bruce Kaphan and Todd Beene, for example, both operate outside the bounds of conventional country virtuosity and, Kaphan says, "on the fringe of the music that's normally played on that instrument"—a personal style is "pretty much all I think I have to offer." This limitation, reframed as individuality, perhaps enhances Beene's recognizability: "because of the simplicity of my style, I think that people who know me would be like, 'That's Todd playing, because I hear one of the three riffs he knows.'"

Rock and rock-adjacent music—because of its valorization of expressiveness over technique and plethora of autodidacts—is a haven for "personality players." As a self-taught player, East Bay Ray "didn't grasp music quite correctly. So I would listen to a song I liked to try to figure it out, and I wouldn't be able to figure it out note for note, but then I came up with my own version of it. . . . I was making mistakes, [and] then [turning] the mistakes into art." Janet Weiss didn't start playing drums until the age of twenty-two, and Quasi bandmate Sam Coomes "encouraged this very personal style . . . really fostering this boisterous approach." When Lori Barbero recorded John Peel sessions, the house engineer (a former drummer for Mott the Hoople) gave her one of "like three compliments I remember in my life," as she describes:

> He knelt on the floor, put his elbows on my knees, and he goes, "I've never heard anyone that drums like you. I don't know what you're doing. I admire you more than almost any drummer I've ever seen." It really meant a lot to me.

> People have asked me to give them drum lessons and I'm like, "I don't even know how to read or write music." I'm so ass-backwards at drumming that I can't even teach anyone what I do, because it's really incorrect.

Their limitations, and the individuality that those limitations highlight, mean that players like this, while they are less likely to be offered *every* gig, are more likely to be hired *to be themselves.* "A couple of my favorite drummers [are] guys who have nothing but style," says Josh Freese. "They really have an interesting voice in the way they play drums, and I have watched them try and sit in with other bands. Or I'll talk to someone and they'll go, 'We hired so-and-so for a record.' And I go, 'You did, oh my God, how was it?' And they go, 'It was horrible. He couldn't play with a click. He just did that one thing the whole time.' And I go, 'But he's so fuckin' great. That guy was one of my favorites.' But that's a testament to him, that he's got such a style and such a presence that you either get him or you don't get him. It's all or nothing. I kind of respect that."[32]

"Usually people want me because they want what I do," says Ralph Carney. "I didn't really get sideman gigs. I was just in bands. The job description was really different." Tom Waits—who Carney compares to Duke Ellington for his tendency to hire people for a specific voice—described Carney's playing as "like a broken toy that works better than before it was broken." Conversely, Carney "got in the tour with They Might Be Giants, and [they were] really way to into perfection, and I'm not the guy for that." Katie Harkin says that playing with other people "exposed" her personal style: "Because I'm self-taught, I didn't necessarily know what the norm was in terms of how far I was deviating from it. [Other people] can sometimes point out things you haven't noticed about yourself—you wouldn't notice things about yourself until someone said, 'You always kind of swing that.' You go, 'Yeah, I guess I do roll my r's a certain way.'" Shahzad Ismaily agrees: "That's one of the things where you can't see your own face. You have to look in the mirror."

Those who take pride in having the chameleonic quality of being able to sense what people want and hand it to them musically trust that their personality will come through. Josh Freese says he doesn't know if he has a distinctive style, though "the times I have been told that is one of the biggest compliments I can get; I think that any musician or artist would agree." He admits to some ambivalence: "'You're such a chameleon, Josh. You can blend in like anywhere.' It's kinda like, yeah, that's good, and maybe that's bad? . . . [But] being a quote-unquote working freelance drummer, I'm glad that I can fit in and out of things, and that I can adapt. If someone says, 'Play more like Ringo on this,' I can play more Ringo; or 'Play more like Bonham,' I play more Bonham; 'Play more like Stewart Copeland,' I play more Stu. I can do those things—not as well as them, but I can do a cheap imitation, for sure." DJ Bonebrake thinks of himself as a chameleon, "but sometimes that's how you define yourself. You're in disguise, and you think no one will recognize you, and then they go, 'Hey DJ, how you doing?'"

Michael Bland's formulation is "I think I have a sound, but I don't think that I have a voice"—and he means it as a positive good:

> One of the very first gigs I did out of high school was with the director of my high school band. He hired me to play a New Year's Eve party with his ensemble, and we were on the gig and it turned from being Real Book jazz to being polkas and what-not. And he leaned over and he said, "Mr. Bland, do you know how to play a schottische?" And I said, "Yes, Mr. Lundburg," and I counted it off, and I played the meanest schottische he ever heard in his life. Now, I'm a Black Midwesterner; I had never been to the record store to buy a polka record; I don't particularly care for polka. But my instructor growing up was the first person who told me, "You got to be ready for whatever call is coming," so he showed me everything I needed to know to be a jobber. That stuck with me, and I knew how not to upset the apple cart; I knew how to hide in plain sight. So, yeah—"*I don't want her / you can have her*"—I was an eighteen-year-old Black kid who could play a polka. I took that as a very valuable lesson. You've got to be ready to play what's required of you. You can't be in music for what you like, not if you intend to survive.

If what we are describing was as simple as chameleonic, flexible mercenaries on the one hand and ponies with one (very interesting) trick on the other, it wouldn't be a terribly groundbreaking analysis. A rarer type is the musician with some training and chameleonic skill, who nonetheless chooses the less lucrative, more idealistic band-person path. "There is that ugly British word 'muso'; we don't have that in the States," says Paul Wallfisch. "But there's actually a pretty small fraternity or sorority of people who can play like musos, and who can fake a lot of different things, fake some jazz here and there, but who don't have that mercenary sense about them, [who] really make it a band—even when it is for hire."[33] Often, these are musicians who have the drive and ambition to be an artist/bandleader in their own right, but not quite the singular vision. "I always had a vision of what I wanted to do, and I never could seem to figure out a way to get my shit together enough to do it," says Meredith Yayanos. "So my default was basically to be the best little auxiliary musician I could be. When people ask me if I was slutty in my youth, I'm like, 'Yeah, I was really slutty with music.' I would get it on with just about anybody who was enthusiastic and passionate and could keep time, anyone who was remotely a good lay. Even kind of a lousy lay—I would still hang in there and give it a go." Wallfisch thinks that this very versatility—having a variety of technical tools in one's kit—can be a disadvantage, "because it is like being faced with a sampler with too many sounds in it. A lot of my favorite guitar players, they can't play really, let's face it. [But they have] great instincts and know where to fit in, and primarily they know *what they can do*. But it is often way easier if you do one or two things, that only you can do, incredibly well."

Like a character actor, some musicians worry about being type-cast—confined or prejudged by music they've done in the past, whether for their association with one well-known band, cultural associations with their instrument, or a distinctive style which risks being perceived as shtick. "Let's say [someone] saw me play with the Stooges, the only time they ever saw me, they're just going to think 'He's a really hard-playing, loud, aggressive rock drummer.' And they would have no idea that I could also score a quartet for them," says Toby Dammit. "I play a lot of different instruments, so naturally there are some people who only see me wear a certain suit," says Peter Hess. "Nobody knows how much you like Morton Feldman when you're playing bebop." When people hear Ralph Carney play "older jazz stuff, [they're] like, 'Whoa, I never heard you [play like that], I didn't know.' Well, now you do. The out-there, wacky, space rock or whatever—that's Ralph being Ralph. And the other thing is me really digging deep and trying to make beautiful music—that's a craft; I'm playing an Ellington tune, I'm not just doing my own crazy thing on top of it."

A musician can use typecasting as a shorthand to intuit the expectations of those who hire them: "Somebody who is a Cramps fan would identify me with a record I made with the Cramps," says Jim Sclavunos, so "they would be going, 'He did *that,* so he can play like *this.*'" Similarly, Rick Steff will "go into a situation and think, 'Okay, am I approaching this as 'Rick Steff from Lucero,' or do I want to be a redneck Brian Eno and use a xylophone and a mellotron patch?'" Thor Harris has embraced a positive take on typecasting: "I'm not a metal fan. I think a lot of metal music is really funny, and I don't listen to it very much. But because I was in Swans, I get work putting weird tracks on metal-related records, or, like, Goth. . . . I do feel a little typecast occasionally, because I'm a big hairy metal-looking dude." He adds:

> But I feel like accepting the typecasting, because a good thing about typecasting is that maybe other people know better what you're good at. . . . When Michael [Gira] put together [that] incarnation of the Swans, I was playing drums in a lot of other bands, and I ended up playing all these other weird things, including electric viola. His idea of what I should be doing was more interesting than me just continuing to play drum set in bands. It certainly forced me out of that comfort zone, in a really good way.
>
> Because of the way I look, and my name, he sort of did typecast me as this hairy behemoth, and I certainly went along with it, banging on huge things in the back of the stage; and, you know, he was right. It was a spectacle that people identified with, or liked, or something. . . . If we think our ideas of

ourselves are too precious to let go of, [we'll miss] out on some opportunities.

If you're worried about being typecast, says Matt Kinsey, there's a simple solution: "If you start doing the same stuff over and over, it becomes your style. And I'm trying not to do the same stuff over and over."

SERVING AND STAMPING

Many players parrot the cliché about "serving the song," but more interesting is their relationship to putting their own stamp on a song: the latter is easy to characterize or caricature as the indulgence of an overbearing support musician, but can just as easily be the signature of the self-aware "unique flavor." That attitude can evolve: the urge to leave one's signature can be the impulse of the brash, arrogant young musician ("When I was younger," says Peter Erskine, "I felt I really needed to leave a big mud stain") as much as the prerogative of the confident, mature artist who's moved through a humble apprentice-ship into an understanding of their skills.

As in other chapters, the example of Tom Petty and the Heart-breakers can serve as a rubric of band archetypes: Mike Campbell, in Zanes's words, being "a guitar player who never used a song as an excuse to show what he could do as a guitar player,"[34] versus drummer Stan Lynch, who—as he put it—"discount[ed] every piece of [pro-ducer Rick Rubin's] input, being the total dickwad that I have to be to sign my work."[35] Or, to put it in more academic terms, we have Adorno and Horkheimer's assertion that "It is still possible to make one's way in entertainment, if one is not too obstinate about one's own concerns, and proves appropriately pliable,"[36] versus Howard Becker's claim that "From the idea that no one can tell a musician how to play it follows logically that no one can tell a musician how to do anything."[37]

Let John DeDomenici serve as a stand-in for the multitude of "serve the song" voices: "Jeff [Rosenstock] pretty much hands me a song 98 percent finished, with every instrument including the bass. I might change things around here or there a little bit, just because our styles of playing are pretty different—but usually I'm just given the material, and it's like, 'This is how we mostly want it to go.' . . . I don't necessarily need to get a piece of music and learn it and then [say] 'All right, how am I gonna to change this to make me shine?' Because that's not what I'm here to do. I'm here to play it and make *it* shine."[38]

Josh Freese has "heard stories the other way around, where guys come in and go, 'This is the way [I'm playing]; take it or leave it; fuck you.' I'm not gonna pull that trip. . . . There are times—it's rare that I do this, but let's say I'm really convinced this person doesn't know what they are doing, and they're asking me to do something kind of silly—I'll smile and nod and say yes, and then I'll kind of do it, but not. And see if, A: they notice it, or B: if they just finally give up. Or I'm going to sort of do it, but I'll do it a little bit cleaner, or a little bit more this-or-that, and try and kind of fool them."

For Nels Cline, "it became a fun challenge, and interesting, to try to do what I call 'making other songwriters' or composers' dreams come true.'" Still, Cline has confronted the difficulty of satisfying artists who have "a sound in [their] head . . . that is, let's say, in some cases not professional-sounding." He continues:

> I started realizing that a lot of songwriters don't want finesse in their music. They're looking for something raw, something immediate, something that stands out, that's a signature sound on a piece rather than a bunch of fancy note-blurs, flurries of notes. That can be a challenge for me—not conceptually so much, but to actually do that so somebody with that sensibility is convinced by it. Otherwise I'm putting on a little hat and pretending. It has to be convincing.
>
> I'm not married to the idea of sounding like I know what I'm doing, so at least I have that going for me. Carla [Bozulich] had an idea on a song called "Trashman In Furs" that she wanted the guitar solo to sound like an earnest 14-year-old boy sitting in his bedroom on his bed trying to play a lead guitar solo, but

not well, he's not good. I tried; and I don't think I got it, quite, on the record.

. . . On the other hand, playing certain kinds of Wilco songs, in my mind I'm going to a classicist kind of approach . . . and Jeff [Tweedy] will say something like, "Please don't be so reverent, 'cause I want you to go against the grain on this." That will be hard for me, 'cause I feel like then what I'm doing is putting my own so-called stamp on it before I've even really learned the song inside out. I don't want to start destroying the song before I've caressed the song.

There is a constituency that moves in search of providing not on-demand service, but what Oren Bloedow calls "a transformative idea." Marc Capelle says that "in a creative environment, being harmless would be nonsense. I really think if you went into a session [where] you're just like, 'Oh, yeah, that's great,' and you just were a yes person, you would never get another session. If you just 'yessir' without putting your sensibility in, I don't think it's going to work." When Bloedow listens to music, "it's extremely common for me to be blown away by the choices that somebody made. It's like nature photography to me—'Wow! Where did that come from? That's amazing'"—and he wants to provide those experiences himself. This approach may not always be welcome: "I might not have prioritized [accommodation] in my career as much as perhaps being the person with a transformative idea. And that may be a failing, because sometimes people [aren't] craving a transformative idea. There have been many times in my music life where I felt like if I didn't throw a monkey wrench into it, that machine was just going to keep on going, and I didn't particularly care for it." Bloedow goes on:

I'm not completely insensate to the values of giving the person— satisfying their objectives. I didn't mean to say that I was always trying to blow everything up. What I was trying to say was that I was always hoping that my contribution would be a really big deal, and that sometimes that would have that effect.

So there have been moments where being easier to get

along with probably would have been more appreciated than hoping to be a big shot, or make a splash by superimposing a different key, or feeling, or some kind of stylistic quotation. I think I've always hoped that if we were working on a wardrobe, that I would be the guy who put the false back on it that opened it to Narnia. You know, that everyone would always remember me, and I'd make myself an immortal. And sometimes people just want you to just nail the back on the fucking thing.

Over the lives of bands, power relations are not necessarily static. . . . Eager apprentices who have yet to define their own musical values may readily conform to a leader's wishes. Experience and the maturation of their own styles increase assertiveness. One career drummer [says], "I feel I've evolved to the point as a performer where they shouldn't have to tell me. . . . Of course, I will still accept criticism from someone I respect, but it also depends how you lay it on me."
PAUL BERLINER, *THINKING IN JAZZ*[39]

As band people age and grow into a personal style, the journey is not necessarily the obvious one from arrogant youth to tasteful elder summed up by Joe Ginsberg: "When you're young, you want to play a lot: 'Look at all these things I can play, and look how cool my part can be.' As you play longer, especially in the professional realm, you start to realize that less is a lot more." Just as often, the young player is insecure, pliant, eager, and suggestible ("I used to be terrified of coming up with my own parts," says Sarah Balliett);[40] the older, confident in their voice: "When I was younger," says Josh Freese, "people would give me a lot more direction. They'd go, 'Think Keith Moon,' 'Think Steve Gadd.' The older I get, it is a compliment to you when people go, 'We hired you for you. You do what you would do. We want that.'"

Todd Beene was an example of confident youth: "When I was younger, I felt like I was really putting a lot into the part that I was coming up with, and I was like, 'This is the perfect thing for this.' And if I got pushback on it, it was like, 'Well, they don't see how good this is.' As I'm older, having pushback on parts or suggestions, I use that as an opportunity to see things from somebody else's perspective . . . and to leave my mark on it—not in the sense of leaving a musical cue or a signature; but I want my mark to be that I came up with something really interesting, that they really, really liked, and it was exactly what they wanted." The hardest thing for Bruce Bouton to learn was "that I don't have to play all the time, that I could lay out for most of the song and maybe just do something that was really cool, and nobody would penalize me for it, and think I was being lazy or not contributing." Some of this youthful exhibitionism is about being noticed, placing a musical watermark: Nate Brenner, on early Tune-Yards, "was thinking a lot about my personal style in terms of wanting some of the bass lines to be recognizable. . . . It's like [when] you hear Charlie Parker, you hear his same licks—a lot of people have their go-to licks—so you can immediately identify them. Growing up in the jazz world, I thought more about that—wanting people to hear the bass and know it's me." For George Rush, learning to simplify his bass playing was a matter of stepping outside his primary instrument to get the necessary perspective: "I couldn't play all this Geddy Lee bullshit on the tuba, just because I wasn't capable of doing it. And it made me realize that, 'Oh, maybe I should simplify the other stuff too.'" Rush continues:

> I did a tour with an Australian singer-songwriter, and there was an older guy in the band who used to very gently say, "Man, you're just playing too much. You are playing too many notes. This song does not need that." So I learned how to pare down [and] lock down bass lines, as opposed to doing my poor man's imitation of Jaco or Stanley Clarke or whatever. And the interesting thing is that when I came back to New York and started doing these shitty little jazz gigs again, people remarked on how much my jazz upright time improved, even though I had been on the road playing electric bass and playing indie pop songs for six months. Because I had developed this sense of consistency and continuity that I hadn't realized was there in jazz double bass playing as well.

Michael Bland's "epiphany was listening to—I can't remember what Motown song it was, but I heard it and I was like, 'Wow! This drummer is doing almost nothing except keeping time, and just marking the different sections.'"[41] Thor Harris "used to think, 'What is my stamp, and how do I get it on this record?' In the last twenty years, it has served me better to [ask], 'What do I wish this music had that it doesn't have?' Like when I listen to Jamie [Stewart] of Xiu Xiu's terrifying and awesome music, I just thought, if I was listening to this, I would want something pleasing and solid to grab onto. So I tried to play solid drumbeats—as much as he would let me." When songwriter Jim White recorded with drummer Jay Belrose, "I said, 'You're playing so fucking great, what are you doing, why does this sound so good?' and this was his reply: he said, 'On your demo tapes, I can see that you really like drum machines, so I tried to play like a drum machine.' This was one of the best jazz drummers walking the earth, and he attached no ego to it. He just understood, 'This is how I can best reflect this artist's vision,' so he played like a drum machine. But he also made it incredibly personal."[42]

Mike Yannich's experience as both support musician and songwriter inclines him towards the songwriter's prerogative: "If I'm the drummer in your band, [and] you're like, 'It should have this type of feel,' I'm usually going to defer to the songwriter." He adds:

Ultimately when you're writing the song, you know how it goes in your head. . . . So in certain band situations with The Ergs, we would have arguments over certain things that would go on the recordings; and I always felt like well, it's my song. There is a famous—amongst our friends—fight about an egg shaker on a song called "Books about Miles Davis." I laid the part down, and as lead percussionist and the songwriter, I thought, why not do this? And Joe, the bass player, and I had a pretty epic fight about it. I definitely lost that fight—but we had a compromise a year later and put out the "egg shaker version" of the 7-inch single. We worked it out, [and] that just seems so funny and trivial now. But at the time—I mean, it was a scary fight, lots of yelling.

INPUT AND PUSHBACK

"A thing that constantly has to be re-evaluated is how much your input is welcome," says Thor Harris. This is the question of creative hierarchy specifically—how comfortable does a musician feel introducing ideas, or questioning musical directions?

As in the question of political democracy in bands, a younger band is likely to be a freeform affair. When Andrew Seward joined Against Me!, "[it] was very much four people in a room playing way too loud; everyone's playing their own parts and coming up with it, and I didn't even really realize what the other people were playing until you got out to the studio. . . . I was trusted that I was going to come up with something cool. I was absolutely confident." Doug Wieselman felt a similar "sense of trust playing with the Lounge Lizards. . . . You were basically expected to do something amazing; and yet there was also a sense that you would be supported."

"As our band's progressed," says Jenny Conlee, "Colin [Meloy] has wanted more and more creative control over the music. So I feel a little bit more like a player. . . . [I'm] a keyboard player, he's not a keyboard player, so I can do what I want. I feel a little bit worse for [Chris] Funk our guitar player, because Colin's a great guitar player and he has ideas for Chris. So Chris is a little less free." At the same time, she says, "I think I've gotten more respectful of the song as the years go by. I came from a jam band scene [where] every single moment in the song is filled; so I came into the band like that; 'Oh, we need piano on that,' and Colin is like, 'Rein in the Bruce Hornsby a little bit.' . . . As our band is getting older, I feel like Colin's giving me more freedom to be a little bit busier—I guess you have to rein it in before you can let her go again."

Long-term band members may feel more empowered to defend a position or give creative pushback. Rick Steff is "pretty forceful. If there is something that I hear that I think would benefit [the song], I ask for the indulgence to just see, and more times than not, it's right, or something that they haven't thought of. Sometimes it's totally wrong, and I just put egg all over my face. But I definitely go with my heart." Michael Gira of Swans, says Thor Harris, "will just say no until he hears something he likes. You might, and quite often do, end up doing your original idea, but you do have to go through this process of him saying no to several things and feeling like he has control. It's a control thing."

Players brought in as hired guns are, at least initially, more diplomatic. "I'll try to pick the curtains that I think look good hanging on the wall," says Steff, "but ultimately it is your house." Generally, says Jim Sclavunos, "you are there to complete a picture that has already been painted." When people "deliver a record that's basically done," says Jean Cook, "then I figure out, what's already going on in the song? What's already going in this record? What makes sense to add to it? Then how do you balance whatever I'd be adding? You wouldn't want it to overpower all the other flavors. You'd want it to blend. So I have to do a lot of listening before I figure out what my approach is going to be with any particular track."

Offering an unexpected take can be a gamble. "Sometimes, unfortunately, people say they want a certain dynamic," says Meredith Yayanos, "but when that dynamic actually presents itself, it's absolutely not what they want: [They say] 'You are not just a hired gun; we want your input,' and then, 'Why do I feel shitty?' Oh, I don't think anybody really wants my input. Well, you asked for it, and I kinda wouldn't have done this project if it hadn't been offered, so, this is awkward." Janet Weiss "did play on a Go-Betweens record, and they were very much not into [her 'boisterous approach']. They would tell me where to put the crash, like very constructed and planned-out sound, no crashes over the vocals. . . . But I adjusted; I just want the music to sound good. I just knew that as a permanent thing, that wouldn't be something I would want to do." "Where I'm unsure, I'll sit upright until I feel okay reclining a little bit," says Peter Hess. "I've definitely been in situations where I thought after the fact, 'Oh, I could have just been me, and it would have been cool.' It wasn't necessary for me to feel buttoned-up stylistically; and paradoxically, they wanted more me and what I might bring. Then I've been in circumstances where I've thought going in [that] I could be a little more of an individual, and I was wrong about that—what they wanted was more stock. It's a real sliding scale."

Still, Stuart Bogie tries "not to make assumptions" about what people are looking for. "I'm very often wrong when I try to do that. A couple years ago I got called to work on a record by an artist [who] was doing this really interesting avant-garde R&B pop music. One minute the melody is shaped like a Backstreet Boys song, then the next minute it's like musique concrete. I went in there and I was doing things that fit in; I was doing things that imitated the vocalist's style. And they kept saying, 'No, you've got to push it harder.' I was like, 'Oh, okay.' So I put the pedal to the metal and gave them all I got; and what they worked out for the record was phenomenal, the saxophone as a juxtaposition to the vocals. So that was a lesson to me not to make strong assumptions about what people want."

Ideally, though, a musician is hired not as a replacement-level operator of a particular instrument, but as a trusted artist in their own right. Almost everyone has their personal exemplar of the support musician who brings a special sauce to a project. For Rick Steff, "Mick Ronson was just the perfect template for how to be that sideman where you can really add something to a record, [that] when you hear it, you go, 'Oh, that's something.'" Scott Brackett says that Thor Harris "brings a distinct flavor that just makes everything better, whether or not it's what you had in mind. For people who have a very specific vision for their material, it's hard to work with folks like that; but when Thor left Shearwater it just wasn't Shearwater anymore, for me." Harris, himself, recognizes that "my strength is in making other people's music sound a lot better; and that's certainly what I'm known for. We don't ever write down our resumés as players, but it's a huge part of how you get your next gig, your unwritten Wiki discography." Having this level of autonomy, for band people, also pays dividends beyond the recording session: "The parts I enjoy coming back to during performances," says Sarah Balliett, "are the little creative parts where I blend into the song in a seamless way, or add interest that you won't hear on first listen."

For Todd Sickafoose, who feels he is "usually brought in to be extremely hands-on," it's not a matter of a bandleader relinquishing control: "I don't even see it as [having] leeway. For a lot of people I work with, they are casting: you bring musicians together, who you are interested in the way that they add to a situation, and the way that the bandleaders control things is by bringing the right people together, then setting them loose." He continues:

> People ask what's it like to keep putting all these different hats on all the time, and I just really disagree with that metaphor. I always have the same hat on in my opinion, because what you are supposed to do as a musician is show up as yourself in a very true way, and collaborate with what is around you, and I don't feel like that changes for me day-to-day and from project-to-project.

If Marc Capelle is "recording something and I hear a harmony, or I hear a part that I think would be effective, I will just say, 'I'm hearing this. Are you feeling it as well?' And more often than not, people will let me run with that. I try to say what I can. I'm really energetic and driven. I try to temper it more than I might have done in the past, instead of blurting out any momentary Edison light bulb that comes across, but I always try to contribute."

There are occasions where a musician may take it upon themselves to salvage a song—or, at least, give themselves something interesting to play. "When [Murder by Death singer] Adam [Turla] comes to band practice with a song I find dull, or too straightforward," says Balliett, "this is usually when I try to throw in something really off-the-wall weird, or I grab a pick and strum the cello to add a slightly off take on rhythm guitar." Doug Gillard "always [tries] to juice songs to try to make them more interesting. There are a lot of things I have worked on where I think the song is poorly written—this is really boring; this is plodding, what could be done to help out a song that really needs some of the fat trimmed, or needs some help as far as some interesting chords." Though, Balliett says, "it is important to remember that you're making a song, and not just trying to entertain yourself."

Finally, there is a class of band people who insist on the parity of their artistic goals with those of the song in the abstract. "I don't like the term 'serve the song,'" says drummer Jim White. "I'm into *not playing*, that's for sure. I'm happy to sit down on the stage and not play, [if] there's nothing to do at the time. I'm also happy to do something, to shake it up because it needs it. Some songs sound boring; but you're there for a reason. I don't think about playing a beat—it's not better than playing nothing. It depends on the situation, but I think the situation is more complicated than just the song." "If that's what you want me to play," says Josh Leo, "I'll play that part. But you'll never know what I was going to play."

One of the most powerful practical differences between a hired support musician and a band member proper is that creative, personal, and business ties binding the group to the latter make them (in theory) harder to dismiss. Therefore (also in theory), they can exercise a veto over creative decisions, on a scale ranging from objection and negotiation to work stoppage. Not that hired guns can't defend certain boundaries.[43] "I only want somebody to back up and let me do my job when, out of ignorance, they're asking unreasonable things," says Peter Hess. "Like when people make some kind of snarky comment about a mistake, when their part is all fucked up and written badly for the instrument—which happens all the time." Where Hess links this to sensitivity about "how I'm perceived, because I want people to think I'm good, and I want them to call me back so I get to keep doing what I do." Peter Erskine's lines are similarly drawn to protect his area of expertise: "I've been in situations where I just say, 'Maybe I'm not the right musician to play this.' Just, 'I can't give you what you're looking for. I'm not able to come up with it.' If I'm a side person, I generally won't take a stand, like 'This is against my musical principles.'"

Sarah Balliett has deployed a veto "only after a song was completely finished and I still hated it. You've got to give a song a chance to evolve, but be willing to kill it if it comes out with no soul. (I've also had my veto overruled—still not my favorite song, but you can't win them all.)" Nigel Powell doesn't like "the finality of the veto," preferring to leave room for reconsideration: "Sometimes it is one of those penny-dropping moments where you've been thinking about it, you've been looking at the mirror from the other side, and you miss what the other person's seeing, and [then realize] 'Oh, of course.'" There are projects, in retrospect, that Peter Hess feels he misunderstood and misjudged: "I couldn't shake what I wished it was, and I didn't ever embrace what it really was. And it was better than what I was thinking of. Everybody in your band thinks they are in a different band."

Carla Kihlstedt says, "I've gotten to the point musically where I like to try to embody that age-old adage of—when you're working on music and you're very opinionated—'hold on tightly, let go lightly.' Meaning that if you really are convinced about something and your bandmates disagree, those kinds of disagreements can be the source of bigger strife within the band. Be convinced of what you think, then if someone has a better idea, let go of what you thought."

PRACTICING AND REHEARSING

There are two kinds of people in the world, etc.:

Do you like to practice (your instrument)? Do you like to rehearse (with the band)?
   Cook: No.
   Bland: Love it.

But seriously, folks: The argument for practicing is that you can work on your skills, shoring up scales and getting new voicings under your fingers and so on; the argument for rehearsal is that the band gets tighter. The argument against both is that they're boring and repetitive. Choose your fighters, presented here on a sliding scale from "no" to "yes":

Sarah Balliett: Band practice is the pits. I hate it. Mostly because we have gone through several member changes over the years and it feels like we are always shrinking our song repertoire for the new member's sake, and we end up practicing songs I have played on stage and off literally thousands of times.

Ara Babajian: If you're a guy that is a quick learner, that's a real plus, because musicians are the last people on earth who want to practice, they just want somebody who can learn something real quick and get on with it.

Ralph Carney: I don't like people that over-rehearse. "I don't need to be here. You guys can do it. I already know my parts." Usually it's because someone's nervous. Generally, I say rehearse for a purpose.

Marc Capelle: Mark Eitzel [had] a great thing, which is practice less, more often. The idea [being] that you get together and you do these little rehearsals more often, instead of creating some traumatic 12-hour "We got to get it all perfect."

Rick Steff: If you are talking about rehearsing for a live performance, absolutely. I think you can overdo it big time for a recording—you can rehearse the magic and subtlety right out of something if you are not careful.

John DeDomenici: If I had my way, I would like to rehearse with the group at least once a week for a few hours, just so everything stays fresh—because on tour, you see songs start to change a little bit as you're playing them for forty-five days in a row, and sometimes it's for the better . . . [B]ut usually that is not an option. Usually it's "Here's the material; we're going to have three days before we go on tour, and we're going to sit in the box for three days."

Ruth Finnegan: Practicing together . . . played a part in band unity. . . ."Practicing" and "playing together" conveyed far more than a routine run through prepared material. The hours spent in such activity formed an act of creation and discovery in which all members of the band participated.[44]

Ralph Carney: I'm sixty years old and I'm actually learning some new notes on the saxophone—*altissimo*. . . . I gig a lot and play, but I don't really practice, and that's something I used to do. Like Stan Getz [said]: "Why should I practice? I already know how to play." There's a point where you just turn on the faucet and it comes out, and you don't think about it.

Janet Weiss: I love playing and I love playing by myself—which I thought everyone did, but I was on this drum panel recently, and a friend of mine who is a drummer said, "I never practice by myself." That just blew my mind. I spend so much time in there by myself. Every time I go to the practice space, there's three drummers in there playing alone. I really get that.

Josh Freese: I definitely don't like to practice by myself. That drives me nuts. I would much rather play with people than play by myself. I'm not a big jammer. I like creating a song and going for something together, and having more of a plan.

I'm [also] not a "Let's rehearse this thing to death" guy. The Vandals, we hardly ever rehearse. We rehearsed two nights before Coachella, and the fact that we rehearsed two nights was a big deal. . . . A lot of this stuff is just like riding a bike.

The band I played with that did the most rehearsals were Nine Inch Nails, but half of that was [because] the production was on such a giant scale that a lot of this stuff was *everyone* rehearsing; not just me but the lighting guys and the guys that run the video walls and set designers and shit.

In the last five or six years I do one-offs with [Sting] when his normal drummer, Vinnie Colaiuta, is busy. They will call and go, "We thought we had a couple of weeks off, so we told Vinnie he could take that tour with Jeff Beck, but now we've got this giant gig that came up, and can you do this gig?" Sting has made enough money where he doesn't want to have to worry about shit. He *shouldn't* have to worry about shit. They said, "We are going to fly into Quebec and rehearse the night before, just do one rehearsal."

I thought, "Wow, he's really putting a lot of trust in me, because I haven't even seen him in two years." To rehearse the night before we headline the frickin' Quebec Jazz Festival, 60,000 people or something. But I think, okay, I'm going to show up and I'm going nail my shit and we will be all right. So I do my homework. We rehearsed for like twenty minutes and he's like, "That sounds great. What are we going to do, rehearse 'Roxanne'?" And we basically went home early, and it was awesome.

Then a year later I got a call, and he had this one-off in Dallas. I hadn't seen him in a year or two again at this point. His crew manager goes, "We're just going to show up, do a longish sound check [on the] day of the show. He doesn't think you need a separate day rehearsal." I went, "Cool." Number one, he's got enough faith in me that he knows I'm going to pull it off, and he doesn't want to show up a day early and rehearse "Message in a fuckin' Bottle" with me. Like why? You shouldn't have to. I shouldn't have to make him do that. So I listened to recent live tapes in case they are doing it slightly different, because he likes to change around the arrangements and stuff. My wife goes, "Why are you listening to 'Every Breath You Take'? Haven't you played that thing a thousand times?" Yeah, but I'm going to show up, and no matter what, I'm not going to fuck up, and then he's going to know: This is great. I can call this guy and *not rehearse* anytime I want, and he's gonna be up to speed.

RECORDED VS. LIVE PERFORMANCE

Until relatively recently, to be a musician was to play live, full stop. For the last century or so (more so as the technology has spread into the home), the job has bifurcated: playing live, and recording. There is surprisingly little consensus on the question of whether the two skills are different. "It is much more mentally taxing in the studio, and physically taxing on stage," says Paul Wallfisch. "I don't totally believe those people" who say they approach recording and performing in the same way, says Todd Sickafoose, "or believe that it is possible. It's a different art form, isn't it?" Michael Bland is one of those people: "I don't give myself any more slack in a live setting than I do in the studio. For some people, that level of restraint may be boring, or a lot less interesting as a live experience, but I want to play the music like it's supposed to be played." Bill Stevenson agrees:

> I don't think [they are different skills]. When I see bands live and they have either drank too much, or done too much coke, or something, and they have tainted what I call the essential DNA of the groove of the songs—this isn't a conservative thing of "they played it too fast," or "they played it too slow." Songs can have a lot of different variations; but when I go to see a band play one of their songs, and they have taken it to some spot [where] it sounds like they got tired of playing it live and it

evolved into some other thing that it is not supposed to be, that bums me out, 90 percent of the time. Ten percent of the time it is, "Whoa, I saw ZZ Top and they played one of the songs like half speed and it was crazy and it was cool," but that's usually not the case.

When I play live, I'm trying to play the fuckin' song the way that it really truly goes, and not get caught up in even the social aspect of drumming. You will go see a band and the drummer is trying to show off and wave his arms around and create a big spectacle for himself, but when you are doing all of that the core of your body is being compromised, so you are not maintaining the groove of the song properly, you are just up there jerking off. The entertainer in me will always give way to the musician in me.

For Oren Bloedow, on the other hand, "they're so intrinsically different, because there's different upsides in each situation from taking risks. If there's ever a time that you wanted to open up a gateway to a new universe on a song, certainly when you're recording is *the* time to do that. You should always be able to move smoothly between playing dangerously and playing conservatively."

Obviously there is a performative, public-facing aspect of playing in a live setting that doesn't exist in the studio—as Sarah Balliett says, "Someone who is good in the studio is a skilled musician with chops and a no-nonsense approach . . . could be a total nerd onstage." "In the studio," says Thor Harris, "I feel like there's absolutely no room for ego." "You don't have to be interesting to put down bass or drums on a record," says John DeDomenici. "Even though it's not your name on the band, you certainly want to look and be engaging." He singles out former Against Me! bassist Inge Johannson: "He's just as exciting to watch as [bandleader] Laura [Jane Grace], and I'm pretty sure he's probably not doing that while recording—but if he is, that's awesome." "If you're not smiling on stage or anything like that," Bruce Bouton says, his boss Garth Brooks has "like eighteen eyes in the back of his head. He'll be like, 'Hey man, what's wrong?'"

Each mode influences the other: Michael McDermott emphasizes the way the perfectionism of the studio can seep into live performance, especially as one ascends into larger venues where "there is no room for 'Ah, that's [just] how I played it tonight.' . . . When you're playing in an arena and you got that many people watching you, they're recording the show, and it's on video and there's audio being tracked, you got to just be on your shit constantly."[45] Doug Wieselman puts the emphasis on bringing the spontaneous energy of live performance "into the recording process, because it can be a little sterile. You want it to be as alive as you can make it."

The basic dichotomy is the familiar one between Apollonian and Dionysian, precision and performance. "Live, I'll go a little more off book," says Jon Wurster. "I have always secretly wanted to be in Black Flag," says Viglione, "so I approach most musical groups with that level of intensity of just 'go for blood' every moment that you are on stage." For Peter Hess, "Live, good enough is good enough. You can't take it back."

At the same time, the question of which mode allows for more risk-taking, and which involves more vulnerability, is not as clear-cut as it may seem. "Depending on the circumstances, in the studio I'll take fewer risks," says Hess. "Sometimes I'll do something I know I can execute, playing a little safer, because I'm literally spending somebody else's money while I'm taking time. . . . [Then] I might say, 'Now that we've got one that could do, let me try something different.'" Band members and long-established collaborators see recording as a place for trying things out, free of audience expectations. For Caitlin Gray, "recording is way more creative—you are building something from the ground up. . . . It's a blank slate, so you have to have more openness to new ideas." When Jean Cook records, she's "creating a part. I'm not playing a part that was given to me, so I approach the process very differently—I'm not a performer, I'm a composer." Paul Wallfisch "will just take a coffee can in the room and throw it against the wall and record that—we can use that for something. I recorded my coffee grinder a few days ago right before leaving, because I thought if I really fucked that up and [played it] super loud, I bet I can use that with Swans. I will walk around the room in different shoes and record that. The birds in my back yard." There's room for experimentation "because you can hear the results instantly," says DJ Bonebrake. "You can define something really quickly. When you're in a rehearsal room, you're playing and you go, 'That might have been good.' You don't really have a reference point. When you go in the studio and you play it back, you go, 'Oh, that part I thought was so creative, it sounds like crap. OK, I see what I have to do.'" For musicians who focus on the studio as a safe space to experiment (as opposed to the pressure of "this is for posterity"), it's in opposition to the vulnerability imposed by stage and audience. For Bruce Kaphan, though, the vulnerability is in that process of studio exploration, so "the trick to working with people in the studio [is] getting everyone to be comfortable so that they're willing to become vulnerable—because that's where exciting performances come from."

While some emphasize the precariousness or anxiety of live performance, for Marc Capelle, "the safest place on Earth is playing on a stage, or an imagined stage." Once you're up there, "that's the whole thing"—that is, there's a simplicity in only having to focus on the execution, and trusting one's preparation. "What's great about playing live," says Scott McCaughey, is, or was, its transience. "It's less the case now, when everybody with their fucking cellphones records every song you do—used to be you just played live and you go 'That was a great show; I don't ever need to hear it again; I don't ever want to worry about it again; I had an amazing time that night.' Which you don't when you're recording—you're thinking all the time, 'This is for forever.'"

It can certainly be a different skill: Eliza Hardy Jones has "played with drummers [on stage], and I'm thinking 'This is the greatest drummer I've ever played with in my life'—then I've played with that person in the studio and thought, 'How come they don't know how to count?'" Mike Sneeringer has concluded that "it takes a much better musician to record"—or at least a more precise one; on stage, performativity and enthusiasm can sell a sloppier performance.

But the microscopic perfectionism that can often infect studio work rankles some. "With the software and technology now," says Josh Kantor, "you can Frankenstein a part together more. I'll do a date and they'll say, 'That was great.' I'll be like, 'Oh, I made like five glaring mistakes on that.' 'No, it's no problem, we'll just fix them.' That was a foreign concept to me for a long, long time. I really want to get at least one take that's really awesome from start to finish. I feel like it used to be everyone's point of pride, and now it feels like it's no one's point of pride." Nigel Powell has sometimes felt sidelined as a creative agent: "Depending on the producer, they'll just fix it in a computer anyway, so that makes you wonder why the hell you bothered showing up in the first place." "It's actually hard to get feedback from [Bill Callahan]," says Thor Harris, "but if you pay attention, playing with him is wonderful, because he doesn't like to fix things. There's no going into Pro Tools and moving drumbeats around. He feels that that's a complete waste of time, and I do too, in most cases." "Capturing something that feels like an honest live performance," says Todd Sickafoose, "with all of its irregularities and beautiful warts, is something that we cherish and that we always feel lucky to have captured. I read an article in the *New Yorker* about a guy who has a Photoshopping gig for all the big beauty magazines. Everyone likes his taste about what he will tweak and what he won't, because his stuff looks really organic and never looks Photoshopped. That's the way we work on digital audio now—that's all you have, your taste about what to alter in a recording that has already been made; your taste about how to put that together, where you draw the line of what's right." Josh Freese says it's easy to psych yourself out in the studio:

I used to go, "Whatever ends up being used, that's it forever, you can never go back and change it." And the older I get, the less I'm worried about going for perfection. I listen to some of my favorite records; if it speeds up, cool; if it slows down, cool; if the guy hits a stick or a rim I go, "That was awesome; that was the best part." Because it sounds human and it doesn't sound like tons of overdubs, or like it was fixed on the computer, or whatever. Some of my favorite songs and records, the drum sounds aren't that good, but it doesn't matter. Then you hear other stuff where the drums sound awesome and they've got all the right gear and the performance is great, but the song sucks, so who cares?

A joke I heard a couple of years ago that I just love is: What's the best cure for a bad snare sound? And the answer is "a hit song." Who cares what the fuckin' drums sound like, if the song is great and the spirit is there? I mean, *I* care. Every time [I'm] going to the studio I'm really concerned with making it sound great. But I try not to get too, too precious about it. 'Cause I know at the end of the day it doesn't really matter. People are either going to like the record or they're not. . . . It's not like I'm playing on some U2 track where you've got to go through committees of people that green light it and tell you it's okay, and radio programmers, or whatever. Being less precious about shit is liberating.

And then committing to stuff. I've been in studios with people where they second- and triple- and quadruple-guess themselves to death and it just kills the project; it kills the vibe; it kills everything. And when I am in the studio with people where they're just like, "That was great, let's move on," I'll be like, "But I fucked up that fill on the end, and you told me not to go to the ride cymbal on the bridge and I went to the ride"—and they're like, "Let's move on." I go, "Great!" And no one notices or cares. The track was great, and we move on to the next track.

One my favorite guys in the world, who I worked for a lot, is Brendan O'Brien. I've had guys put four different mics on their snare drum and go, "You want to A-B which one is the best?" And Brendan will go, "Well, bring up the fifty-seven first. Let's listen to the fifty-seven." I'll hit the snare a couple of times and he'll go, "That thing sounds great. I'm not looking for anything else. It sounds like a snare drum, let's cut this thing. I'm not worried about what the other four microphones sound like." And I go, "Right on." It sounds great, let's fuckin' do it, then have lunch.

I have worked with so many people who have all the right gear. They go, "We go to these kind of preamps and these kind of mics and this kind of board," and then the track sucks and the song sucks and you go, "Why are we doing this?" Congratulations, you've got a bunch of gear that you read that you are supposed to buy. Who cares? I'm definitely not a gear guy at all. I did an interview recently and he says to me, "You're known for not really caring about gear." Well, it's not that—I know the difference between good and bad, and DW makes great drums, and the fact that they make great drums [means] I don't have to worry about it; there's other things to worry about. "Cool, I've got a great drum set. Now what?" I'm not going to sit here and chase down vintage snare drums all day long, because I've got other interests and I've got kids to raise.

Drummers often acclimate to the studio earlier in their career than other musicians, because of the way records are typically made: the drums are tracked first, so the drummers are under more pressure to figure out how to execute so the record can move forward. "I'm really comfortable on a click now, but it definitely took a lot of practice," says Benny Horowitz. "That and learning how to actually play a tambourine and a shaker and stuff like that and actually keep it on time. It's trickier than it looks."[46] The drummer in the band is often not the best choice to do the auxiliary percussion. "Someone said that to me during the first session [when] I was having a hard time with it, and my competitive nature went fucking nuts. I literally took a tambourine, and I drove home driving with my left hand on the wheel and my right hand doing the tambourine. When the producer was like, 'Maybe let someone else do it,' I was like, 'No! These are drums. Drums are mine. This is my department. Don't touch it!' I seriously practiced for like a week. I'm actually pretty good at it now, but it did take that to get me there."

For drummers, the studio may be their first or only opportunity to play quietly, and to explore the dynamic range and tonal possibilities of their instrument. "You adjust your style," says DJ Bonebrake. "It's more restrained, and it's more architectural. Drums are tuned differently for the microphones." When Peter Erskine started recording, "I didn't know how to play to a microphone, and I didn't understand about finding my own dynamic range and [my] own compression range, so that everything tracks and is picked up by the mic and sounds good. Recording takes some discipline." Violinist Jean Cook, too, points out that "you don't have to project when you are recording. You have to think a lot about quiet noises."

There are, broadly speaking, two schools of thought about recording: one says that it should aspire to simply reproduce, in documentary fashion, *the sound of an artist or ensemble* exactly as they sound in performance; the other that this is a unique opportunity to *create the ur-version of a song*, with all the children's choirs or tubular bells of the artist's imagination. The studio, in the latter conception, is an opportunity to create unreproducible parts from overdubs. Daniel Hart will "put on a shitload of string parts. I'll just track violin after violin. . . . I certainly can't recreate that live, [but] I try not to think too much about the live aspect of it when I'm writing or recording or producing, because I don't want to limit the possibilities." Similarly, Glenn Kotche thinks more "in terms of a percussion section when I record—here's my main idea, but I might want to also make that idea more stripped down because I want to add a second pass with a slightly different sound, playing mallets and putting these things on the heads instead. Then there's a shaker part I want to put here, but I don't want to make it sound like a store-bought shaker, I want to make it sound like an interesting shaker that I messed with somehow. So I think in terms of layers. Then when it comes to playing it live, I always try and challenge myself [to] do a composite part and cover all of those things myself."[47]

From a compositional point of view, Peter Erskine urges a player to consider a macro view over the course of a recording session—that risk-averse playing which leans only on what a musician is confident they can execute can expose their tropes and repetitions:

> It involves keeping track of what you're playing. For an album, it pays to be aware of the fact that someone is going to sit and listen to this thing. I was just listening to a recording yesterday, and the drummer was giving his all on every tune, throwing everything including the kitchen sink in terms of rhythmic choices, and basically over-playing. I could see his wheels spinning, like when he could slip in the next impressive lick. Which maybe on one tune is okay, but these performances are

all going to be put together. It's like a film—if you've got an actor who's rolling their eyes every time, you know they're the bad guy, and they let us know they're the bad guy. It's like a grotesque vaudeville performance.

In recording, you have to imagine the arc. I may not know what order the tunes are going to go in, but I have to quickly figure out where this might fit in the overall scheme of things. I meet each piece of music on its own, and yet I'm aware of how they all relate to one another, so I can't play the same lick on every tune. I can't use quote-unquote improvisational devices, or rhythmic connecting devices, that become redundant for the person listening to this album. A lot of times you don't have much control, because you're not sure which take will be selected; so you have to keep tabs on what you're playing.

Live, that's an easier process, because you're not doing multiple takes of one song, and it's easier to perceive the arc of the evening because you're right in the middle of it. So recording is a bit like working in television or working in film. There's a different long view involved.

Shahzad Ismaily thinks that the idea of recordings as a simple documentary of a live event, while conceptually appealing, is a mirage. Recording, he says, is as "a much more dark art form, in the sense of being unknown how it exactly works—it's more of a black box." He elaborates:

Because what saddens me is that there are a lot of recordings, that when you hit play, it's emotionally flat, and it's like a bad photograph of a live band. And nothing compelling or special or moody is happening in making the recording. So it has become clear over the years that you can't make a good record simply by walking into a recording studio and playing the material.

And I started to wonder why that was. I started to simultaneously wonder why [it was] that certain records just completely envelop me. It wasn't genre-based; it wasn't geographic. It was just sometimes, you put a recording on and the music would surround you and consume you, and sometimes you would put it on and it was just a flat physical object that was happening in the corner. So because of being aware of that, I have a very different mentality when I go to a recording studio. What I'm aiming for, what my ear is looking out for, or what my sensory mechanism of this static collection unit the human body is looking for is, "Is something happening right now?" Is there something special, moody, enveloping, happening right now in the recording?

Sometimes that means that you make very odd choices in the studio. For example, a songwriter comes in; they have a plan: the music is supposed to be the guitar part, the vocals, electric bass, drums, saxophone, etc. Everybody comes in; they record the song the way they practiced it; we go into the engineering room, and let's say accidentally three of the mute buttons are on and all that's playing back in the speakers is the saxophone and voice. And if you are open to it, in that moment, you experience—oh man, this is hitting you really hard. And then you turn to the band and say, "I know this is crazy, but I think this song could or should just be the saxophone and the voice." It's an absurd thing to turn to a band and say, because you have a five-person band. I know what it is like to be in a band; I know how important it is to you to play your part you have practiced. But in the recording studio, the most important thing you are looking for is, is the recording doing something special?

I started to feel that it was similar to painting or visual art—of course this is romanticized; I'm putting myself in the mind of the painter—you are looking at the painting, and the main goal is that the painting is an evocative piece of art. So you walk up to it and you put a red line diagonally from one corner to the other. Then you step back and look at it, and then you add a little blue square, and right at that moment something profound is happening for you. Then you go up to it and you put a figure of a human being in the lower left-hand corner—and all of a sudden that moment you had a few moments earlier, where something was taking place, is now destroyed. And now nothing is taking place when you look at it. It's that kind of awareness that we need to have in the recording studio.

JOINING EXISTING BANDS

Even in bands which have a defined hierarchy and explicitly hired members, the artistic and personal chemistry that can only develop during long hours of travel and rehearsal can be fragile, and the integration of a new member is a vulnerable moment for everyone. Some members may wish to take the opportunity to reimagine power relationships, others may not; and the incoming member may have their own agenda. In addition, fans can have attachments to the personality and/or playing of departed members—whether or not that attachment is shared by the remaining members—and both sentiments need to be honored and balanced. "I definitely start with who was there last," says Michael Bland, "whoever did the most successful job before me. A lot of Soul Asylum's music has to do directly with the influence that [former drummer] Sterling Campbell had on the band's sound. Generally, my approach is his approach." Glenn Kotche will "stay pretty close to what [former Wilco drummer] Ken Coomer did because I like those parts." Katie Harkin thinks "part of learning [existing] parts is learning someone's physicality and how they approach an instrument. . . . It's almost like learning their language or their regional accent; you can anticipate how they're going to say a phrase you've not heard them say before." On a tour on which they were playing the Sugar album *Copper Blue*, Bob Mould told Jon Wurster that he didn't have to copy the drumming on the record. "Obviously I listened to the record and learned the songs," Wurster says, "but I didn't try to duplicate anything really. There were a few crucial drum fills I would try to duplicate.[48] But [on] the last show on the tour, we were playing somewhere, and I'm playing along, and there's this kid in the front row air drumming . . . and every time I got to a specific thing, he did this air drum fill that I never did—and I thought, I guess I didn't learn that one, and I felt like I was letting him down a little bit."

When we spoke, Michael McDermott had recently joined the Joan

Jett band, replacing their long-time drummer Thommy Price, who was battling cancer. "If there's another drummer that they've been happy with—like the situation I'm in now—you just try to honor that previous drummer. You try to make the situation the least uncomfortable for the people as possible. Because they don't want to have to have somebody else. They liked Thommy. They love Thommy. They've been playing with Thommy for twenty-eight years. So I want to make the transition as comfortable as possible. So you try to play what he played, you play it smart and you listen to his records and you go on YouTube and you try to look at videos and how he played it and what he played, what kind of fills he played, and why he played them where he played them, and you just try to do that." In fact, for most of McDermott's career, he has been preceded by "in most cases, really good drummers. [So] when I get into a band, or I start to work with a band, and have to learn their catalog. It's almost like a mini-master class that you get to take." Mike Watt experienced filling in with Porno for Pyros as "not just a shop floor, it was a classroom too—what can these cats teach me?"

Often, musicians find themselves joining bands of which they've already been fans. When Mike Yannich joined a band called the Kung Fu Monkeys, "their drummer before me was an obviously self-taught guy who played really cool odd fills, and . . . when we were writing new songs, I would throw in fills that I thought he would play." Katie Harkin joined Wild Beasts and Sleater-Kinney to fill out the live performances of already-recorded albums, but necessarily "also to play on songs that I had loved for years, [which was] like getting the skeleton key to some of your favorite records—and equally, once you're in there, you don't want to break anything." Mike Watt was so in awe of the legacy of the Stooges that "I had nightmares, seeing a gravestone, and all that was written on it was 'Fucked up Stooges song,' 'Fucked up the Stooges gig.'"

Sometimes the pressure is reversed: Bill Stevenson "felt like in Black Flag my job was to just do the best I could to do the stuff how Robo had done it, or on newer material to try to do it how Robo would have done it, because I loved Robo. Robo is one of my heroes, and he kept getting deported. Okay, Robo can't be here; but I'm here, and I will do this how it is supposed to be done, how he would do it." He goes on:

> But as we progressed in Black Flag, oddly enough, as we moved into new material . . . Greg [Ginn] made it really clear to me that he had not been fond of Robo's drumming. He wanted me to play a more strong, sturdy rock beat. So to me, I was underutilized in that band, because Greg had this idea that the beat should be strong and simple. By contrast, before me, Robo is from Colombia and he brought this *cumbia* influence to Black Flag, that probably no one in the whole world even knows what I'm talking about—but if you listen to the way he plays, his high-hats come in little sets of threes and this is a cumbia thing, like *jink jink-jink sha jink-jink jink jink-jink sha*, so he brought a flair to the music that made Black Flag sound how they sound.

Josh Freese was such a fan of Cheap Trick that he turned down the gig:

> A couple of years ago, Bun E. Carlos finally had his final falling out with the Cheap Trick guys. A friend of mine who was working with them called me and said, "Hey, [there was] a huge blowout with the Cheap Trick camp. Rick Nielsen's son's the drummer, but he is in Europe with his band, and they are playing Austin City Limits on Friday. . . . You want to do it?"
>
> And I went, God, twenty years ago, I would [have died] to be in that situation. Of course! Then I went, "Dude, Bun E. Carlos was such a voice and a presence in that band and such a big piece of that puzzle." I was like, I don't wanna see me or fuckin' Dave Grohl or *anybody*, I don't care who the drummer is, I don't want to see someone playing drums in Cheap Trick other than Bun E. Carlos. If it was me, I would be sitting at home going, "Oh my God, Josh Freese's playing with them, that's so lame, what are they doing," you know what I mean? I'd bum out if I saw me playing with Cheap Trick. So I respectfully declined, out of respect for Bun E. in that band. I don't want to be the guy

doing that. I'm not going to take the heat for [people asking] "Where the hell is Bun E. Carlos, why do they have that dude who plays with everybody playing with him?" Sounds like fun, but no thanks. I can't believe I'm gonna say no to this, I say no to so few things; but I don't want to put myself in that position. I don't want to pretend like I'm going to fill Bun E's shoes. It felt like sacrilege.

In the end, they ended up getting Rick's kid, which is great, that's the only way they could have done it. He's a good drummer, and it's Rick Nielsen's kid; you're not getting some session drummer, you're getting the dude's kid, you can't bag on that.

As these fresh relationships deepen and evolve, though, the new(er) members accrue the trust to assume their own voice in the band. When Doug Wieselman joined the AHNONI band, he was "stepping into someone else's shoes. I had to phrase specifically either how they had been previously hearing these phrases, or how the other person was playing it. But once I was able to do that, and they started to hear what else I could do, they really gave me a lot of freedom." It was the audience that Jon Wurster felt he had to be mindful of when he joined the Mountain Goats. The band had never had a drummer, and their ardent fans "had a very specific idea in mind when they would come to see the band, and seeing a drummer up there wasn't something they were maybe wanting, or it wasn't something they foresaw when they bought the ticket for the show the first couple tours, so there really wasn't any map to follow."

When Narducy joined Bob Mould, and Jay Gonzalez joined Drive-By Truckers, it was on instruments which weren't their primary tools—Narducy on bass, and Gonzalez on keyboards (both were, first, guitarists). Bass "wasn't an unfamiliar instrument" to Narducy, "but to play a ninety-minute Bob Mould show, I was in no shape—I really worked hard that summer. I actually set up my garage as if it were a sound stage, with a full PA and a bass rig, and played at full volume for months to get ready for playing bass like that on stage." It was, he said, a "leap of faith" on Mould's part, but "he just trusted [me]; and he knew that once he asked, I would immediately start working very hard at it." Gonzalez realized when he moved to Athens that guitarists were "a dime a dozen; and keyboard players, certainly there were some, but not a lot. So that's why I moved back toward [keyboards] . . . and of course to end up playing keyboards in a rock band, it's not radically different, but I had to learn how to arrange it and simplify and find holes, but not get in the way of the two guitarists playing really low power chords." The Truckers hired him, at first, to cover the parts Spooner Oldham had played on their record.[49] For Gonzalez, this also meant "three or four years" before he felt like the band's fan base, accustomed to a certain level of turnover, began to think of him as a member as such: "Especially [then], there were more people in the band, and I was tucked away in the back. When I started playing guitar, it became a little bit more noticed that I was in the band—but it was still vague, and it takes a while."

The most difficult, but least visible, aspect of joining a long-running band is sensing, and maneuvering within, the web of established relationships—Katie Harkin describes it as "navigating through a dense mist that slowly clears. You can't force those kind of relationships. . . . There are some things you only learn about people when you've sat next to them in a van for 4,000 hours." Brian Viglione went into the Violent Femmes, a notoriously fractious group, "cautiously," but with the hope that he, as a fresh and enthusiastic presence, might be able to rejuvenate their relationship:

> I had to tread lightly and not rush anybody into anything, so I would very gently suggest things—perhaps we can do more to up the activity of what the band is doing, and the level of money and shows that we were generating. I hadn't worked full-time with a band of the stature of the Violent Femmes, who had been around for thirty-five years and had a long history and wide international fan base. But joining that group with two guys who hadn't spoken to each other in close to eight years, I tried to bring them together and point out that things could change. Those guys, Brian and Gordon, were taking separate vans to and from the gig. The road crew was nervous and walking on

eggshells around everybody, and it was just a very intense scene, where nobody wanted to say the wrong thing or rock the boat.

I thought, somebody has got to break the ice between these guys, and remind them that this can be fun, and that doing shows does not have to be a burden. So I spoke on the phone separately with each of them and said, "You guys have earned the right at this point to enjoy your band. You guys have locked yourself into a power struggle, which doesn't need to exist. You are operating in this outdated paradigm. You had all this time away from each other, and the band is now reunited, and you have a new drummer who doesn't have any of this past baggage of any of the other guys, and we are just getting together to have some fun and play music. So maybe there's a way we can collectively learn to let the past go and get back to why you guys enjoy playing music in the first place."

That helped a lot. And fundamental infrastructure things I tried to help with—getting the band's social media up and running—at [that] point they had zero presence except for a couple of fan pages on Facebook. It was bizarre to me that there was no way to offer even a T-shirt online. So I put them in touch [with] a new online merchandising company for the band.

And watching Gordon Gano, who normally was a little bit stoic on stage, begin to say things to the audience, like "I forgot how much fun this could be," and smiling and bouncing around; and everybody was lightening up and the mood just lightened up—that was a really rewarding thing, and I was happy to be a part of that.

Unfortunately—spoiler alert—it didn't last. "They basically gave me [an ultimatum] cutting my pay by 70 percent, and saying, 'This is what it is going to be, take it or leave it.' So I decided to leave it and move on. I also realized that it was not my job to repair thirty years of dysfunctional behavior between two guys."

EXTRA-MUSICAL SKILLS

"Like other free-lancers," wrote Robert Faulkner, the musician "competes for jobs in a market where his ability, reputation, tact, and social contacts determine the nature and volume of his work. He is a musical entrepreneur."[50] In a job market, the terms of which are often dictated by non-professionals, there is tremendous pressure on the musician to conform to certain standards beyond simple instrumental proficiency—which can vary from group to group, and are not always explicit. Then there are the aspects of (for lack of a better word) self-care which allow a band person to survive the physical and psychological pressures of, especially, touring, creatively intact. Besides being perceived as clubbable and uncomplicated (Jimmi Mayes quoted his mentor Joey Dee, "Be a gentleman and be on time"),[51] what are some of the skills that make a good band person?

"If you are a working musician working for other people," says Shahzed Ismaily, "the classic stuff [is] always be on time. Never put anybody out. Take responsibility for everything. Take care of yourself; take care of your health. And, always, always, always put your best foot forward in every situation. Know all the music extremely well. Play well. Be a really fun and engaging and pleasurable person to be around." Doug Gillard adds "being organized, packing light, [and] patience, a lot of patience." Caitlin Gray mentions a "level of self-promotion . . . like being able to maintain a website and social media. And keeping a good calendar, keeping track of your receipts and mileage—there's a lot of organizational stuff that people take for granted." Rick Steff suggests, "Listen first—on every level, not just musical. But really wait to figure out what water you are swimming in before you jump into the pool. Try to assess the situation. It is important to be supportive, to know when your opinions probably aren't necessary. Old tricks, like if you are playing with a bunch of people from different places, try to figure out who has been there the longest, and figure out why."

John DeDomenici emphasizes preparation: "I always want to be the person in the group that knows the songs the best. . . . When I was on tour with Laura [Stevenson], we played with Against Me!;

and their drummer Atom Willard was a dude that just showed up super ready to work. I remember that band before he joined and after [he] joined—they sounded completely different. They sounded like a huge, huge rock band, now, with him—and it's just a different drummer, that's really all that changed. Just watching how he prepares . . . was very, very inspiring. I said, 'Wow; that's why this guy is so good—because he wants to be.' I'm sure a lot of that's born talent too, but [it's] just as much that he comes ready to work and is super prepared. He was definitely one guy that I've sat and watched for forty straight days and was like, there's a reason this guy works so much. There's a reason this guy's in every band."

Almost everyone emphasizes the importance of being able to maintain a steady keel through the physical and, especially, psychological stresses of touring. There is more emphasis in the twenty-first century on the importance of maintenance of mental and physical health on the road than in the past. "I used to lose my mind on tour a little bit more before I started running and going to yoga," says Gray. "Emotional coping skills go out the window when you're drinking every night and eating crap food, so being able to remember how important it is to take care of yourself, and doing what you need to do to maintain some sanity—because there's not a lot of stability otherwise, so you have to do whatever is in your control." You learn to monitor yourself, says Marc Capelle: "You become more judicious about what's [working]. What am I making? Is it making me sad? Am I contributing anything? Do I have to go to a chiropractor in order to work? Because you can play god-awful music for eight hours and get paid pretty well, but it could ruin your mindset and your body-set for a month. There's an athletic aspect to what this is."

"It's such a strange way to live, on top of four or five other people for months at a time," says Mike Yannich. "You can easily not be able to think clearly. You learn, okay, let me step back from this situation, go take a walk or something, and that will clear your head. It's learning boundaries, like knowing, I'm going to leave that person alone for a while." "Mentally and emotionally," says Sarah Balliett, "everyone has varying levels of need and empathy. To get along in a band, you need to be able to meet your own needs, and have enough empathy to see the people around you and what their needs are. These dynamics are often in flux, so it's good to have at least a couple of band members who are highly empathetic and good at communicating or even mediating when necessary. I find this person is often a sideperson—someone for whom ego can take a backseat."[52] Putting that ego in the backseat is also part of the work. Mike Sneeringer "used to not be easy to tour with. I could be very moody; I could be very demanding, and I look back at it now [and think], 'I'm so above that.' But everyone has bad days, and how to deal with a bad day is a big deal. The maturity has been both on the emotional side of dealing with the rigors of touring, and on the musical side being able to swallow my pride—being able to [say], 'Hey, this is what this [bandleader] wants. I'm here to help them deliver their vision.' It's not my vision. And that's part of the beauty of a sideman, because I can focus on the job, and not be so sensitive about it."

Thor Harris—whose list of "tour rules" went viral—finds the hardest part of touring the way "it forces sedentariness upon you, which isn't very good for anybody. One of the worst times, that's just so hard to really make anything of, is the time between sound check and the show. But what I love about that kind of time is, because at home I'm such a goal-oriented busybody, tour forces me to sit down with a sketchbook or a book and occupy my time in ways that I don't do at home. So it does a lot of really cool things to my brain . . . that wouldn't have happened if I hadn't been stuck in an airport for eight hours here and there. I've read way more books than I ever read in public school."

That downtime is often—especially in early touring—filled with alcohol. On low-level bar tours, there may not be a hotel to relax in; you sat in the van all day; there's no green room; the bar doesn't offer food, but you have drink tickets. Band policies (usually unspoken) on drink and drugs vary considerably. In some, being a "good hang" necessarily includes drinking; in others, especially those with sober bandleaders, it may be explicitly off-limits. Jimmi Mayes expressed a familiar dynamic: "If you were a star, you could get as stoned as you wanted because the band had to follow you. But you couldn't get stoned if you were in the band, because you had to follow the leader."[53] The bottom line is reliability, says Michael Bland: "If you get your swerve on, do your job, man. I'm not here to judge you for your drinking, but if you're messing up—if you're making the gig a clam fest because you can't hold your liquor, then we've got a problem."

To be reliable, says Bloedow, is "like a football player—this guy should be open at that point, and you put the ball right in his hands, and it's a touchdown." A tolerance for, and ability to, repeat oneself is a necessity: "Some people are just incredibly talented, and they have a million ideas and they're awesome, but they never do the same thing twice. For me, there's a certain amount of repetition that is necessary, so I need people that can repeat. But I also like people that can write and delineate—not only can they repeat *a* musical line, but they can come up with maybe ten musical lines for a song, each of which is appropriate to what's already there, and they are willing to keep those more or less in the place that they are, over the course of a tour. Then you can speak to them over breakfast in Switzerland and say, 'Actually the seventh event—you should just play the first half, and leave the second half out.' Then that night, the thing has continued to adapt and evolve and grow. And the person actually enjoys doing that with you, so it's a constant process of arrangement. That's how rock bands eventually, arguably, come to rival great composers."

Efficiency has helped Josh Kantor: "I don't mean to sound immodest, but I cultivated or developed or acquired a reputation for being a musician who can learn a lot of songs quickly, and that's a skill that was developed from my work at the baseball games. I get a lot of calls where it's like, 'We're putting the band together, and the show's in two days, and we just realized that we actually need a keyboard player.' The keyboard comes often as an afterthought. So they're like, 'Can you learn twenty songs in two days and come to the rehearsal tomorrow and do the show on Saturday night?'"

Appropriate volume comes up regularly: "I know early on [that] the way that I started working a lot in Chicago, getting asked to play with a lot of people, was because I could play quiet," says Glenn Kotche. "There's a whole world of sounds I could get with brushes." In general, says Jon Rauhouse, "I play well and also *know how it works*"—by which he means the smallest aspects of being in a working band, which fall below the level of having to be explained, but are immediately understood as signifying professionalism: like getting gear quickly on and off stage, or coiling cables correctly. Michael McDermott has occasionally taken it upon himself to mentor younger musicians: "A couple bands that I worked with down in Florida, I had more seniority. . . . In that situation, you take on a role where you're like, 'No, this is how we load in. This is where we put our gear. This is how we get on the stage and get off the stage'—that dad mentoring role."

Those with the necessary skills—contracting, transcribing, transposing, arranging—in the popular music world can often make themselves invaluable as music directors, translating between the "trained" and "untrained."[54] This can be an informal role: Rick Steff joined Lucero "coming from a different, journeyman place, as opposed to more [self-taught] artisans like the four original Luceros are. . . . Trying to learn every chord in the book was never part of the thing for them, so when we are going for pre-production and stuff, I'll suggest chords, or suggest transitions, or anything like that" (a teacherly function he compares to the one Garth Hudson filled in The Band). For John DeDomenici, it can also simply mean leading rehearsals in the leader's absence, or taking responsibility for musical discipline on stage: "When we're playing, [Jeff Rosenstock]'s doing his thing and I am sometimes leading the rest of us, or just watching over some tempos. Or [if] someone's getting a little lost, they'll look at me, because I'm usually the one that knows the song the best and holding it down, because I'm usually the one that's been there the longest. There is a slightly rotating cast, but I'm usually the guy that's been there for a while, so I am the anchor, I suppose."[55]

Gerry Leonard has worked in the more comprehensive capacity of musical director for Duncan Sheik, David Bowie, Rufus Wainwright, and recently, Suzanne Vega:

> She's constantly getting asked to do things, and she needs somebody like me to come on board and sort it out—in the creative sense—with her, and protect her interests, and make sure that she's well represented in terms of what she needs to do and her preparation. Management can make a deal with

the idea of "Let's do two orchestral shows in Tel Aviv with the Symphony Orchestra there." It's a great idea. But there's a lot of dots to be connected between us going there and playing those shows successfully, and the initial spark of the idea: charts have to be created, rehearsal time, dealing with the conductor over there, dealing with the arranger here, coming up with arrangements and making sure that they're appropriate, finding the old arrangements and having them re-orchestrated, and stuff like that. And if nobody connects those dots and you go over there and you're not prepared, it's a bad situation for everybody. Because the orchestra, the conductor is embarrassed, the artist is embarrassed, and the show is [only] okay—whereas if the work is done, then everybody is happy and we have a great show. . . . There's a lot more work involved, so it's more responsibility and you can get a little more in salary and that's good for me—but believe me, there's plenty of hours I'm the one still awake writing the charts when everybody else is off.

This can be more effective when the music director is acting as a bandleader surrogate: that is, as a proxy for the single artist/star with a hired band. "With Antibalas," says Stuart Bogie, "we explored a whole bunch of different roles. For a while my role was as music director, which meant I was [writing] set lists, playing the rehearsals, and helping with the sound check. I enjoyed it, but I did run into situations where it was like 'Man, if you don't like the decisions I'm making, you can do this job. We can switch jobs; I can take your job'—which didn't work out either. That is just a difficulty in group dynamics."

BOREDOM AND ROUTINE

"I liked one band's music, but I couldn't have spent five years playing it," a bass player maintains. "It was a lot simpler than other bands." . . . A pianist complains in a similar vein, "I've been in situations in which I've been terribly bored. . . . I learned from that . . . especially on the road. . . . When the music is the only

thing that you have to look forward to during the day and you
don't look forward to it, it's really treacherous."
PAUL BERLINER, THINKING IN JAZZ[56]

What for them is routine, one night like another, is for their fans
a special event. . . . Simply by being at work when other people
are at play, all professional musicians . . . are distanced from
their listeners' lives.
SIMON FRITH, SOUND EFFECTS: YOUTH, LEISURE, AND THE POLITICS
OF ROCK 'N' ROLL[57]

We musicians are supposed to show enjoyment on the band-
stand whether we feel it or not.
DREW PAGE, DREW'S BLUES: A SIDEMAN'S LIFE WITH THE
BIG BANDS[58]

Some tolerance for repetition is a must, and an under-discussed
challenge and skill for touring musicians is preserving a sense of
freshness in and attention to touring repertoire. Beyond the "acting
as if"—a skill common to any successful performer ("I think great
musicians who can play the same thing over and over somehow can
embody the spirit of that solo every time like a good actor," says Jenny
Scheinman)—I asked players whether they find themselves getting
bored with the music they play and, if so, how they deal with, or
avoid, that feeling.

The first category of tedium is uninspiring material. "I've backed
up songwriters whose songs basically do nothing for me," says Oren
Bloedow. In those situations, he focuses on technique: "There's always
something to work on: how long you're playing the notes, relative volumes; maybe there's a different passing tone to take on the way to this
chord—just work on perfecting shit." Toby Dammit closes his eyes
and thinks of the paycheck: "You just think, 'Look, this is going to
go on for so long, and at the end of this it's going to be X amount of
money, and I've got to find something in this that is satisfying enough
to have a good time.'" You focus on finding something to look forward

to, says Peter Hess; for example, "in the Tommy Dorsey band, there were some really amazing Eddie Sauter charts in there."

Todd Sickafoose prefers not to "impl[y] that it is the music's fault," and if he can't find that "redeeming element" he believes he's just not looking hard enough: "I can't remember working on a piece of music that I didn't think had a redeeming element to it, so the job sometimes has been to just start over and go back to whatever that redeeming element is, and take a fresh approach to highlighting that." Brian Viglione had to find a route to working within stricter parameters than he had been used to: "[In] Jesse Malin's band, I felt a little bit under-stimulated at first, and that it was very constricted. He was very rigid in what he wanted me to play. That was my first experience with that, but it was a good learning experience, because I found that [within that] very tight set of parameters that he wanted, I could find my personality and my voice."

It's all part of building a career, says Peter Erskine; not every gig can be exhilarating: "When I was younger, [and] we're on a road band playing the same things for weeks on end, and that's kind of 'What the fuck are we doing?' because we were aspiring to something else, [and] I want to get to do *that*. Well, this sucks, okay? Get on the bus and have a beer. It was a gig, and we were still struggling trying to find our voice, trying to just find out how do you play this instrument."

Jean Cook used the experience of tedium playing certain people's music as a handy data point that "made me realize I didn't want to work with them again." There's always that option—"I have the ability to not play on records that I think stink," says Scott Spillane. "If someone gives you a piece of music and they're like, 'Hey, see if you can figure out something to this,' and I don't like it, I just say, 'I really can't think of anything. Maybe you should get a flute.'"

The second category is the routine of a repetitive set list from night to night.[59] This is the more troublesome problem, since it's usually a side effect of a secure and long-term gig. "It's hard to not get a little bored with songs you've played thousands of times," says Sarah Balliett. "Sometimes you're just punching the clock, there's no doubt about that," says DJ Bonebrake. "When I was doing the Broadway show [*Fela!*]," says Stuart Bogie, "I did find myself going a little crazy. Not because the music was boring—I had the best gig any saxophone player could want, playing in that show . . . but after three hundred shows, it starts to turn into Groundhog Day, and you start to really space out." But, says Nels Cline, being able to recreate a routine is part of being in the entertainment business at any level—and, to some extent, the nature of musical structure generally: "Many of my improvisor friends either ask me directly, or they ask other people who know me, how I can play in Wilco, 'cause 'Don't they play the same songs all the time?' Or 'Don't their songs have the same arrangements every night?' Anyone who knows me really well should know that this is not an issue for me. For one thing, Wilco doesn't play the same songs every night. . . . But yes, they have arrangements; and yes, I play those parts. Some songs that Wilco plays I have a lot more latitude; other songs I have really set parts. To me, that's what music is—it's just a combination of freedom and limitation, or freedom and rigid structure."[60]

People have a range of mechanisms for introducing variety: Balliett "push[es] for playing a few old ones here and there"; John DeDomenici says that "luckily with Jeff [Rosenstock]'s band, he's constantly writing new songs; we're playing new songs all the time." With Superchunk, Jason Narducy is often "learning three to five songs at sound check, because Mac changes up the set list more than anybody else I have ever worked with, and he is not afraid to throw on songs that I have never heard." New material keeps things interesting, agrees Bonebrake. "Sometimes X will go, 'Let's do this song just for fun.' We were on tour last summer and we said—just as a fluke, we never do cover songs—we said, "Let's do 'LA Woman.'" And it's a long complex song, for the stuff we do—it has three sections. We rehearsed it at soundcheck, and we played it backstage, and it was like, 'Wow, we felt young again. I'm young! Blame this old cover song.'" Every Mountain Goats tour cycle, says Peter Hughes, "there is definitely a conscious effort to [say], 'All right, these songs get cycled out; we are done with these for a while. This one is spent, and there are a handful of songs that we play that are staples; but definitely, let's have half of our set be new songs. Also let's have a bunch of other old songs that either we have never worked up as a band, or that have just been sitting idle for ten years now.'"

Players focus on detail work. "Sometimes I talk about rolling a rock up the hill every day," says Jim White, "and the sun is different, you see something else, and you push it up." "Within the pop-structured rock songs that get played live," says Doug Gillard, "I like seeing improvisation, different fills, different drum fills, different guitar flashes. . . . I'm always trying to think of, 'Can I join here? What chord voicing can I throw in here that will not disrupt the band, not sound too weird for the band that I'm playing for and distract them, but also be interesting to the crowd?'" Caitlin Gray "still take[s] lessons a lot, so I'll try to use what I've gotten from the lessons and try to focus on my technique." You wait for the songs to evolve in productive and interesting ways, says Todd Beene: "Let the songs breathe, live and breathe, and by the end of a tour maybe the song is a little different. It's the same song, but everybody's version is a little bit more refined and interesting." Janet Weiss has "been lucky to have been in bands that improvise on stage, whether it's interludes or certain sections of songs that we leave open. . . . If you have to stay on your toes, stay engaged because there's a part coming up for you, you get to really stretch out. I try to play different fills in some songs. I don't script everything out. I don't know exactly what I'm going to play. The element of surprise is important." Grace Potter, says Eliza Hardy Jones, will spring surprises on the band mid-set: she has "talk-back mics on stage where she can talk to us—it's in our ears, but the audience can't hear it—she will give us these directions [like], 'When we come around to the B part, I want everybody to do a jungle groove.'"

No, says Bill Stevenson: "I think what I play on the record is the right thing to play; that's why I chose it." Instead, you try to entertain yourself and your bandmates: "You can throw little things in live—like Charlie Parker, for two bars he would quote that Woody Woodpecker thing . . . live, I may just throw in a couple little Woody Woodpeckers for fun, to keep myself and my band guys amused, get a little chuckle from Karl the bass player if I do something funny."

Not every gig includes the possibility of even these low-level moments of improvisation. Jim White made a duo record with Nina

Nastasia which featured elaborate arrangements. To reproduce them live, he prepared and played along with overdubbed and pre-recorded tracks: "I suddenly realized after a handful of shows, basically there was nothing to—[it] was the same every night exactly. It was just a representation, just a presentation, rather than an event. I was kinda like, 'Ah shit.' . . . I never did it before or since." When Bruce Kaphan "was with David Byrne, I felt a lot of pressure to be *on* every second of every show. And when you're touring the world, and playing many nights a week, and not able to stop long enough to pick up a lot of new material—the repertoire does get to this point where you're on the high wire, and really the only direction is down. It was just a matter of having to do . . . flawless execution night after night after night; and that pressure built up on me a lot in that band, and I think it was because there wasn't much in the way of improvisation and there wasn't much freedom to explore." Similarly, Bruce Bouton on the Reba McEntire gig "had no opportunity for improvisation; I mean, very little. 'Blue jean cabaret,' we used to call it, because of the discipline of really, really having to play it perfectly every night. The challenge was 'Tonight we'll see if I can make the tone of this note be just a little bit richer, or let me see if I can nuance this phrase just a little bit better. Maybe I'll let this note die out on the second beat.' You just make up little games, to play with yourself and to keep yourself entertained." Bouton continues:

> In the Garth [Brooks] situation, we are working a lot, but the crowd energy is totally different. . . . Garth spreads it around; everybody is their own personality on stage. So you have to be on—I end the night every night with a gold top Les Paul on the last chorus of the song; the last phrase of the song Garth and I are hopping around the stage, twirling. It's pretty wild, it's acting like a twenty-five-year-old. The discipline is still the same. I still try to play things precisely. I still try to play something with some meaning and emotion behind it. So I don't get bored, I don't fall asleep. And the energy of playing to fifteen, twenty thousand people every show—he leaves the first three rows open until the show starts, and then they go way in the back

and get rabid fans to come down into the first three rows. So there's plenty of energy to go around.

To some extent, repetition is built into touring itself. "What you do every day is exactly the same," says Hardy Jones. "but it's totally different. That's what makes it possible—you need to have that routine, like 'This is what my day is going to look like every single day,' but you're in a different city, and the crowd is different, the set is different." Benny Horowitz says he has to be "pretty stoned on tour sometimes just to get through the days. The days fucking kill me on tour. I'm a hyper guy. I'm a busy guy, and I'm so run down from traveling and playing that I don't really have the energy to go out in a city and do something crazy and then come back and still play a show. But I have this natural restlessness; sitting in a backstage for fucking eight hours or something—there's not many things that I know how to occupy my mind. . . . I wish sometimes I could be the type of person who is like yeah, fuck it, Munich again, cool. But I'm not. I get bored." And repetition is especially necessary for bands still introducing themselves to people: "Strand of Oaks basically played the same set for a year and a half," says Mike Sneeringer. "It will change, it will evolve—but then iteration B will be run for like six months. We were . . . a band that is being discovered by most of the people we were playing in front of—it's a lot of new audience, so you want to have a good setup; and when you have a set that flows and a set that the band knows really well, you can play around [with] the segues and things feel really seamless. And that's great, but you do have to fight the boredom with that because it is so predictable. [There's] no danger."

More established bands have, on the one hand, a core set of songs concertgoers may expect to hear every night; but on the other, a deeper catalog and a more-or-less guaranteed audience. Scott McCaughey came "from the school where my favorite band that I ever saw, and still have ever seen, is NRBQ—a band that went out there every night without a set list, and could play any of five hundred songs," adding:

> I absolutely refuse to go out and play the same set two times in
> a row. I don't understand how bands could have the laminated

set list for a tour. I understand the reasons for it, but that would drive me crazy. Luckily, even when I was playing stadiums and arenas with R.E.M., they still wrote a set list two hours before the show every night and tried to mix it up. There are certain songs, of course, we had to play, but they still changed it up every night. We would maybe play twenty to twenty-five songs a night [out of] seventy-five to choose from, so that kept me from going insane. Because I'd have a really hard time being in a band that only played the same songs over and over. . . . I need the spontaneity, and to have every show be different and special.

The [Young] Fresh Fellows . . . went for most of our career without having a set list, but that can be a complete disaster. You go out there, and if you're not inspired, you stand around looking at each other—but that only happened to us maybe one out of twenty-five shows.

For the musicians who don't confront this issue, the tradeoff is acceptance of a certain amount of uncertainty and even potential chaos—as Jon Wurster says, the benefit of a consistent set list is "you get really tight and the show is pretty effortless."[61] For Lori Barbero, though, "every night is different, and we don't care about perfection. When we just played Primavera in Barcelona, [Babes in Toyland singer/guitarist Kat Bjelland's] strings broke, and our tech wasn't with us that night, so a stage person put 'em on, but they put 'em on upside down. It was being recorded live, and there was probably thirty thousand people, sixty thousand people there. Huge festival. And Kat had to just fucking go with, 'Oh, the strings are upside down.' But some people said they thought that was unbelievably great when shit like that happens, [not] 'Yeah, it was exactly like the last time I saw 'em.' We're playing the same songs and stuff [each show], but we have a different energy." Drive-By Truckers and Fugazi both improvise(d) set lists onstage, which offers the nervy energy of the unexpected—"to the point," Jay Gonzalez says, of "we haven't played this in five years; are you seriously going to pull this out during the show?" For the multi-instrumentalist Gonzalez, this adds the logistical challenge of "figuring out how I'm going to get to the guitar in time, or back to the keyboard, within the two-bar intro or whatever." Joe Lally supplemented the "extremely open and exciting feeling before you go on stage" with a compulsive routine of self-distraction on stage: "To keep my mind open, I had to remove pieces of paper on the stage, anything that might catch my attention while I was playing. Somebody left a water bottle; somebody dropped a pick—I started getting those things off the stage. Anything that would continuously draw my eye while I was playing fucking annoyed me. It was a very meditative experience, because it was really about not thinking, and tuning in. Oftentimes you would collectively understand what the next song was going to be. So that doesn't leave a lot of room for just going, 'Oh, this song again.'" For Marc Capelle, the sheer terror and euphoria of performing is thrill enough: "You're trying [for a] gigantic huge victory celebration, and then somebody's pulled the floor out from underneath you, you are going into a shark tank of sadness—it's the swing between those two things. It's a motivator. You could ruin some people's lives, including your own, over the course of the show. [Alternately], you could make yourself, and a bunch of other people, really happy."

And, says Mike Yannich, there's always the support musician's freedom to light out for new territory, Huck Finn–style: "A cool thing about playing in so many different projects [is] if something got boring, it was only a couple more weeks until I was playing in another band."

ABOUT THE INSTRUMENTS

I had never before thought of how awful the relationship must be between the musician and his instrument. He has to fill it, this instrument, with the breath of life, his own. He has to make it do what he wants it to do. And a piano is just a piano. It's made out of so much wood and wires and little hammers and big ones, and ivory. While there's only so much you can do with it, the only way to find this out is to try; to try and make it do everything.

JAMES BALDWIN, "SONNY'S BLUES"[62]

A musical instrument is in itself a piece of musical language.
LUCIANO BERIO[63]

More troublesome than a stale set list is the frustration that can set in with one's instrument—one can, in theory, walk away from a monotonous gig, but frustration with the limitations of one's instrument, or with one's limitations on that instrument, is more existential. One works with the available tools: one picks up an instrument, or is assigned one by one's parents. Diligently, one acquires first skill and then a job. "[Violin] is mostly a way of getting what is in my head out," says Jenny Scheinman. "I don't know if it matters what the instrument is. I started violin because my parents made me, so I just ended up playing it. It wasn't like I was always in love with the violin." But a consequence of mastery is the discovery of boundaries, and the greatest piano player can't make it bend notes like a guitar, or give it the timbral variety of a saxophone. And by then, you're stuck with the damn thing. How do musicians face down the limitations of the physical instrument—or their own limitations as a musician?

The pedal steel is "a bastard instrument," says Bruce Bouton.[64] "I get incredibly frustrated by it. It's a tuning compromise. I'm always playing at least three pedals and four knee levers, so it's very mechanical. It's a machine. Everything's gotta work right. You're bending, you're raising and lowering strings so much. . . . I told somebody the other day, 'I think I've been tuning longer than I've been playing.' I've been fighting that instrument for forty years." Bouton, at least, represents the mainstream of pedal steel technique. Guitar players have a variety of models—you can play like Ron Asheton instead of Eddie Van Halen if you want to—but there isn't an established alternative school of pedal steel. "You can forget that the instrument is really new," says Todd Beene. "We're talking about something that's only been happening since the '40s, and there's a lot of room to innovate— but it's definitely got this traditionalist's view: Nashville-style virtuosity is one way to do it, and that's 'the way;' and if you start doing some goofy shit with it, there are people out there that are going to say, 'What are you doing? That's not cool.'" It produces, among the non-traditional pedal steel players of the indie and rock worlds, a distinct imposter syndrome. "You know when you first start playing guitar, and then you figure out power chords, and then you figure out you can play along with anything with power chords—[that's] how I feel on pedal steel right now," says Beene. "It's really exciting, but I'm going to be learning about that thing for the rest of my life. It's frustrating when I feel like I'm plateauing, or I get frustrated with myself if I can hear myself relying on the same things over and over again in certain situations. . . . The frustration is not necessarily the instrument as it is my laziness about progressing."[65]

Violinists, meanwhile, carry the baggage of the *classical* tradition, and its stifling pedagogy. "I have such a push-me pull-you relationship with my violin," says Carla Kihlstedt:

And in fact, I'm at the point now where I feel equally dedicated to—or maybe more dedicated to—my craft as a singer than I do as a violinist. I was as schooled as one possibly could be in the violin, [up to] the point where I veered off. Everything else I learned from that point was a result of unschooling, learning from my peers, learning from my surroundings, taking what I knew already and trying to use it in a different context as a singer. I tried to teach myself about breath control from what I knew about bow control—I tried to use the tools I had in one area and apply them to another. I think as a result it took way longer than it would have if I were a schooled singer or a schooled composer. [My experience] both as a composer and singer all came after my formal schooling was done. . . . I felt very restricted by the violin, so my response was I would distance myself from it and then dive back into it and try to find other models. Like, what happens if you listen to a Marc Ribot solo, and try to replicate that angularity and that chordal thickness? What happens when you play in a band with two heavy metal guitars, [and] you try to apply that to the violin? What skills do I have that they don't have? What tools do I have that they don't have? What tools do they have that I can't currently access? I think I learned more about how to play the violin from looking at non-violinists than I did from looking at violinists. . . . So as a result, my violin playing is very distinctive, because I didn't really have the right violin heroes. All my heroes didn't come from the violin camp.

Jenny Scheinman picked violin because "it was so much more of a naturally collaborative instrument, ergonomically, [in] that you can move around, and the body language is so much stronger and more precise with violin. Playing in bands and playing chamber music on violin was so much more gratifying because of all the interaction. As a musician playing at home, one of the most magnificent things ever [is] to play classical piano with charts—[but] you are stuck behind this big thing."

The very strengths of an instrument can be a trap, especially if it's seen as exotic in the rock context. "You'll meet people who think that your instrument is one color in a paint box," says Stuart Bogie. "And when you train on an instrument, you train to think of your instrument *as the paint brush*, and the colors are the different tones and harmonies that you employ—it's a very different way of looking at things." Daniel Hart is "primarily a violin player. I can't think of a band that I've been in where I wasn't playing violin, and that can be limiting or boring. In Other Lives, one of the main guys in the band . . . just wanted me to play violin on every song. And I thought, that's kind of boring—there's some songs where on the record there were no strings, and I was looking forward to an opportunity to play something else. . . . It's what pushed me to try and find things to do with the violin that aren't as commonly done, and to go more into the pedals to create alternate sounds. [It] was a good exercise, but still I wish I didn't have to play the violin all of the time."

"I get frustrated by [my instruments'] limitations," says Peter Hess, a multi–winds player. "Some of them I'm still just trying to beat into submission; and others I'm trying to push their boundaries—specifically alto saxophone. I really want it to be an analog synth, and have that cutting sine wave power that could slash through anything and make one note be everything, because I don't love that sound.

Does anyone really love the sound of the alto saxophone? Unless it's Johnny Hodges. So rather than 'tired of them,' I'm trying to make them really, really speak."

"The thing about saxophones which is a drag," says Ralph Carney, "is the reeds, the mouthpieces, and 'Is your horn working right?' Is there some little leak that comes up out of the blue and you have to deal with? . . . I remember reading Barney Bigard['s] book, years ago. [At] one point he said, 'I don't want to play the clarinet anymore. I've done it enough.' Why? You're so great! But I can understand that 'I'm tired of that darn thing.'" Doug Wieselman "stopped playing tenor sax years ago, because I didn't like the choices I was making on it, and because of the baggage that goes with the tenor sax. Then I started to play it again [when] I felt like I could bring something new to it, and that is more exciting."

Multi-instrumentalism, for those who have the option, is a common reaction. If you're frustrated with one instrument, says Joey Burns, "Drop it and pick up something else. That's the beauty of having other instruments around." Katie Harkins thinks that "because I play a few different instruments, that hasn't happened. I get frustrated with myself—if I feel like there's a limitation, I don't blame the instrument, I blame the workman." When DJ Bonebrake gets bored, he takes up the vibraphone: "It can happen in any situation, if you're playing with a band too much. You go through periods—people get tired of their instrument. They go, 'I don't know if I like playing music anymore.' And then they're enthusiastic the next year. It goes in waves." Thor Harris "was really tired of the rock beat, the *boom-chick*," and on Bill Callahan's *Dream River* "tried not to play drum set. I tried to play congas on the whole thing, with a kick drum and a clave on my left foot. . . . There is something about that sort of nervous exploration, when I'm playing an instrument that I'm not very good at, that is far more interesting. When I play drums, the trouble is there's a lot of tried-and-true tropes that just come out of me—because I'm a musician of a certain age who listened to certain drummers—and I do consciously try to pluck that stuff out and not play a bunch of clichés." For Peter Hughes, it was getting a *different* bass that renewed his enthusiasm:

For a long time, I wouldn't really play [my bass] much. I would come home from a tour and put my bass in the case or hang it on the wall, and literally not touch it again until it was time to go on tour again, or whatever the next thing was. . . . Two years ago, I bought this Godin fretless semi-acoustic bass. I had never played a fretless before, and I didn't really know if I could. It is such a beautiful instrument and it feels so great to play, and because it is fretless, it is totally different. It got me really excited. So when I came home, I found myself wanting to play this bass all the time, which was really novel. I would walk around the house just playing this bass, because it feels good, and it is forcing me to learn new ways, and a more traditional vocabulary on bass playing that I had never really bothered with, playing scales or whatever. . . . That was a mini-renaissance for me: "Ooh, I'm playing the bass, but it is a totally different thing. I like playing the bass."

"Trumpet is a monophonic instrument, you play one note," says Scott Brackett. "That's one of the main reasons I enjoyed having other things to do, because . . . with a piano or a keyboard, you've got essentially two quintets at your disposal. That's the real out for me, that I play a lot of different instruments, so if the instrument that's my main breadwinner is not my favorite, I can also work some other stuff [in]—sometimes it's just about rotating the crop." He continues:

Adam from Murder by Death asked if I would start considering banjo. I was like, "I don't want to carry a fucking banjo around, man. I've already got an accordion, a keyboard, a theremin." I started messing around with the mandolin, [even though] I don't know how to play mandolin. And that was like discovering guitar all over again. I wasn't thinking about chord changes or inversions, I was just following my ears. Picking up a new instrument is a good writing tool, because you don't really know what you're doing, so you start using your intuition, and end up writing some cool stuff.

Jon Rauhouse, as it happens, did start playing banjo:

> And I didn't play that thing for five years, because it got to be
> so limiting. . . . But Neko [Case] found out I played banjo, and
> she said, "You got to bring it out," and I ended up completely
> changing the style of what I was doing. I got the greatest com-
> pliment from some dude in Seattle one time: "You play the
> creepiest banjo I ever heard." I was like, "Thank you, that was
> what I was trying to do," but I didn't realize I could do that until
> somebody forced me to do it. We were playing murder ballads,
> songs about horrible subjects, like, "I gotta make this sound
> strange"—I plug it in to a Vibrolux and slap a ton of reverb and a
> little bit of distortion on it and play it really hard and slow.

Doug Gillard treats the guitar itself, with its variety of traditions and
comfort with sound-altering pedals, as a multiplicity of instruments:

> That's the sole instrument that I play; I tend to think of it in
> terms of arranging different guitar parts within the same song:
> "On this rhythm thing we will do this; okay, this little part will be
> here, but it won't be like the other lead part; then the acoustic
> part is going to come in the middle, but only on top of electrics."

Bass players tend to be quicker to acknowledge the constraints of
their instrument. Says Todd Sickafoose:

> The bass has its limitations, so sometimes I have a little bit
> of envy of the way that other people can interact with music.
> But also it's those limitations that [are] the beauty. Sometimes
> I may love music with no bass. I understand why people have
> bands with no bass. It makes a lot of sense to me. Sometimes
> people come up in airports and see me carrying the bass and
> say, "Oh, bass is my favorite instrument." And I'm always glad
> that they are saying that to me, but maybe bass is not my favor-
> ite instrument. I love playing bass, but I would never say that
> about bass. But I feel weird saying that out loud.

At the same time, bassists are profoundly interested in the expansive ways the role of a bass player, and a bass part, can be interpreted. "It wasn't enough [to be] a bass player," says Melissa Auf der Maur, "which is why I ended up making solo records." She goes on:

> But in terms of the creative process, I became a really good bass player by playing within limitations. I actually don't even really like bass players—I do love one bass player: Eric Avery is the only bass player I ever noticed, put it that way—[but] in playing simple music like Hole, I learned how to become very layered and elaborate and busy as a bass player within the whole confinement.
>
> If I had just done free jazz, alone, forever, I couldn't have necessarily learned—which I ended up liking learning—how do you make A C G exciting? As a drummer and a bass player, that is fucking boring. So I got to really figure out how to make it more dynamic and more exciting and evolve. . . . A whole song is either one riff or two riffs, and they all involve the most simple chords. So I would manage to—by the end of the song, I'm never playing the same thing I ever played at the beginning. I never play that verse the same way again. So that was the challenge of being slightly stunted, or occasionally bored.

Similarly, for Peter Hughes:

> John [Darnielle]'s songs, because . . . they were simpler in terms of chord progressions, they left a lot of room for me as a player to come up with different things. Part of the challenge was, because so many of the early songs were pretty simple chord progressions, like I-IV-V type things, a lot of my job was—I don't know how much of this was conscious; I think Franklin [Bruno] actually pointed it out to me that I was doing it—but I was finding ways of taking these songs—[which] were pretty similar, and the songs sounded like all the other songs—finding ways to take these songs and differentiate them texturally or rhythmically, or hiding the I-IV-V progression by not playing root notes.

Playing bass is like you are steering the ship. I always had this metaphor in the back of my mind, even then when I was sixteen years old. The drums are the engine making the ship go forward, and the guitar and the singer and whoever else are all up on deck, showing off and performing a show, and the bass is the thing that is steering. Because if I'm just holding an E, we are going straight ahead. If I start to add some other notes, we are going in *this* direction, and nothing that you can do is going to change what I'm doing to go in *that* direction. I liked having that control, and being the person who is mediating between the thing that is pushing us forward and the stuff that is going on top. That role in the band is a really satisfying one for me.

"The way I perceived bass in a song," says Joe Lally, "was that it had more of a lead role in it than traditional bass playing, working around the root. I tended to try and find a memorable riff, very much like a guitar. I see myself as being much more influenced by guitar players than by bass players doing traditional bass playing." His approach was more simple, he says, than bass players he admired (Rick Danko, Paul McCartney, and funk/soul/R&B players like Larry Graham), "but it was probably more apparent as a bass line—you're aware of what the bass line was, instead of going, 'I didn't notice it,' sneaking around under the song the way that a lot of traditional bass lines do." A shared fandom of Joy Division and Public Image Ltd. with his first writing partner gave him "a ticket into understanding the role of the bass in a song, and that it didn't have to be complicated, that in fact it could direct the course of the song."

There is, says Mike Watt, a political economy within a band that privileges certain instruments over others, and to overturn that hierarchy—for example, to think of the bass as a melodic instrument—is a radical act. Watt had perceived and accepted a sense that the bass was held in low regard: "[I] didn't really have the idea it was lower in pitch, but definitely lower in status. I put a picture of [Richard Hell] on my bass, because I could not believe that the leader of the band was a bass man. It seemed like bass was where you put your retarded friend, or was like right field in Little League, where nobody hits the ball." He shared with Lally an interest in R&B bassists like Graham and James Jamerson (because, he says, you could actually hear them on the records), but Minutemen leader D. Boon encouraged him to consider *why* those players had more room to work:

> The politics dealt with in the Minutemen wasn't lyrics. D. Boon called that thinking out loud. He thought what made Minutemen political was the way we structured the band. He was influenced by the R&B guys, and trebly and clipped [guitar] playing, and he thought that left more room for the drums and bass. He thought there was hierarchy—we come from the seventies, arena rock, so it seemed like the guitar players dominated it. He wanted to make a more egalitarian way of doing a rock band, so that's where the politics actually was. He didn't really do power chords; he asked me to be up front there. . . . We were trying to make a three-way conversation.

According to Watt, the title of his first solo album, *Ball-Hog or Tugboat?*, was his way of asking:

> What is the bass? Does it aid and abet? . . . A farmer, he'll tell you, if you want a good crop, use a lot of manure. So the bass— there's a lot of manure there. The bass is still on a quest to find itself. I don't think it's a fake guitar. I really think it's more like drums. It's [in] a very interesting place, this instrument, very mysterious.

The non-canonical rock instruments (that is, instruments other than guitar, bass, and drums) share the additional frustration of permanent outsider status in the rock context. "I played the clarinet almost exclusively between the ages of ten and twenty-five," says Stuart Bogie.

> I had a fucking clarinet, and I wanted to rock! I'd go to hardcore shows. I'd go see Fishbone. I wanted to *play*. I'd listen to Neil Young. My clarinet—I couldn't fit into any of those worlds. My

whole life has been this weird identity crisis. I've never identified with the basic clarinet repertoire. I love it; it's beautiful; I
admire so much of it, but I never felt like it was for me. I didn't
feel like I was at home performing a music other than original
music. I developed an original music that I felt very comfortable with, but playing someone else's, another style of music
like jazz or blues or something—I never felt comfortable with
that, until I found Fela's music, with Afrobeat.

I wish I could play drums; I wish I could play guitar. I also feel
[that] if I had developed those skills more, I might have found
myself as a member of a band. Playing a horn, it's like I specialized in this antiquated profession that didn't feel antiquated at
all when I was studying it, but you never hear about the guitar
making a comeback, or the bass making a comeback—it's a
pillar of the music. The rock quartet stays what it is. It's like we
[winds] are stuck on the outside because of choices we made
when we were younger. I wish I had played other things, so I
could be in a band like Grizzly Bear or something, and I could
have. I was in Antibalas, and that's a great band, but there's
twelve people in it—so it's fated to what it is.

This is not to imply a general penis envy of guitars and drums, but
to point out the inherent limitations that certain instruments place
on the ability of their player to engage with the band experience, or
the creative process—drummers, for example, are often structur-
ally excluded from the financial backstop of songwriting credits. Jay
Gonzalez remembers the core members of Drive-By Truckers "saying they liked the way the keyboards were working," which, to the
new member, was both a meaningful and backhanded compliment
because "they are not big fans of keyboards. In rock, they don't necessarily want it on everything." A pervasive, reactionary notion in
rock remains that keyboards don't belong, nominally a conservative
response to '70s prog-rock and '80s synth-pop—"which is hilarious,"
says Gonzalez, "when you think of the basis of rock 'n' roll, Little
Richard. The saxophone gets the same rap. Saxophone and piano
were the roots of rock 'n' roll!" He adds:

> I feel like the Truckers [felt] that maybe there is that stigma, but I felt like they had been together long enough where they were open-minded to it, and I don't think they were ever against it. But when it's your music, you want it to be the right amount; and when you are a guitar-heavy band—as most bands are—it's a matter of how it's going to fit in. It can work, and obviously does.

The pressure is towards humility and reticence:[66] "Even the bands I was in before," says Gonzalez, "they wanted a keyboard player, but nine times out of ten the thing in recording or coming up with parts was peeling back the layers and honing it down to the very minimum. I spent a lot of time trying to figure out how a little could go a long way. . . . That sort of self-editing really helps with [the Truckers], because there are very few songs where I'm providing the rhythm pattern or playing straight through. Whereas The Band [a group with two keyboardists], if you listen to them, [guitarist] Robbie Robertson is hardly ever playing; it's almost like fills." Gonzalez has gotten a longer leash as the band became more comfortable with having him around (although that has coincided with his assuming third-guitar duties). "It was really tough the first six months. I wasn't in the monitors. I was in my monitor, but I was pretty sure I wasn't in the mix. I know no one else could hear me—[which was] for the better, because they just gave me a stack of CDs, and we didn't practice. . . . I've got to give them credit for not being like, 'Well, this is not working,' right away. The real strength Patterson [Hood] has is that he knows chemistry, and he also knows it takes a little while to get into the groove of something."

I've left drummers for last, because drummers—perhaps because they stereotypically combine a support role with a performative physicality[67] (the drummer as star stuck in the back), or perhaps because of their built-in limitations around harmonic and melodic content[68]—are unusually articulate and eager to talk about the peculiarities of their instruments and their roles as drummers. Some like the feeling of power and control, of being "the engine room"; some say it's like being the goalie in soccer, where you're crucial but you only get noticed if you screw up; and some struggle with their perception that the drummer is at the bottom of the traditional rock hierarchy. "I can literally go from one [feeling] to the other in a day," says Benny Horowitz, "because maybe I'm a little sensitive and moody like that." He continues:

> I think the thing that drummers struggle with—and it's something that's pretty fresh in my mind at the moment, and I'm really careful of my words because I don't want to sound ungrateful, because I'm not at all. I love my life, and I love the fact I became a professional drummer in rock bands. It's the coolest shit ever. But there is an aspect of it—and I guess it comes from a human's [need] for validation, and from some level of ego or something, I'm not exactly sure—but the idea that people think I don't contribute to the thing that is literally my life's work is a little demeaning and a little frustrating. I would like to sit here and say I make art sheerly for the fact that I make art, and I find such validation in the creative process that that's all I need, but it's not. Be fucking real. I'm the type of person that works really hard at something, presents it, and I appreciate the validation if it's good. It feels good, and there's a level of that that does frustrate me about being a drummer.

While he feels the power of the drummer in the live setting—"My finger is on the pulse of the whole thing. I can slow it down if I want to. I can speed it up if I want to"—he's resistant to exercising that kind of fiat in a democratic band. "Being giving artistically may seem like an altruistic or generous state of mind, but it's very self-serving, ultimately," says Peter Erskine. "I'm the puppet master. The drums—by shaping the dynamics, by controlling the rhythm, I can pull a lot of the strings of the music, and that's satisfying." He elaborates:

> Drummers, by nature, we're the bus drivers: "Hi folks, get comfortable in your seat. Don't worry, I'm going to get you where

you're going." It doesn't make us the most important person on the bus, but we determine where everything is going. That's what you want from a drummer. That's what you want from an airline pilot. You want someone who knows what they're doing, who's confident, doesn't take too much bullshit, and will get you there safely.

Glenn Kotche points out the advantages of the wide-open field of what constitutes percussion: "I am lucky because I'm a drummer. The voices of a string instrument, a brass instrument, a wood instrument are very specifically defined. Historically, percussionists in the orchestra get handed everything that, like, 'What the fuck do we do with this? It's a siren. It's horse hoofs. It's a wind machine. It's a box that you close, you slam on the ground. Give it to the percussionists!' So now percussion is anything, to me, that isn't one of those other instruments. It encompasses all sorts of noise makers and sounds, even recordings and other things. It's such a broad family of instruments that I could never really get bored." Kotche continues:

> In college, sure, I got frustrated learning marimba literature. But then I'd go over and learn Afro-Caribbean music on drum set, and figure that out. Now I play a lot of drum set, [but] Wednesday I'm going to be playing a lot of mallets, [which] is something that I'm comfortable with, but maybe that I don't flex that muscle all the time. So it's fun to float between these different areas of percussion, different styles. I imagine if I was in a band and I just had a four-piece kit and I played the same type of groove all night long and that's what I did, yeah, I would get frustrated and bored. But luckily the situations I'm in are so different, so varied, that I think it'd be impossible for anyone to get bored or frustrated.

Jim Sclavunos agrees: "There's a whole set of tonal scope there that you can integrate into a drum kit or into a recording session that you have been called in to do as a drummer, and that can be anything from gongs to tympani to tubular bells to tambourines and maracas. . . . I have gotten tired with my own limitations and I seek to go beyond them, but all I have to do is listen to someone like Max Roach and I know that there is a whole palette of sounds that can be drawn out of the instrument that I have yet to explore. They aren't part of that signature sound that people identify with me, but there is always room for expansion—I can write a bigger signature, or a signature with more curlicues." Jim White wants to write drum parts that are "intrinsic in the songs. I want drum parts that the songs wouldn't exist without."

That's not to say the drummers don't pass through fallow periods. "For some reason, last night," Jon Wurster says, "I just wanted to play along with some country records, because that's very meditative and therapeutic for me, to just kind of tap along with a Charlie Rich record or something. I don't really play that much when I'm not on the road, or I'm not in the middle of a project, because I do get tired of it. If you are a mechanic, you don't want to come home from work and start working on a car again. If I'm playing a lot for a month on end, I won't touch the drums for a couple weeks, because then when I come back to it I want to be excited; I want to be inspired to do it again." Viglione, for a period, associated drumming with "a part of my identity [that] had become a curse that I just wanted to get away from. I couldn't even look at the drums; I didn't play drums for close to six months [because] the drums made me feel the sense of failure and disappointment and hurt that I felt around being in a band." Sclavunos "never felt corralled by playing drums. I feel more corralled by people's attitude toward drummers than I do by drums. There is a thing in the media, for example—most media is quite celebrity-obsessed, and if they are talking about a band they will always focus on the singer first and foremost, and whoever they perceive as the second-in-command. And it's usually going to be somebody who isn't the drummer. . . . It didn't used to be that way. I can remember when the Beatles first came out, they were all considered equally important. They all got equal coverage in the media."[69] Michael Bland points out that the physicality of drumming means "there's a lot more ergonomic issues than for anybody else. Drummers have physical issues, arthritis, carpal tunnel. I've got to stretch. I read when I was a kid somewhere that being a drummer is tantamount to being like a triathlete. You're putting your body through the grinder. . . . You give your life to this thing, and you take your dings. You've got to just navigate and survive it all without too much nerve damage, not too much psychological baggage."

In any case, says Bill Stevenson, there is, for him, no such thing as drumming absent a group context: "I have never been a *drummer* drummer. I rarely even listen to the sound of drums without being accompanied by other instruments. The drums drive something, and whatever they are driving, I want to hear that too." Horowitz says, "The only thing that frustrates me about being a drummer is that I don't have independence in music. It would feel good to me to create a song by myself on a guitar, and then build the whole thing. But it's gotten to that point that I'm offended sometimes by people who, like, in their thirties decide to do their solo records, and they've never played these instruments in their life. I really think you would be better served staying focused and staying disciplined. Even if you're maybe a touch bored with your instrument, to actually continue building on like twenty years' worth of work, then going and getting *sort of* good at a bunch of other instruments—even if I ever had that instinct where I think, 'I should do this or that,' I want to go, 'Play drums more and just get better at those.'" The communality of group music-making resolves some of the instrument-specific issues, as for Ruth Finnegan's musicians: "Players who had chosen instruments unsuitable for solo work particularly valued playing in a group. As one drummer explained, a band gives 'comradeship in music-making—the ability to use talent that could not be used individually.'" "The bass is like glue," says Watt, "so if you don't have something to stick to, you are just a puddle. So you got to find [group] situations." "I wish there were more cellists out there," says Sarah Balliett. "The other guys always have tour-mates they can talk to about guitar, bass, drums, or keys. I'm [jealous]."

Still, "it's a constant struggle" for Gerry Leonard. "I was watching a movie about a chess player and they're saying, after four moves in

chess, [there are] 300 billion possibilities. With music, and any instrument, you make your opening moves, and then you open it up for the
amount of variables and possibilities."

"Let's say I pick up a guitar," says Ismaily, "and there's something
tiring in that experience for a split second." He continues:

> I feel like all I have to do is think about anything. If I close my
> eyes and I think about two-step dance, two teddy bears, two
> stuffed animal bears sitting on a shelf staring at each other,
> or staring forward but sitting next to each other, and I think a
> little bit about the architecture of that. I think, okay, teddy bears
> are inert objects that are trying to mimic life, or imitate life. So
> then I would pick up the guitar and I would think, literally let
> me imagine that this guitar is trying to imitate the actual life
> of a saxophone—it isn't a saxophone, it's just an imitation of
> it; and there's a childlike quality to it because there's a teddy
> bear space, and it's a kid's room. Now I'll just sit and play from
> that perspective. Then immediately it's an entirely new instru-
> ment, and it feels really live and really fresh. I can do that at any
> moment, so I never felt dead on any instrument in that sense.

"I love the instrument," said Nels Cline. "It's not the instrument's
fault that I suck ass half the time."

4

THE FAMILY BUSINESS

Musicians with Children

"Leaving [my daughter] Julia for a five-week tour when she was three weeks old was just about the hardest thing I've ever done," says Ara Babajian. "So my playing was informed by a sadness, ferocity, and love that was at times extremely difficult to live with. I used to sit in the back of the club after the show writing letters to the future Julia, explaining why I was out doing what I was doing, and hoping that she would understand some day."

Many studies of the lives of working musicians presume an all-male milieu in which family life is a nuisance, if not an active handicap. Writing about jazz musicians in 1963, Howard Becker took as a given that "membership in families binds the musician to people who are squares, outsiders who abide by social conventions whose authority the musician does now acknowledge. . . . Marriage is likely to turn into a continuing struggle over this issue; the outcome of the struggle determines whether the man's musical career will be cut short or will continue."[1] Robert Stebbins, in 1968, relegated the musician's family to the status of "peripheral institution"[2] in the structure of his life—prioritized after gigs, jam sessions, after-hours social life, the musicians' union, and "cliques": "The number of jazz musicians who are legitimately married, with or without children, is not known, but they are probably in a minority. The status of 'married' in the jazz world is a liability rather than an asset. . . . The jazz musician finds he must put jazz first when he marries. . . . Certainly," he added drolly, "this situation must increase the jazz musician's interest in the less legitimate forms of marriage."[3] It's no picnic for the imagined spouses, either: "The initial glamour of being married to a musician," wrote Bruce MacLeod, "wears thin once the realities of making a living in music become clear."[4]

Of course, far from the dope fiends and "deviants" conjured by Becker, desperate to squirm loose of the shackles of "square" society, many of today's working musicians are simply trying to secure a stable and sustainable life, including long-term partners and children. Not that they don't have familiar worries: "You have to be with a woman who really understands [that] you're not always going to be present," says Michael Bland. "The woman I'm married to now understands it much better than the one I was married to when I was dealing with Prince." A sense of financial insecurity haunts Stuart Bogie: "I have never really felt stable enough to jump into [parenthood]. I always felt like 'tomorrow I'm going to start earning some money.'" And there's the freedom to accept work, or opportunities, or simply adventure: "If I just need to jump on the plane tomorrow and go to Australia or Brazil or Norway, or wherever, I can," says Toby Dammit (who still says he and his fiancée plan to have children). "I can make that decision myself, on the spot, without having to consult, or be concerned about 'who's going to take care of little so-and-so' or the cat or anything else like that." "If I had kids or was married," says Jon Wurster, "I wouldn't be able to do it like this." He continues:

> I watched this great documentary last night about Bobby Bare Jr.; he's on the road, he's doing this summer tour, which is just deadly, going through Arkansas and Oklahoma. He's got three kids in this [vehicle]. He has just had a new baby and he's trying to keep this new relationship with the mother of the baby together. And I was just thinking, I would never be able to do what I do if I was in that situation. I do make a good living,

thankfully, at this point. But if I was doing it like he's doing it, making 350 bucks a night, I would have to quit, because I'd have three kids I've got to support. I guess I'm trying to say that I'm lucky I don't have those things to worry about. My life has been pared down to basically just looking out for myself financially and not having those other kinds of concerns. Otherwise I wouldn't be able to do it.

Many, though, do choose family life. In many ways, for musicians to talk about how becoming a parent affected their relationship to their work is simply to summon up, as Joe Lally says, the "enormous amount of clichés" that accrete around parenting in general: the reordering of priorities, the "higher stakes," the erosion of narcissism, the gratitude for a patient and pragmatic partner; and, especially, the financial imperative, and the consequent focus on music as a *job* as much as a calling. "Once I had kids, I had to make more money," says Babajian. "I loved having a purpose, but I also hated the amount of money I had to make at music if I wanted to continue playing." Bruce Bouton "had to work harder. I was really lucky; right after I had my son, I had a really big album cut as a songwriter, and it made a whole bunch of money. . . . I was a good provider."

For Peter Erskine, the financial pressures of parenthood freed him from the tyranny of aesthetic judgment. "I, of course, had to take a lot of jobs—pretty much anything that was coming along," he says.

I remember I was in New York City, and I was walking back to my hotel after having dinner or something, and these three young hipster jazz guy musicians, gig bags on their shoulders, [say,] "Hey, you're Peter Erskine, right?" Yeah, hey fellas, how you doing? And the alto player comes up to me and says, "Can I ask you a question?" Sure. I turn back and we're facing each other. [His] question is "What the fuck are you doing playing on a [smooth jazz pianist] David Benoit record?" That was his question. I just shrug my shoulders and I said, "Paying the bills, boys."

But not every musician/parent doubles down on their bookings. Those, especially, with more traditionally professional partners often find the irregularity (and nocturnal nature) of their schedule re-branded as a benefit: they can be the flexible parent, available during the day for doctor's appointments, daycare pickups, and cancelled childcare. In fact, the role of stay-at-home parent can be a congenial one. "It's a good lifestyle for a musician," said Ralph Carney. "You stay at home and then you go out and work at night. We would play music when [my daughter] was really little, just for fun, little toy pianos and stuff. It didn't put a damper on my playing." (As long as, of course, you're not out so late you can't respond to a 6 a.m. wakeup call from an energetic three-year-old.)

Musicians, as workers in the culture industry, occupy overlapping and sometimes conflicting roles: as skilled craftspeople, whose technique requires years of focused, repetitive exercise and maintenance; as crowd-pleasing entertainers at the mercy of the market; as self-employed small business owners, employers, and contingent employees (often simultaneously); as artists cultivating and protecting unstructured creative time; as rentiers, union members, day laborers, independent contractors, and members of self-organizing collectives. The profoundly ordinary ambivalence of parenthood—its abstract benefits and concrete disruptions—must be filtered, kaleidoscopically, through each of those roles in shifting combination.

For one thing, music creation can't be walled off: parenting can't help affecting the content of the music. "I spent the last forty-five minutes driving kids to school listening to Taylor Swift," says Jenny Scheinman. "And I was thinking, 'Wow, this is going to come out on my next three records.'" More fraught is the question of the insistent new demands on one's time, and the pressure to be productive in the limited time one has. Gerry Leonard says family life improved his creative efficiency: "I think back to the days when I would just wake up and have the whole day to myself, and I could go and sip a coffee, and write in my journal, and all those things. Now I'm making dinner, I've got a track open in Pro Tools, and I can run back [when] I've got an idea and I can lay it down in twenty minutes and get it done before the pasta boils over."

Children simply take up an overwhelming amount of the mental space, once casually available, that parents don't notice or appreciate until it's irrevocably gone. Scheinman mourns her loss of focus amid the haze of obligations: "Violin is such a pain in the fuckin' ass, because you have to play it so much to be able to sound decent. There was a time in my life where I was able to practice all day and gig all night." Children, among other demands, have made it "very hard to maintain my technique, much less actually improve." She adds:

> I just don't have as much time to daydream about it. Before I had kids, if I was biking across the Brooklyn Bridge, I was most likely working on a tune, whether I liked it or not. I was probably singing a song and figuring it out, or thinking about [one]; I was working all the time in my head. Now if I were to bike across the Brooklyn Bridge, I would probably be thinking about whether Bellamy should take the first or second soccer camp, and whether Rosa really ate all her carrots for her lunch. It absorbs my psychic energies. That has affected my music. It has divided my time.

Glenn Kotche compensates for the distractions of home, and its drain on mental energy, by taking advantage of a tour's downtime to reclaim some working hours. "I do probably, say, 80 percent of my composing on the road with Wilco, because [on tour] I work three, four hours a day, tops. So I have all that other time, and I can't be distracted [by] 'OK, I have to pick up this birthday present, and then I have to go to the store to get this, and then we have to go into the bank, and then we have to go to the dry cleaner, and we're definitely going to the park for an hour.'" Meanwhile, he brings more concentration to those three or four hours of band work. "If I'm three thousand miles from my kids right now, I'm going to make sure that everyone who leaves the show tonight is blown away. . . . 'Cause I'm not going to be out here wasting time, or going through the motions, if I have to be away from my family."

The main concern for musician parents, of course, is not the opportunities[5] but the demands of touring, and the time necessarily spent away from their children. "I tried to get a road case with a blow-hole for [my son] when he was smaller," jokes Marc Capelle. Time on the road away from family occupies an emotional position between guilt and obligation. "Sometimes music feels like the enemy, because it takes me away from the ones I love," says Babajian. "You embrace both sides," says Michael McDermott. "Embrace what you have when you're home, and feel fortunate enough when you're out to be able to do what you love to do."

Some—mostly men—tour more to provide; some sacrifice or temper their earnings and ambitions in the name of emotional responsibility. Erskine "was traveling a lot when the kids were young . . . to keep things afloat financially; then you're missing their growing up. And when you get home, you've just got off a three-leg flight from somewhere in Europe. You want to read them a book at night and you're so tired, you pass out after two pages." Lally took himself off the road after a few years: "I just started to feel like an absent father, and that feeling was much worse than any good feeling about what I was doing." Carla Kihlstedt "used to be on the road ten months a year. Now [it's] a few weeks a year. I do many more one-off gigs." Bill Stevenson turned toward more studio work: "I took the show quantity from, let's say, a hundred and fifty shows a year down to seventy-five shows a year, just so I wouldn't have to be an absentee father. And I supplemented that lack of revenue by starting to focus more on engineering and production . . . [so] I could still be working, but not be in New Zealand or somewhere, but here in my studio, and maybe every once in a while make it home for dinner and do some math homework." For Jason Narducy, the last two weeks of October are non-negotiable blackout dates "because my two youngest kids have birthdays then, and it's Halloween, and you can't, as a parent, recreate Halloween."

Still, as for any parents, the specific frustrations are balanced by benefits no less meaningful for their nebulousness. "My playing seems to be colored by a deeper love, a richer tapestry than it was before I became a father," says Babajian. "When I hit a drum now it speaks volumes; I can write a novel in a brush stroke, rather than push and strain to say too much like I may have done when I was a younger man." "Wiping a kid's ass," says Kotche, "somehow basically I grew stronger." He continues:

> Toddlers are the ultimate improvisers; you never know what they're gonna [do] next. So that has to be good for your skills as a musician: to be able to react, and react in the right way. Just looking at things through a kid's eye, the things they notice, the things they find are funny, keeps an open-mindedness to life which *cannot* hurt creative people. Looking at things from the unobvious way, appreciating little things, noticing little things—those are all really important skills for any creative person, and when you're around little people who are doing that all the time, it's gotta rub off.

Scheinman, who had children later in life, doesn't feel like she's missed opportunities. "On my short list of people who I always wanted to play with, I played with many of them. . . . I didn't feel like [children] interrupted something that was just about to bloom." In fact, she adds, becoming a parent freed her from the outsider pose that many young musicians adopt out of affectation, mannerism, or obligation. "I feel finally like I am a part of society, rather than some[one] at the periphery, making comments about it without any real first-hand experience." Peter Hess shares her sense of a greater connection to and stake in the world: "Making music is my contribution to the way I wish the world was, instead of what it is. . . . I want [my daughters] to inhabit this more beautiful world, and this is my contribution to it."

5

THE ARTIST AND THE ARTISAN

Money and Credit

Many times . . . when we are pleased with the work we slight and set little by the workman or artist himself.

PLUTARCH, "LIFE OF PERICLES"[1]

Participants in the making of art works, and members of society generally, regard some of the activities necessary to the production of a form of art as "artistic," requiring the special gifts or sensibility of an artist. . . . The remaining activities seem to them a matter of craft, business acumen, or some other ability less rare, less characteristic of art, less necessary to the work's success, less worthy of respect. They define the people who perform these other activities as (to borrow a military term) support personnel, reserving the title of "artist" for those who perform the core activities.

HOWARD BECKER, ART WORLDS[2]

The fundamental dilemma for the working band person goes beyond celebrity and attention, since many of them prefer to work unnoticed. Rather, the music worker occupies an uncertain place between the artist and the craftsman—let's say artist and the artisan, to avoid gendering—roles which can seem mutually exclusive in their expectations. The artisan privileges function, virtuoso skill, adaptable versatility, and reliable reproducibility, whether the product is horn charts or ceramic mugs. The artist must be a vessel of unique expressiveness. How musicians place themselves on a continuum between these poles, oscillate between them depending on context, operate as one within the confines of the other, or reject the formulation, is a window into how they think of themselves as musicians. "It's a meter with a rapidly flickering needle," says Peter Hess. "It depends on the day," says Ara Babajian. "Today I feel like a tired old whore. Some days I feel like a god. Most of the time I feel like an ambitious T-shirt salesman with entitlement issues."

I borrow this binary both from common understanding and from Howard Becker's *Art Worlds*, which uses the terms "artist" and "craftsman" (or "technician"), and concerns itself with the problem of art works which are produced collectively, or with a large network of what he calls "support personnel," but which the conventions of art and the necessities of copyright ascribe to a single "artist":

> Members of art worlds . . . recognize that making art requires technical skills that might be seen as craft skills, but they also typically insist that artists contribute something beyond craft skill to the project, something due to their creative abilities and gifts that gives each object or performance a unique and expressive character. Other people, also skilled, who support the work of the artist are called "craftsmen," and the work they do is called "craft." The same activity using the same materials and skills in what appear to be similar ways, may be called by either title, as may the people who engage in it.[3]

The division is by no means exclusive to any creative mode—the workshops of artists from Da Vinci to Koons are a tradition in the visual arts. "The film business," wrote Becker, is so "confused about which people are artists and which are support personnel that the latter often think of themselves, and are often thought of, as artists in their own right"; he cites film editors and composers. "The confusion is chronic in music schools, for almost all the students who hope to become . . . virtuosi will end up as, at best," section members, teachers, or ex-musicians.[4] But the demarcation—enforced, again, by the legal necessities of copyright law as much as by the audience's desire to admire a sole creator—has a tendency to reinforce a specialized division of labor: "Support personnel with permanent positions in a stable organization develop motives different from those of the artists with whom they work. While the artists worry about the work's aesthetic effect, as well as its effect on their reputations, support personnel consider their activity on a given project in light of its overall effect on their long-term organizational interests. Support personnel, hired for their ability to perform one function, spend all their time doing that one thing and develop a guild pride or a protectionist attitude about it which conflicts with the production of the overall work. . . . Conversely, they may feel trapped in that function, the way ambitious symphony players fear being trapped as section players . . . or repertory actors fear being typecast in character roles."[5]

In the old paradigm of big bands and club-date groups, the hierarchy was easier to parse: there were bandleaders and hired bands, contractors and session players. It was one of the relationships clarified by money. Or was it? William Bruce Cameron, in "Sociological Notes on the Jam Session," wrote that "two things are simultaneously required of the jazzman on a session: he must subordinate and integrate his musical personality, as expressed through his instrument, into the general group. . . . On the other hand, as a soloist, he must produce startlingly distinctive sound patterns which are better, if possible, than those played by any other member of the group."[6] It is this tension, between standing out and blending in, which complicates the professional lives of creative workers in ensemble industries. It is too simple to think of the work of even the most industrialized musician— a functionary in a film-score orchestra, say—as a card-punching cog. A musician, during their long practice and apprenticeship, is nudged toward ideals not always compatible with what turns out to be their work. Robert Faulkner wrote:

The social context in which he learns and performs (his role models, repertoire, and personal success) awakens desires for artistic fulfillment and creativity in work—values often forgotten, ignored, or even not defined by many professionals and white-collar employees. . . . The fracture between dream and reality seems particularly severe for those who are taught one set of values in their training and who then, in due course during their careers, find that these cannot possibly be fulfilled if they are to earn a living. . . . [Music] was portrayed not only as a prescribed career line, but a glorious endeavor. It was a calling. The most bitter views of this calling were held by those who reflected on the sharp distinctions between the investment and effort put into this career, and the slim rewards received. . . . They attained their goals, but the concrete manifestations of those goals—lack of pay, poor conditions of work—set up a wide discrepancy between principles and practice.[7]

"The notion that musical performance can be regarded as a craft or skilled trade rather than an 'art,'" wrote Bruce MacLeod, "is unfamiliar to the lay public, and it is also difficult to accept for many musicians."[8]

In general, band people—whose formative musical experiences tend, to some degree, toward the ideal of collective creativity—find it difficult to maintain a purely utilitarian relationship to their playing. Todd Beene was primed to adopt the day laborer attitude towards music: "The [session guys] who came up in the generation just before me," he says, "their whole deal is 'I get up and I go to work and I don't even remember half the things I've played on; it's not important. I'm there to build a house, I'm there to hammer nails with the guitar, basically.'" Michael McDermott describes this sort of work on a commercial session: "They're like, 'There's just some guy in there,' and [the producer is] just like 'Read the chart'—that's all he cares about; he doesn't really care what you've done or where you've been or who you are or how nice you are. He just wants and needs to get it done, in a timely fashion, and you're just there to work. You're not a name. You're not even a face. You're just a drummer, just play." "For me," says Beene, though, "that is not what music is, [though] I fully respect that style . . . [but] because I'm personally so emotionally invested in it, I always want it to be art."

It is true that not everyone feels called to foreground their personality: "I have an artistic side, but that's not the side I lead with," says Michael Bland. "When I was eight," said bassist Garry Tallent in an interview, "I wanted to be Elvis; when I was fifteen I wanted to be John Lennon, then along came Jimi Hendrix, and I thought, 'I'm never gonna be that' . . . and I said, you know, it's pretty cool being Noel Redding. Just being in a band was cool enough. And you don't have the personality that really wants that kind of attention."[9] There is also the matter of who is the boss. Artie Shaw—who knew from rebelling against creative frustration—pointed out that "the bandleader and the musician who makes his living playing in other men's bands . . . are working for different kinds of employers."[10] Put another way, which is the more vulnerable to musical compromise: the musician who answers to another musician, or the musician who answers to the public? "Good work is good work," says Katie Harkin. "There is a democracy to design in your mass-manufactured furniture. . . . It could be that the furniture-maker in the next village makes terrible tables." And someone needs to execute the innovations, Benny Horowitz adds: "If you had a bunch of people . . . broadening the horizons of how people make tables . . . you need artists that are disciplined enough to create and manufacture final products, [who can say] I know how to perfect this design; I have the discipline and the tools to make it perfect every time." Scott Spillane agrees: "I'm a tool that they're using, and I try to be the best tool possible to fit that situation."

Practically speaking, musicians drift along a continuum over the course of a long career. In particular, the more professionalized technicians feel the pull toward personal, creative work. "I definitely started as a craftsman," said Nate Brenner, "and at a certain point I was like, 'I don't want to just be shredding scales every day.'" More troublesome is the tendency of musicians, as Andy Gill and Kevin Odegard wrote, to "suffer from a kind of aural myopia that prevents them, when listening back to a recording, from hearing anything except their own contribution,"[11] and even a player who understands that they are doing work-for-hire can feel the sting of alienation. Toby Dammit recalls a "blitz run" of a session, "working with people who are going to use you . . . as a database for constructing something later with loops and samples. I have no idea what [they'll] do with it in the end, but it probably won't sound like me."

In general, the musicians who began their careers already self-conceptualizing as artists never quite find themselves comfortable in a hired-gun mentality. As a drummer, Michael McDermott sometimes feels like "just a human monkey and beating machine, but there is some art to it." "A craftsman implies a technical ability that has been honed over the years," says Janet Weiss. "I have been playing for thirty years and it is something I work at, and work at regularly; I practice, I try to gain more tools to my trade so that I can communicate better. But in the end for me the focus is always the emotion of the thing, the feeling, the vibe, the music. How well did you communicate the emotions and the ideas? Someone who plays very little, has very little craft and skill, I still think can be very communicative and very artistic. . . . To be an artist, it seems like something that's so cool! A craftsman sounds like, with enough work and enough practice anyone can do that—but not anyone can be an artist." In fact, they may be flabbergasted to find that other musicians prefer to engage with music as a job, rather than a calling. "Only recently am I understanding that not everybody in music is an actual artist," says Thor Harris. "Some people don't do anything else artistically or creatively." He continues:

> The other day . . . I said, "Man, all these people come to [music] to make something new and fresh, [but] they all use the same tools: bass, drums, guitar; verse, chorus, bridge—why not just avoid those things, and then you'll have something that sounds different?" And Jordan [Geiger of Shearwater] said, "Do you really think that they are trying to do something new?" And that had not occurred to me. I just assumed, because of my motivation—[it] hadn't occurred to me that they weren't all trying to do something new.

There is no clear boundary, says Jenny Scheinman, between the work you do as a hired player and more personal work: "I don't think of . . . the weddings and bar mitzvahs and the movie scores or studio gigs as your day job to support the music that you actually write. I remember a friend of mine had a bumper sticker saying, 'Real musicians have day jobs,' meaning it should all go into their art. I have always just enjoyed being a laborer, a musician-laborer, and I'm constantly thinking of how I can contribute to society through music. And one of the ways is just collaborating with people, playing with people, and being open to different kinds of music—I can be part of the social fabric a little bit more." For Joe Ginsberg, one can also be "in a process of practicing my creativity, as odd as that sounds, which is part of the craft too"—the fact of being a professional songwriter, going into an office every day to write songs, is an approach that necessarily combines both modes. "I am legion," says Meredith Yayanos. "The musicians I admire most in the world have this beautiful balance between their craftsmanship and their unique, magical unicorn-ness." Brian Viglione squares the circle: "I consider myself an artist, one who is a passionate and involved collaborator."

"We as artists, so-called," says Nels Cline, "quite often have craftsman envy. You look at these people with insane musical ability and wish we had it too." But, he adds, "I had a really weird epiphany in the '80s, playing in this band BLOC and realizing, from close work with certain kinds of other players, that there are people out there in the world who have insane musical ability skill-wise and can play any style, they can read anything, they have a really firm working knowledge of some of the most demanding disciplines that music can ever come up with or offer—yet they never do a single original thing. And they never write a piece of music, they never start their own group. I couldn't believe this. I was stunned." He goes on:

> Because I spent so much time thinking that the whole point was to do your own thing—at least eventually—that I couldn't believe that people could get that good at playing music without being so-called "original" or "artists." . . . But I hadn't pondered this at

all until I was confronted by two of the members of this group I was in. They cornered me, and the question became, "How come you and your friends, and your brother, think you're good enough to put out your own records, when you're obviously not as good as John Coltrane?" And I was completely stunned by this. I said, "The only reason we're doing it—we're not trying to stake a claim on genius, we're just trying to get our own music out there so we can play it!" . . . Maybe these people . . . have a high degree of suspicion for anybody who claims that their music is worth listening to, that's not so-called genius. God, if I spent my life measuring myself against Jim Hall or John Scofield or Wes Montgomery or George Benson I'd probably never go out and play guitar!

TALKING MONEY

The taxonomy of support musicians begins to seem more an artifact of the influence of capital and copyright in the culture industries than a definition of a role ("Most terms used to describe art and music-making are tarnished by romanticism," says Toynbee).[12] In this sense, the "artist" is the figure to whom *aura* and *credit* accrues—the figure who, sometimes, trades compensation for status. Becker locates the graduation in status from artisan to "artist" sometime in Renaissance Italy, signaled by the gradual removal of the utilitarian justification for their works in favor of an idea of art as an end in itself (Becker refers to its "sublime purposelessness").[13] But while "we accord people who have [that title] special rights and privileges" which are not extended to the support personnel who are crucial to their production, those rights and privileges are a double-edged sword.[14] Engineers, producers, arrangers, and session musicians can expect a salary or work-for-hire rate, while the "artist" is compensated in a more theoretical (if potentially more lucrative) way. According to philosopher Régis Debray, "The writer retains ownership of his work . . . since, and because of, the French Revolution which, in recognizing private ownership of land and of goods in general, also legalized literary and artistic ownership. . . . More accurately, [the writer] is a *rentier*, for copyright may be likened to rent in the broad sense of a premium deriving from a monopoly situation. . . . For the majority of artists . . . adopting the status of *rentier* in the name of 'independence' of the creative artist means permanently receiving a remuneration far inferior to the value of their labor power."[15]

So are salaried musicians in a better position than copyright owners? To address the question, we must turn to the fraught question of credit, in its legal and financial sense: who *owns* the credit for music that is almost necessarily the product of a group of people and a division of labor?

We come, finally, to talking about money. How does one ask for it, how does one value one's labor, how does discourse around money organize the power structures in a band? More existentially, how does one's comfort level in talking about money map onto one's comfort level in thinking of oneself as a working professional laboring in a culture industry? How was that comfort level affected by one's socialization as a musician? Does squeamishness about money perpetuate the class dynamics quietly at play in most music scenes? The foundational figures of punk and indie DIY who set its anti-capitalist terms were more likely than not to be suburban children of the professional class. As Simon Frith wrote, "Rock music is capitalist music. . . . The music doesn't challenge the system but reflects and illuminates it. Rock is about dreams and their regulation, and the strength of rock dreams comes not from their force as symbols, but from their relationship to the experience of work and leisure: the issue, finally, is not how to live outside capitalism (hippie or bohemian style), but how to live within it."[16]

This is true as much for musicians as for consumers of music. No response was as universal in my conversations as some variation on Scott Spillane's "I hate talking about money. It's a horrible, horrible thing." "If [musicians] were better about [money], we would be accountants," says Rick Steff. The question very quickly becomes a proxy for self-esteem—"I don't know how to value myself," said Mike Yannich—followed by the imposter-syndrome classic (voiced here by Paul Wallfisch), "Some people are just good at that; I wonder if that is because they just feel better, like they are worth more." "It's not the fun part," says Caitlin Gray; and like many, she leaves it "until I'm more comfortable with people, or until we have to." For Katie Harkin, "It gets easier the more you do it, when you realize how important it is. There's so many practicalities that you just have to have those conversations"—and, adds Eliza Hardy Jones, the earlier the better: "Some bandleaders are so uncomfortable talking about money that they are just like, 'Don't worry, I'm going to take care of you.' And you're young and [say] 'Okay, we'll work it out'; and then at the end of the day they're like, 'Here's fifty bucks,' and you're like 'Wait! No! I feel mistreated.' . . . The idea [that] 'if I don't make it uncomfortable, it'll make it easier for you'" is a mistake for both sides.

Musicians retreat quickly to jockish platitudes of gratitude: "I don't know that I've ever asked anybody for a raise, or said I was dissatisfied with the money that I got or anything," claims Scott McCaughey. "To me it's all gravy, because I just feel really lucky to be doing what I'm doing, and to have fallen into this life that I could have only dreamed of—and in fact didn't even probably dream of, because I just didn't think it was possible." Daniel Hart "never made a whole lot of money touring, but certainly more than I would make working at McDonald's. . . . I have shied away from asking that question because I didn't want to be perceived as difficult, or too concerned with the money, because that wasn't why I started doing it in the first place. If I wanted to be rich, I should have done something else."

Band people do welcome the opportunity to talk to their peers (when it arises). Stuart Bogie finds it "very easy to talk about money with other session musicians, because I've been in their shoes. [We] are discreet, but tend to share what we're earning, and that is very important. You've got to be open with your friends." Jay Gonzalez likes "talking to other musicians who have been in a similar situation—I am curious logistically how it works with other bands." Peter Erskine disagrees: "I don't ask musicians what they're making, generally, and they don't ask me. . . . You come up with something that works for you, and whatever anyone else is getting or not getting is really none of your business." But money can be a necessary intra-band conversation, too, says Ara Babajian: "It's almost like it's a separate language within the band. . . . Especially now, there's variance in the band—some guys aren't doing as well as some other guys, so it's always an issue; we have to play as many shows as we do per year in order to make sure that whoever has the least amount of money in the band is still doing well, because if that guy falls off, then the band can't continue." "The other band [members], yeah, we talk about it," says John DeDomenici. "In that way it's like any job—talking to your boss about how much money you make is always shitty, because no one ever thinks they get enough. I think even the bandleader would say, 'I don't make enough either,' and I don't think I'm being paid less than I should be. We just all would like to make more, of course."

The idea that openly discussing money is coded as "uncool" is one of the tells of economic privilege ("It is not done in polite society," says Jim Sclavunos), especially in indie rock. "It is the curse of this façade of indie rock or independent music or alternative," says Doug Gillard. "'It's so not cool, man, it's about the art.' Like, wow, he's sniffing around about money; he's not cool." He goes on:

> A lot of musicians are from backgrounds where their folks had some money, and they don't think in terms of music as a way to make a living. When you read about Motown, it's interesting to hear about behind-the-scenes things—the musicians would always come in and demand their checks from the receptionist, and they would swear if they didn't have a check. It was like, "Well, James is unhappy. Okay, we will get him a check." If you do that in a band situation, or in this so-called indie rock world, it's really not cool—"Oh man, you had better look for someone else." Unfortunately, it's mostly not articulated at all. You have to say something to the manager or the manager won't bring it up; they want you to bring it up. . . . I think I have lost out on a lot of money over the years by not being more demanding. Then again, I might not have been working those same things had I said anything about wanting money.

As Cyndi Lauper warned us, money changes everything—better to have the conversation about financial arrangements before there are real stakes. ("It's easy to talk about money when you're not making any money, and it's hard if a band starts to reach success," says Nate Brenner.) Once again, the financial dispensation within Tom Petty and the Heartbreakers over the years was a cautionary tale of malleable and hard-nosed pragmatism, as Petty biographer Warren Zanes wrote: The proto-Heartbreakers band Mudcrutch "had been egalitarian in terms of splitting the rewards and the money . . . and that spirit remained unchanged." "'[Petty] was making a solo record,' explains keyboardist Benmont Tench. 'Then he got us for his band. But the agreement was that it was all for one and one for all.' . . . Tom Petty and the Heartbreakers could never be a democracy, but Petty was trying to give everyone a reason to stick around."[17] In late 1978, though, new manager Elliot Roberts urged Petty to break up the equal-shares scheme, saying, "The drummer and bass player never got called except to tour and record. And they're getting an equal share?" Roberts "called the band meeting to let the members know that things were about to change. Petty left it to him, staying home that night. . . . [Tench] 'felt blindsided. I was furious. But you're absolutely fucked, because these are the guys you want to play with. . . . It took years to accept.' . . . The band settled into the realities of . . . the new financial split, which found Petty moving toward a life that would look somewhat different from the others' lives."[18]

Just as often, though, musicians who have the option of using management as a buffer in financial discussions experience it as tremendous relief. "At a certain level," says Hardy Jones, "you never talk to the artist about pay, because you do want to separate that relationship from your artistic relationship—which I totally appreciate. So when I got hired for the Grace [Potter] thing, she called me on the phone and said, 'Can you come out to LA next week?' And I said yes, and she said, 'Management will be in contact with you about details.' She and I didn't have to have that negotiation. Management sent me an email and they said, 'This is what it is, and when you get paid.' Everything is extremely standardized. . . . It's all above-board and very transparent, which has been wonderful." "That's why I have a manager," says Glenn Kotche. "I'm so bad at it; I'm a wimp with it."

Realistically, there are only a handful of financial arrangements available to a band: equal splits of net profit, day/week/per-show rates, à la carte work-for-hire, and the ever-rarer salary or retainer. Janet Weiss made a weekly salary as a hired drummer for Bright Eyes; Jon Wurster has gotten an equal split of "touring money" (an imprecise term) from the Mountain Goats and Robert Pollard. "I feel strongly that every touring musician, while on the road, has the same job and should be paid equally," says Sarah Balliett. "Touring is a job, and it's just as much work for everyone doing it. . . . There's one quick way to have major problems and resentment on the road, and that's to pay one person more than anyone else in the van."[19] Mike Sneeringer agrees, calling it "the curse of the side person, in that I'm not earning any royalties or licensing fees or additional income that comes when you are not on tour; so I have to tour to make money. . . . I've always felt that touring money should be split more or less equally; and I don't think that's a popular opinion, especially on [for-hire] situations. With Strand of Oaks, it was a weekly rate that was discussed initially and has been renegotiated one or two times, and could probably stand renegotiation again. That's a weird feeling too, where you have to be a bit of a bulldog—you have to say, 'Hey, let's talk about this again.'" (Sneeringer often doubles as tour manager, so he's in a unique position to "know how much money is coming in—typically they are handing you all the accounting.")

Lucero paid Rick Steff and its other members a regular salary, "so when we are off [the road] we make exactly the same as what we make when we are on." Andrew Seward and his bandmates "were all members of the [Against Me!] corporation. We were always smart about money; we always put money away for rainy days, or [if] something happened, like getting sued. But it also meant you never saw the money. You never actually saw the fruits of your labor."

An underappreciated dynamic in bands that have been together since their youth is the subtle shift that necessarily occurs as a childhood friend slowly morphs into an employer. DeDomenici has been working with artists like Jeff Rosenstock and Laura Stevenson since they were all teens. "They understand that as you've gotten older this has become a significant source of our income and also our livelihood, so they understand that they're feeding me, essentially. It becomes a weird dynamic."[20]

"I've always found it easy [to talk about money]," says Jean Cook. "My bandmates have rarely found it easy." Then Cook reconsiders.

Well, that's not true. One of the people I work with—everybody splits everything equally for everything, and he always makes sure to do the accounting right away. So I never carry a balance. There's two bands that I work with where they're like, "I know you want this much. I can't afford that. Will you consider X or Y?" It's not about us splitting at all, and that's fine too.

Then there are a couple of people that I work with that are chronically terrible about money. One of them will very happily talk to you about it, and discuss it, and say everything's fair—but will never pay you, because it's honestly just difficult to try and systematize anything in his life. It doesn't mean he's not good for the money. It just means that you have to get him at the exact right time to make it happen. But we've actually figured out a system that works really well [for what] was a really problematic thing: now I send a monthly invoice. It gets paid eventually. There's a minimum payment every month, and then there's like five percent compound interest every month. That gets assessed on any balance that gets carried over. We figured out that system, and it works really well for me. Every month I have the responsibility of putting together the invoice and sending it in, and then they have to pay me—anything; it can be anything. If they don't pay me anything, that triggers the interest, and I feel like it's a fair amount of interest. I feel like it's a fair system. They think it's a fair system. So that's better than what we used to have.

The other person who's also like that actually has an emotional problem with money, where because they're so terrible at it, they're super sensitive if people get upset about [them] being terrible at it. You have to be super direct and super straight-forward. That's the sort of thing that you learn over years of working with somebody. But now we're straight. When I got pregnant, I went to the two people, who owed me thousands of dollars, and [said,] "Look, [I] have no income for I don't know how long. Maybe we could settle our debts, like, this is exactly how much you owe me." And they both—well, one of them paid right away. The other one we're still working on it, but we got pretty close.

Most band people operate on a sliding scale. This has the benefit of allowing them to work on poorly financed projects which provide artistic gratification or the barter system of shared credit, but the drawback of compelling them to be enforcers of their value. "As an Englishman," says Nigel Powell, "you're always cautious about over-valuing yourself. And I'm aware that you could line up drummers around the block who can play better than me and are working shitty day jobs and playing with cover bands. . . . So it's balancing that sense of knowing that you're doing better than a lot of other people, and that you shouldn't take that for granted or be hubristic about it. But at the same time looking at what's around you, and the money that's being generated, and getting what you think is fair recompense for contributing to the generation of that wealth." There's a certain comedy in the way musicians describe what in most contexts would constitute an entirely banal business negotiation—exemplified by Josh Kantor: "Occasionally, they'll say up front, 'This is our budget; this is the dollar figure we have budgeted for keyboard overdubs.' But more often than not, someone will contact me and say, 'What's your rate?' And I still don't have an exact answer to that question. It's become a bit more standard over time, so often I'm the one who ends up throwing out the first number. . . . Oftentimes they say, 'Okay, that's fine,' and there's a small part of me that wonders, oh, maybe I should ask for more. Then other times they say, 'We can't quite go that high. Would you do it for this?' And if I'm interested in the project and the people, then I'll typically say yes. Most of the time the stuff that I get offered is stuff that I'm into. On the rare instance when it's not,

I might throw out a really high number figuring they'll almost certainly say no, or if they say yes, then at least I get a good pay day out of it. I try to keep that loose and friendly and cordial and informal."

"You play a wedding, and the leader underbids," says DJ Bonebrake, "and you go 'okay'; you get $300 or something. But you go there, and you see it's the fanciest place; the cake probably costs ten times as much as the band. And you go, 'God, we're suckers.' Musicians are really good at doing that; they don't know how to bid."

The fact is, most musicians *want* a reason to take the gig, they just want to know they can trust the person hiring them. The ethnomusicologist Timothy Taylor described the entry-level Echo Park indie rockers he studied as motivated primarily by the use-values—for gas, to fix an amp—of the limited money they made.[21] My subjects, older and more established, are more likely to focus on a sense of being regarded as something more than an interchangeable employee. It's a position that attaches value not to outward-facing, Bourdeausian, symbolic reputational capital, but to a private and mutual exchange of respect which accrues to their bank of personal dignity.[22] "There are people who think they're doing a favor to you, when they're really underpaying you, and then people who know that they couldn't possibly pay you enough," says Peter Hess. "Especially with people I like—and even with people I don't like—I will tell them, 'How much this pays is actually the least important part to me, because I really want to make music first, and I want to do the best work I can on your record or on your gig, [regardless of] what you're paying me. At the end, yeah, I want to be paid appropriately, and as long as you understand that, I'll work for a dollar an hour.' If I'm being appreciated, and with absolutely no resentment— if it's really *me* you want—I'll give you three thousand percent for eight cents." Bonebrake has "certain artists where I know they're going to pay me fairly, so I don't even ask them. Someone like Peter Case, he'll go, 'Hey, do you want to play McCabe's? Do you want to make a record?' And I go, 'Great, I'll be there.' Because I know he'll always pay me what he can pay me, and it will be really fair." All's fair, says Meredith Yayanos, "if those are the parameters that are set down. ... The Walkmen paid me with Chinese food to record violin on the title track of *Everyone Who Pretended to Like Me Is Gone,* and then a couple of months later signed to Sony. And I was so stoked for them, and I had no problems with that."

Even the highest-end session players would rather say yes to work. Bands tell Josh Freese:

> "God, we couldn't believe that we were able to hire you to make our record." I go, "Well, that's what I do." People call me, and if I'm available and the money makes sense, and you guys aren't assholes and the music is halfway good, then I do it. As a matter of fact, there's times the music isn't that good and I'll do it. If it means two afternoons with you, and I support my family playing the drums, I'll go do it. If the music's not that good, I don't want to join your band or go on tour with you for a couple of months; but I always say sluttin' around behind closed doors for a night or two with someone is no big deal. By the time they drive you crazy, you're gone. But if the people are all right to be around, and the money is good, I'll do it. Or if the money is not good, but the music is great, I'll do it.
>
> People will say, "I heard that you cost an arm and a leg to get to the studio, and you won't get out of bed for X amount of dollars." That's not true at all. I play for people for dirt cheap all the time. I do stuff for free for people. Now, you've got to be one of my closer friends, or someone I completely love, and really want to play on your stuff, to do that. But I don't only do big money gigs by any means. Just like an actor you might see go do some dumb Disney film—they go do it so they can go do the three little indie projects over here that they want to do.

The first time Mike Sneeringer ever said, "'Okay, this is my rate and this is what you have to pay me to go on this tour' was actually with friends. I didn't charge much—honest to God it was like $250 a week— but I was like, you have to pay me at least this much to go. . . . That was my first experience saying, 'Okay, I'm not going to leave unless it's this much,' instead of just 'I will take an equal cut of whatever it is.' This is so I don't come back and I'm evicted. And I enjoyed that.

. . . It was nice to leave my door knowing that I would at least come back with enough to cover rent and all that shit." "I remember coming up," says George Rush, "guys always used to talk, almost in hushed tones, [about] certain musicians that very early [in their careers] were just very, very blunt and very frank about how much they needed to get paid: 'Oh, this guy won't come out of the house for less than a hundred bucks; who does he think he is?' Well, he's the guy that's getting paid a hundred bucks [instead of] twenty-five."

"The more creative freedom you are allowed, the more prone we seem to be to lower our price," says Brian Viglione. "If they are just hiring me to be a robot, I'm going to charge the standard rate because I don't have any [creative input]. . . . That's funny in a way, because you would think sometimes it would almost be the inverse; the less mental energy you have to expend. . . . [But] musicians take great satisfaction in feeling a sense of themselves in the project."

Over a career, it can get easier to have frank conversations about compensation, especially as one develops—quoting Todd Sick-afoose—"a reputation and a body of work that people respect, [hence] a little bit more confidence about . . . not being so modest or shy." However, the counterpoint to that confidence is that one aspect of setting one's price is that, in a market economy absent guild systems, (in Becker's words) we "rely on market mechanisms to weed out the talented from the others"[23]—so the price one can command becomes a marker of one's worth as a musician, not just as a negotiator: "Am I going to find out that I'm not worth very much?" says Todd Beene. Shahzad Ismaily says that for a large part of his childhood, his father was "not interested" in Ismaily becoming a musician. "And it was clear," he says, "that one of the ways he valued work was getting paid for it. . . . So I made a pretty uncomfortably hard, permanent [mental] equation between getting paid and being valued."

Certainly some musicians simply find it easy to talk about money—the business requires it, and being frank early avoids unpleasantness later: "I will go through an uncomfortable situation if it means coming out of it [with] some clarity," says Mike Sneeringer. "There's no point in getting weird and squirrely about money," says Viglione. "I know how to balance a checkbook," says East Bay Ray, who rejects "the cartoon [of] either you're a spaced-out musician or some suit record label bean counter." Jon Rauhouse has been "trying to at least talk to some of the younger musicians, and telling them they have got to quit doing stuff for nothing. The second you give something away, it is worthless. You can't take that back . . . are the caterers doing it for nothing?" Gerry Leonard, interestingly, "found that when I came to America, the nice thing about doing business here is people are pretty upfront about things like that, and they don't mind discussing it ahead of time." As a producer, Leonard likes to "do things in what I like to call 'building blocks,' so that if there's any point somebody's getting nervous, then they can bail out, but they still can take their work with them. . . . It's not good to be in a situation where you feel you're not being properly paid for the work that you're doing, because resentment develops, and once that starts, this negativity festers. [This way,] you can always go back to the table and renegotiate if you find the workload is a lot more than what you [signed up] for."

Money changes everything in another way: a bigger pie takes the pressure off the cutting and distributing of slices. The fall of the hegemonic power of established labels in the twenty-first century simultaneously undermined the agreements those entrenched powers had with the American Federation of Musicians (AFM). After this corporate understanding evaporated, it became—perhaps counterintuitively—more difficult for musicians to talk about money. Since the ground rules by which most musicians played had evaporated, terms had to be renegotiated case by case. Musicians who were able to experience union-rate sessions—in, especially, Nashville, California, or New York—lived in a world with ground rules. Everybody knew where they stood: you got your scale; you got extra for playing an extra instrument.[24] "Money [now] is much more veiled and nonspecific and unfortunately not really codified in any way," says Marc Capelle. "You really have to come to the table with your own rules, like here's our card game, this is what we're gonna play. That's a bummer. . . . The old version of paternalism—'You do this, you get this, and if you bring another instrument, you get paid this much more'—that was a nice model. . . . The bell, it stopped ringing in 1996 to '98, and the rules just changed."

"I was really lucky," says Bruce Bouton, "because I moved to Nashville in 1978. . . . Being in the union all those years, all those golden years of Nashville recording, the late '80s all through the '90s, it was you sign the card, get paid, get your pension paid, get your health and welfare paid." He continues:

> In the '90s, I'd get album cuts from guys like Mark Wills—back then he sold a million records. You sell a million records, that's ninety grand in publishing money. A publisher gets twenty cuts a year; he's got money; he can pay for demos. The demo sessions would pay for the farm teams for the musicians. Back in the '90s, a good musician could make fifty, sixty grand a year just doing demo sessions. That's what's gone.
>
> . . . It's the wild west again right now. I have to do a lot of internet overdubs. People call me for a project and they'll go, "Hey man, I don't want to do this union. How much would you charge?" I say this much, and they go, "Wow man, I can't really afford that, so-and-so will do it for this." Everybody's desperate to play, and everybody's got a studio. There's kids around that will sit there and do a whole band in the box for $200–300 a song.

"Record budgets have shrunk," Freese agrees.

> There was a time when I was getting paid a ton of money to record. Then it got to a point where I was going, "Man, I'm playing on more and more hit records and stuff, but I'm not charging any more." Then I went, "Shit, I guess the fact that I'm getting to still charge the same is a huge deal, right?" But I worked with . . . a legendary multi-platinum artist who has been around since the late '70s, and one of the biggest stars in America—and his people called me in 2012 or '13, and they asked for a discount; like, "Hey, can you come down on your price a little?" I'm thinking, this is one of the most famous people I've ever worked with, one of the most successful dudes in rock and roll, and they're asking for a deal. And not that I was

charging so much! It's just that no one wants to pay anything. [As] a friend of mine who has worked on a lot of records used to say, "I don't give rodeos to millionaires."

But I actually did give him a discount! Because at the end of the day, they know that I probably wanted my name on that record—and I did.

SONGWRITING AND OTHER CREDITS

If talking money is at the crux of the interaction between creativity and business for a working musician, and if, as Bernard Miège wrote, the "cultural industries are at the origin of important inequalities between artists,"[25] then nothing is more the origin of inequalities than the way songwriting credit and royalties are apportioned in pop music. Many bands in the recording industry's golden age only found this out when they had a hit, and all of a sudden the singer and guitarist turned up for tour with designer luggage: "We didn't realize," wrote The Band's Levon Helm, "that song publishing—more than touring or selling records—was the secret source of the real money in the record business."[26] The most fractious grudges in rock history (like Helm's with Robbie Robertson),[27] and perhaps the least intelligible to the layperson, center around songwriting and publishing credits— as New Yorker writer Adam Gopnik likes to say, "All biographies of pop artists . . . seem to end up being studies in the music-publishing business."[28]

The original sin of song copyright in America is that it wasn't set up for a context of collective creativity. "Songwriting . . . is the only instance of creativity that is singled out for special payment,"[29] wrote Deena Weinstein. "Writing songs is a form of domination [in which] the egalitarian myth of bands is almost always violated."[30] When the collectives that enforce song copyright were initially established (ASCAP in the US and PRS in the UK were both founded in 1914), popular songwriting was the domain of professional songwriters, or partnerships of a songwriter and a lyricist. As a result, while bands are, of course, free to split percentages as they please, the traditional split has been 50 percent ownership to a lyricist and 50 percent to writer(s) of "the music." "The music" is historically defined as a melody line and chords, as notated on a "lead sheet." Band people who are instructed about publishing by industry professionals are likely to be presented with this traditional arrangement, which even in an equitable split between instrumentalists enforces inequality between the primary lyricist and their bandmates (e.g., a five-piece band in which a lyricist receives 50 percent of a song and the others take 10 percent each of the music).

Further, in the economics of the institutional music industry, a freshly signed band can expect to receive two advances: one from a label (advanced against sales royalties), and one from a publishing company (advanced against songwriting royalties). The label advance—while in theory split between band members—also has to pay for the actual recording of the record, even before they share whatever's left over. The publishing advance has no such built-in overhead: the primary songwriter(s) just receive a check for songs they've already written.

Then, when the record comes out, the record royalties (which are shared by all band members) have a built-in convergence between the debt to the label that has to be recouped and the eventual fall-off in sales as a record reaches its market peak. Publishing royalties, meanwhile, continue to accrue as long as the song is being played: on radio, on television, on the internet, as covered by other bands, etc.

So if a distance is opened between credited songwriters and the rest of a band, that distance only grows with time: while a band's income from records and concerts has a tendency to decline or disappear if they stop touring, publishing and songwriting income continues: musicians call this "mail money" (i.e., checks that turn up in the mail). Credits on a song that remains popular even as an act breaks up or retires are as close to a 401(k) as a band person is likely to get, and an important source of stability as musicians age. "Paying dues may be a collective affair," wrote Simon Frith, "making it is not."[31]

Bands have various ways of addressing these inequalities. Some songwriters—at their discretion—split half of their publishing advance between the other band members. In the days of physical singles, since royalties were based equally on both A- and B-sides, bands might offer B-side placement to secondary songwriters (the Pogues, in the absence of original songs by other band members, would often record a traditional number in the public domain and share the royalties). Some work out a stable partnership—Jagger/ Richards, Lennon/McCartney—which prevents disputes over whose songs make the record, but which doesn't preclude a disgruntled third wheel (George Harrison didn't want to write B-sides for the rest of his life). A few—their rarity perhaps explains the frequency with which they're cited—decide, before there's real money at stake, to split their credits equally in the name of unity. Semisonic's Dan Wilson, remembers drummer Jacob Schlichter, by offering an equal split, "surrender[ed] two-thirds of his songwriting income in order to put the band on equal footing. . . . It would require sales of a huge number of records before our recoupable debt could be cleared. Until then, we'd get by on songwriting royalties."[32] Money goes a long way toward engendering loyalty.

Bill Stevenson's Descendents go even farther, demanding contributions from each band member for each album:

> If you ask some random fan, they'll tell you that [singer] Milo wrote every Descendents song. But if you know anything about the band, you know it's very much a four-way thing where we all contribute equally—almost to a fault. If you look at our albums, each guy wrote four songs. When I say each guy wrote four songs, they could have written two full songs and parts of four others. If everybody has got the same amount of skin in the game, you go far in terms of maintaining issues [dealing] with people's pride. Let's say they are up there playing songs that they have no real vested interest in—that's the stuff that either breaks up bands or turns bands into this solo project that is propping itself up as if it were a band. The world is full of those, but Descendents are not one. We are a real band.
>
> Even if you are functioning as a "real band," but one dude is writing all the songs—if that one dude doesn't include his band members in the sharing of the mechanical royalty income [and]

publishing income, income generated by songwriting, then I think the band is going to break up. So as we have gotten older and wiser, when we do a record all the money goes into the bank and whatever money is in the bank, we write checks for equal amounts to each guy. You keep it that way; you keep it clean, and then you've got yourself a band.

If only it were easy to clearly identify, in a band context, what constitutes songwriting as distinct from arrangement.[33] Many musicians have a pet example of an instrumental part that's so distinctive that it comes to define the song: for Jon Wurster, it's Hunt Sales's drums on Iggy Pop's "Lust for Life"; for Brian Viglione, the mariachi trumpets on Johnny Cash's "Ring of Fire." "The guy that played bass on 'Walk on the Wild Side,'" says Joe McGinty, "probably should have gotten songwriting credit. But some people consider the chords, the melody and the lyrics—that's the song; everything else is arrangement." (For his part, Herbie Flowers, the bass player in question, is more pragmatic, having devised the distinctive doubling of electric and acoustic bass in order to get a double union fee: "You do the job and get your arse away. . . . Wouldn't it be awful if someone came up to me on the street and congratulated me for *Transformer*?")[34] "It's the kind of thing that's often difficult to ask people," says Nigel Powell.

> There's lots of people I would love to sit down with and say, "So what did you do on this record? I know you came in for a session, and did that feel like that was publishing, and were you offered any money for it?" . . . At what point, who decides where the line is, and how do you gently negotiate your way across that line?

At its root, the music industry has no meaningful standard for crediting collective creativity (copyright law, for example, is limited in its ability to address collective improvisation). There is a robust literature (especially by Miège,[35] Becker,[36] and Stahl[37]) exploring the relations between capital and creativity in the culture industry, and music in particular, which emphasizes a Marxist interest in exploitation and alienation from the products of one's labor and underscores the pressures that urge even the most egalitarian bands towards a hierarchal star system. The 1960s turn in Anglophone popular music, away from external, professionalized songwriters and arrangers and toward singer-songwriters and bands as autonomous creative structures, reinforced a romantic idea of a Barthesian "Author-God," as Jason Toynbee wrote: "[In] jazz and rock . . . the author cult has been renewed with a vengeance. . . . Authorial genius was . . . inscribed in the record-text [and] a new style of journalism then deepened and reinforced the legitimacy of this form of *auteurism*."[38]

Even as the music industry reinforced a legal and financial ideology of individual (or dual) creativity, it valorized a parallel ideal of collectivity: the all-for-one gang of the band. The two ideas are, in a crucial way, irreconcilable: "Works of art," wrote Becker, "are not products of individual makers, 'artists' who possess a rare and special gift. They are, rather, joint products of all the people who cooperate . . . to bring works like that into existence. . . . The reputational process systematically ignores, by accepting the theory of reputation, the contributions of others to the works on which reputations are based."[39]

But unlike other businesses in which capital is tied to copyright, musicians are not salaried: Miège makes the comparison to science and industry, in which scientists and engineers sacrifice their patent rights to employer/producers in exchange for regular, contractual wages.[40] Support musicians, instead, have the worst of both worlds: they give over the rights of their labor, consciously or not, to copyright holders (who themselves are subject to uncertain royalty-based compensation).[41] Laws and regulations protect a category called "artist," not a category called "performer," and widen the divide between the two—while reinforcing a star system generally.

"Creative cultural-industry workers," wrote Stahl, "are positioned more or less precisely at the 'point of alienation'"—certainly close enough, he says, to know "that the placement of the line between those who can be considered authors (and who on that basis may be eligible for ownership of the intellectual property they produce while at work) and those who can't is essentially political and subject to struggle and negotiation."[42] The legal definition of songwriting is clearly defined; the reality of it is not. Between that Scylla and Charybdis the band must navigate without losing too many shipmates along the way.

Musicians themselves are hardly unanimous on the question of who is entitled to songwriting credits. Sleepytime Gorilla Museum, according to Kihlstedt, was so uncomfortable with the topic that "to this day I don't think any of us actually registered any of our songs." Melissa Auf der Maur "just took what I was given." Scott McCaughey is "pretty old school. . . . I feel like unless you directly contribute to the lyrics and the chords, that all the rest is arranging, basically. If I came up with a really cool bass part for a song, it might make the song really, really cool; but to me, that's not songwriting, that's not worthy of a credit." Nigel Powell describes it as a "background tension" in their group, but "not one we've broached" with the primary songwriter, who "doesn't like confrontation; and discussions [about money] always either have the potential to get tense, or actually do get tense, when you have them—which is something he doesn't enjoy. And that makes it difficult." Many take the general stance of being happy not to have to ask, and happy to take credits if they're offered. "It's almost easier to ask somebody with whom I'm not close," says Peter Hess, "because if we're authentically close and they didn't think about it, then it's weirder to ask than somebody with whom I'm not that tight and they *did* think about it."

Glenn Kotche says that when he is hired for a session, he doesn't expect to have a piece of the songwriting: "Even if the song changes, even if the drum part has a big impact, I know that legally all that stuff comes under the umbrella of arrangement. . . . [It] would ultimately be [Jeff Tweedy's] decision. . . . When there's been a song where my part has changed the character of the song, I've been offered writing credit. So a song [like] 'Art of Almost,' or 'I Am Trying to Break Your Heart,' things like that where the drum part is distinctive enough that it definitely had an impact, I do get writing credit. Or if my field recordings are used prominently in a song or something like that, I get them."

Generally, a room can be read, says Michael McDermott: "If you're in that situation where you have to be worried about songwriting credits or not, those are going to be the kind of people that are like, 'Hey man, words and melody, and you don't have either of those." If a contribution is significant enough, Rick Steff says songwriting credit "comes naturally. To me, showing transitions, or passing chords or little things like that, is not true songwriting collaboration. So I wouldn't any more think to do that than I would think of asking for a songwriter credit if I played the line that happened to be the hook at the beginning of the song. If you start slicing pennies, you can get really frustrated with it, but I hope that whatever I do on a record is an asset enough that I will be asked for another record." For many musicians, avoiding a breach of etiquette that might threaten future work takes precedence. "In a work-for-hire, I used to [ask]," says Stuart Bogie, "but that's the ticket to never get asked to work on parts with someone again. If you come out and say, 'Hey, I wrote this melody here and it's a good part of the song,' you really need to have some clout in order to get points on it." And songwriters are notoriously protective of their prerogative: "In most cases," says Toby Dammit, "it's not worth jeopardizing your relationship trying to shove your name on something."

For some musicians, I tried reframing the question: do you feel a sense of *authorship* over your parts? Sarah Balliett makes a distinction between her work within Murder by Death and outside; that *membership in a collective* imbues the members with a sense of ownership by virtue of sweat equity and investment: "I have been working on this project for so many years; if I didn't feel that way, it wouldn't be a fulfilling job for me. Adam [Turla] writes songs. Songs begin as skeletons, and when the muscles and the nervous systems have been added, that work was done by the band Murder by Death. If it were any other group of people, they would sound much different (for better or worse)." For Brian Viglione, in the Dresden Dolls, "there was such an immense moment-to-moment correspondence musically in that project, that I would say, yes, I feel a great deal of authorship over those parts." Arrangement exists in a legal gray zone, one which is at the core of the sonic signature that makes specific lineups special, but which is hard to quantify. "A lot of bands just wouldn't be the same without everyone involved," says Mike Sneeringer, "and that is a hard thing to measure at the time, and a lot of people are looking back in hindsight, 'Oh shit, maybe I should have been a little bit more liberal with all sorts of income,' if that person was really part of the beating heart of that band."

"In a colloquial if not a legal sense, creative workers sometimes understand themselves as authors," wrote Matt Stahl. "This is why the bald appropriation of their work, although legal, can strike them as outrageous."[43] Meredith Yayanos tells the story of a project in which she "was getting paid, but not terribly well":

> I was coming up with a lot of my own parts, because frankly the guy who wanted to write the parts for everything and was claiming to be in charge of all of it could not compose for violin. And he took full credit when the album came out. That pissed me off, and when that happened, I did want my stamp on it. If we had had a financial arrangement where he was going to take credit for everything that I composed or arranged, that would have been one thing, but it wasn't, and he actually tried to blanket take credit for all of my arrangement work. In those kinds of circumstances, I do get grouchy, and I want my credit.

Some emotional and musical investments simply can't be quantified—or, the quantification itself sours the experience. "On paper," Scott Brackett says, "we ended up getting a decent shake with the Okkervil thing. It was like a percentage breakdown, so the side players got a much smaller percentage, and Will [Sheff] got the lion's share, because he wrote all the lyrics, his songs, his concepts. But part of that just felt shitty, because putting a number on it doesn't feel great—'I wrote five percent of this song'—that's not really how I feel about it, but that's how we have to work this out. Trying to put a monetary system, an industry, on top of art—it's not clean." East Bay Ray became involved in a notoriously bitter lawsuit after the breakup of the Dead Kennedys, of which songwriting splits were only a piece: "Back when we started, I suggested to the band that we give 25 percent of the publishing to the band [for the arrangement]. I got that idea, I think, from the Talking Heads—they did a third to the band, a third to the melody, and a third to the lyrics; and Los Lobos did something like 20 percent to the band, 40 [music] and 40 [lyrics]; so I talked the band into doing 25 percent for the musicians—we call it 'the track,' which is the drum, the bass, and rhythm guitar. It's just the basic feel of the thing, which is what the songwriter really doesn't write; the musicians make it up. But unfortunately, we offered [Biafra] 50 percent for his lyrics; then in the court case he wanted to deny the 25 percent—he lost on that one."[44]

There is the one legendarily clean solution: "I have a lot of respect for bands like Radiohead who just split their publishing five ways equally," says Viglione. "They go, 'Okay, we may all contribute varying levels here and there, but we are not going to muck around with different percentage points on all things. We're all contributing to this project and the success of it and the musical outcome, so here it is,' and they just split it five ways." Sleater-Kinney has chosen to split their songwriting equally—it is, said Janet Weiss, "a very collaborative band; it's part of the reason it's so rewarding to be in." Superchunk also shares credits, "which is very generous on Mac [McCaughan]'s part," says Wurster, "because when I joined the band, Mac pretty much wrote the songs . . . but we never had a huge hit, so it hasn't amounted to a fortune for any of us."

Even in uneven splits, generosity engenders generous feelings: "Gaslight [Anthem] is split up that way," says Benny Horowitz. "But at the same time, I need someone like [singer] Brian [Fallon] to do what I do, you know what I mean?" In the Dresden Dolls, Viglione's portion (while not what he hoped) "was far greater than some other people in other bands I've met who have had far more successful careers than I"; and the Violent Femmes gave him "a much higher publishing percentage than I was expecting—sometimes you're pleasantly surprised." In the Decemberists, says Jenny Conlee, "the musicians get a percentage of the songwriting royalty. That's a choice that [singer] Colin [Meloy] made. We get a much smaller portion than him, but he's respecting the fact that we do put our creative input in there. This came from [another band we were friends with]; they don't split their publishing up like that, and the band members were quite upset. . . . It does feel difficult when all the sudden one band member is making a lot more than the others. But then again, he's the creator."

Conversely, an insecure leader can experience the slow spread of credit as a threat to their hegemony. Paul Wallfisch was a member of the band Firewater, but "it was really just [bandleader] Tod A. . . . There was a clear hierarchy there. He *wanted* a band; that's why he didn't use his own name; that's why we always recorded together as a band and everything. But only on the fifth album did I get songwriting credits on like two or three songs, and the guitar player on one song, and that was rather grudging. . . . And that was actually the demise of the band, or at least that incarnation of the band—it was just too much for him."

In the professionalized world of Nashville songwriting—which might be assumed to be cutthroat and transactional—"everything's split equally, so it's not even a discussion," says Joe Ginsberg. "If you're in the room and the song gets finished, you're splitting equal ways. It's not an issue in Nashville. As far as in LA, it can be a little different, because sometimes someone's working on a track and you send it off, and people are toplining on top of it, and that's where splits can get a little trickier"—a problem which, in these more corporatized worlds, can be outsourced: "I just let my people handle that."

Outsourcing can cause its own complications, though. Stuart Bogie recorded with a group who had a big record deal and a new, inexperienced manager. "My manager at the time . . . was like, 'You should get X amount, and if you write any of the parts, you should get an appropriate amount of the writing credit,' which could mean one or two points—not anything that is going to alter the economics of these peoples' lives. But the point is they have a whole big business [they're] building, [whereas] that one day is all the money [session players] are going to see from it forever." Bogie continues:

> And we played the session, and I made a mental note and wrote down a little chicken scratch of any of the ideas we contributed, and they put [the parts] together. And they switched managers before they cut the check. The new manager came in and [said], "No way, this is too much money. You shouldn't have promised the horn players this much money, and horn players never get writing [credits]."

. . . When they sent the part, I was like, I know we made that up, because there's melodic shapes that I've taken from other stuff that I've studied, that I know they hadn't studied. There's a vocabulary in there that I knew they didn't know, and I remembered conceiving of the part.

But when they said no points, I wasn't surprised, and I was fine with it. We didn't get paid what we were promised, but we got paid very well and I was happy. I didn't feel ripped off, I didn't feel wronged; I just felt like it didn't go our way. Sometimes people are going to be generous; sometimes they're not, and I'm not going to let that affect my emotional state.

As an addendum to the story, it did go through the Musicians Union, so I have been paid since then for additional use on the recording; money that I very much needed to keep the lights on, to pay rent. . . . That's just an example of how things can be confusing. But it's important not to make it into a whole social justice issue, because you will drive yourself crazy.

An obvious benefit of the union-town settlement is that terms don't have to be renegotiated in each new room. "Back in the day," says Marc Capelle, "you would sign a union sheet and you would get royalties, and I still have a mild royalty stream [from those sessions]. I feel really lucky that the music industry was more structured on that level, and it impacts my life. It used to be, 'Oh my God, all this mailbox money has come in and I can go on a trip.' Now it's like, 'I can get a nice dinner' . . . I caught the last wave of that in the '90s . . . and that's like, 'Tell me another story, Grandpa.'" In work-for-hire situations, Doug Gillard says, "It's more fair to ask if there are songwriting credits you can get" in lieu of the benefits of a longer relationship. In fact, credits are commonly a bargaining chip in a work-for-hire session, in exchange for up-front pay—"I don't have much to pay you now, but here's points on the song(s)." It's a lottery ticket musicians are often happy to accept.

The position of drummers in this discussion deserves particular attention. Drummers are at a structural disadvantage in copyright law which only recognizes harmony and melody;[45] which is a matter of frustration for some. "Drums are often, because they are not a harmonic instrument or melodic instrument, sidelined by people who write songs, and I don't see that that is a justifiable position," says Jim Sclavunos.

> If you start playing a beat, and then other people join in, and then they go, "Oh, we've just written a song." And you say, "Yeah, me too," and they go, "No!" You are the actual person who initiated the flow of ideas and your part has not changed, and it is the part that is part of the song—why is it not considered part of the composition? It is saying that what the drummer contributes is not as important as what a guitarist might contribute . . . if that drumbeat was part of the natal condition of the song.

Mike Sneeringer has used that disadvantage as a negotiating position: "I get an equal cut of all money for touring, or I don't go. I was willing to say, 'I'm not writing songs, but I'm also not asking for any publishing or licensing.'"

"Certain drumbeats are signature beats," says DJ Bonebrake. "Like with X, 'Hungry Wolf' is kind of a signature beat. You could say it's a Gene Krupa lick, but it's a floor tom thing that goes *dut dut dut, dutdutdutdutdutdut.* And as simple as that is, it's kind of a signature, so I'm really torn about the legal part. Obviously as a drummer you think, 'My part's really important, and it contributes something.' But on the other hand, from a practical point of you view, you go, 'Well, can I copyright 1-2-3-4?'" It depends on the creativity of the part, says Brian Viglione: "I don't know if I would say putting a regular four-on-the-floor beat to a Ramones-y sounding song is necessarily considered authorship, because it's fairly self-explanatory."

The split-it-between-whoever's-in-the-room model has the appeal of simplicity and conflict avoidance, especially for collaborative projects which prize spontaneity. "I made a record in 2003," says Freese, "[with] a bunch of folks—the *Desert Sessions, Volumes 9 and 10.* That's the kind of thing where everyone is in a room. . . . I played drums on some stuff, and I played bass on some stuff. But everyone [is] working on these things very spontaneously and real quickly, so everyone gets a cut of everything that you play on. There's a song that the Queens [of the Stone Age] ended up recording on the next record, called 'In My Head,' and that was my riff that I brought in, but even though I wrote that riff, everyone got writer's [credit] on it. And maybe the next song I played drums on it, but I didn't write any of the notes to, I still got writer's credit because I was sitting in there with them while it was being born and materializing."

Gerry Leonard recommends insisting on clarity. "It used to be like, 'Oh, you'll get points on the record,' through this mysterious 'back-end.' You'll hear people talk 'You'll get paid out the back-end.' My phrase to all my friends was, 'There is no back-end.' . . . My philosophy is, don't look for what isn't there—get paid appropriately for the work you do, and if you end up writing, then you should get a part of that pie." Even up-front clarity and mutual trust between collaborators is no guarantee, though. "Years ago," Stuart Bogie said, "I had worked with a friend a lot, and he specifically said, 'I want to step up our work together.'" Bogie goes on:

"I want you to start producing with me and start writing with me." And I'm like, "Do you mean working for back-end?" He said, "That's exactly what I mean." And I was like, "Yes, this is the greatest day of my life!" Because I never cared about today; I always cared about tomorrow. All I wanted to do was get in a room and make as much creative beautiful things as I could and have enough of a thumbprint on it that if it was successful, I would see a little bit of mailbox money. And hopefully that would fuel whatever else I was doing in the future. My friends had worked for Mark Ronson, and he had been giving them little bits of back-end here and there, which made a huge difference, which allowed them to enjoy a middle-class lifestyle. . . . I was like, "Holy shit, you bought a car? How do you guys pay your rent and everything?" They were getting little bits of back-ends here and there, just little ones; but it was adding up, and it really made a difference in their lives.

He was into that idea. And as work came and went, I ended up doing a lot of creative arranging for no money up front. Then out of the blue, I got a letter from his management, asking me to release any creative work that I had done.

I spent hours—maybe even a whole day—trying to sculpt the perfect email to say, "I love you; I love working with you; I want very much to be a partner in the music we're in, and I'm not asking to be a 50/50 partner. I'm not necessarily even *asking to be a partner*, but I want you to be open to the idea that I can hear the music"—because they didn't send me the music; they didn't send me the final product that they wanted me to sign off on—"If you would send it to me, then I'll know, and then I want to discuss it," and I tried to find the most loving appreciative way of saying that, and they were immediately incredibly responsive. They replied and they were so wonderful, like, "Here's the record; listen, we'll talk about it; [we] want everything to be good." And I was like, "Oh, thank God."

And I listened to the record, and I said, "Oh, no, I didn't make any of this stuff." I did some original arranging, but they were just horn bumps and little patterns that are well within the vocabulary of horn arranging. [I said,] "No, thank you so much for indulging me, but I don't request any writing credit on your record," and that was cool; I signed the form—and I never heard from the guy again. That was the last we worked together.

And it felt very tragic. That was the functional end of our relationship, and it makes me feel so sad. All I wanted to do was be a partner. It's like there was a glass ceiling there. And I've seen other people knock on that door, and I say, "Ah, don't knock on that door!" It fucks with my head so much, because the people who put this together, the indie rock world—they are the children of professional and successful immigrant families, and all these people who had to work together, who had to have unions and more socialist ideas to construct what they were doing. . . . When you are talking about what's supposed to be alternative society music, you want it to have more ethics.

For Thor Harris, the issue is credit in the general, rather than the legal, sense: "A lot of people don't even know I'm on a lot of records that they listen to; people aren't reading liner notes like they used to do. . . . If the parts are distinct enough and I feel really proud of them, I want to at least be listed in the credits. That's more important to me than being given songwriting credit."[46]

The root of the split between performers and composers, wrote Miège, lies in the fact that until the development of recording technology, only the underlying composition could be widely distributed and commoditized ("published"): recording "eliminated the formerly ephemeral character of performances" and made them newly eligible for a royalty structure—but copyright protection for performance has continued to lag behind that of the composition.[47] There does exist a royalty for performers equivalent to songwriter royalties, which in theory would go a long way toward alleviating this inequality—just not in the United States, and not for broadcast radio. Performers can get royalties for satellite radio and internet broadcast (SiriusXM, Spotify, and the like—though only for recordings made after 1972), but not when the recordings are played on terrestrial radio (a $16 billion a year industry built on the back of popular music recordings). A bill called the Fair Play Fair Pay Act has been kicking around Congress for some time, aiming to close both the terrestrial radio and the pre-1972 copyright loopholes (I was among a group of musicians who traveled to Capitol Hill to lobby for its passage in 2016). But the ferocious opposition of The National Association of Broadcasters—that is, big radio, ClearChannel and the like—has managed to squelch what would be a valuable lifeline for non-songwriting musicians.

ACCOUNTING, BUDGETING, AND SCHEDULING

The profession, too, breeds insecurity and a sense of isolation in its own indefiniteness. . . . His employment follows no set cycle, and although he is paid well when working, his popularity may vanish overnight; he must travel . . . and engagements are generally short . . . and last, he may suddenly find himself, for one reason or another, physically or mentally unable to play. Further, he is not covered by the Social Security laws, he is seldom a member of a group insurance or health plan, and he is seldom in a position . . . to put money in the bank, or to insure himself, in any way, against old age.

ALAN MERRIAM AND RAYMOND MACK, "THE JAZZ COMMUNITY"[48]

[Robert] Curtis cautioned that the unusual freedom enjoyed by people in music "may also include . . . inopportunely . . . the freedom not to work."

MATT STAHL, *UNFREE MASTERS*[49]

An underappreciated challenge for even relatively successful band people is budgeting and scheduling. For physical, psychological, familial, and logistical reasons, even the most hard-touring bands don't stay on the road permanently; for most bands in the digital era performing is the source of the majority of their revenue. Since most bands don't keep their members on salary or retainer (though some do), musicians are incentivized to keep downtime to a minimum: time off the road means reduced or negative income ("If you're not playing, you're paying," as the maxim goes).

Some musicians are able to patch together local gigs, recording sessions, and intermittent labor. Others will try to balance working relationships with more than one band. This can be a dangerous game: one risks jeopardizing a job with First-Priority Band if one commits to a tour with Second-Priority Band during scheduled FPB downtime—if a late-breaking opportunity for the FPB presents itself, the musician is put in the position of disappointing one or the other. Some bandleaders are more understanding in these situations than others. "For a long time," says Peter Hess, "when I was involved with Balkan Beat Box, I had to put them at the top of the food chain. I didn't have a sub—it wasn't really subbable. They didn't have me on a retainer, but I had to leave them at the top of the food chain, so when they gave me a date, I pretty much had to take it or fuck them, and the exchange is 'Here's all this work; here's all these great shows.' I don't think anybody ever said it out loud." Hess continues:

I'm a part of Slavic Soul Party now, and the leader of that band hired me after I was already a part of Balkan Beat Box. And he sussed out early on that I had to [prioritize them], and that his band was going to be second to me—not because that's necessarily how I wanted it to be, but when you're working for somebody else, you sometimes don't get to pick and choose exactly what you do when, if you want to hang on to the job. And I also saw that [BBB] had a long ongoing drama with a couple guitar players who were putting their own things ahead of that band, being different degrees of explicit about it, and causing massive headaches. And I never wanted to cause them those massive headaches, because I wanted to hang on to the job.

Eliza Hardy Jones knows that "if a last-minute show gets booked with Grace Potter, I have to go. [For example,] I have been invited to go to Russia—which I really want to do, but I have been told that I have to block out my schedule to October, and I'm like, 'I know that I won't be on tour for the next six months. Can you just tell me one way or not when we're going to be on tour?' And management is like, 'We have no idea, you just have to be available.' So that's been tricky."

Different genre ecosystems have different standards. Nels Cline has—in exchange for "a small retainer, nothing super dramatic"—made Wilco his priority. "The only thing that makes that difficult . . . is that the rock-and-roll world seems to book things far closer to the actual engagement date than the improvised music and so-called jazz and so-called legit world. Those things get booked really, really far in advance. So quite often if somebody has asked me to do something, say, at a jazz festival in Europe months and months and months or maybe a year from now, the Wilco world can't always sign off on it, because we aren't sure exactly whether or not we're on tour, or what we're doing, and that person will wait for me until he or she can't stand it anymore; and then they usually get somebody else to play those gigs."

Thus, the typical band person is in the position of having the responsibility and commitments of a salaried worker with a contract and benefits, without the security. The self-employed have often found themselves in a state of, as Matt Stahl puts it, "flexibility leading to radical insecurity." Budgeting and planning for time off is a crucial and hard-earned skill, "the learning experience of my life of being a musician," says Michael McDermott. "There's great times; there's times where you're like, 'I'm going to tighten my belt.'" "I [would] eat pasta for two months, and just not go out," says Mike Yannich. "I made sure that I was living very cheaply, knowing that [I've] got to get through two months with this $300." John DeDomenici works "literally as much as possible" when at home: "Over the last year in the fall I worked something like fifty straight days in a row, just to hoard up enough money so when it's the slow season for work, I'm not starving. And then when I go on tour, in case the tour doesn't do super well, I'm still okay."

"Between December and April," says Michael Bland, "everything slows down during that trimester. So you gotta be like animals in nature and start getting it, gathering it, and saving it as the year comes to a close, because you know that winter is coming." Luckily, when Bland was in Prince's band, he was on retainer and on call: "Which meant, in his case, I'd just call him at two o'clock in the morning and get up and go out to Paisley Park, and sometimes he'd be ready to work. Other times, he'd be watching *Last Tango in Paris*, eating popcorn in Studio A with the lights out. I come in, and we'd talk for seven or eight minutes and he'd say, 'We're not going to do anything, man, I'll see you later.'" Very few bands have the luxury of buying blocks of musicians' time, though, and a lack of attention to these dynamics can strain and break bands. When Will Sheff moved to New York, says Scott Brackett, the rest of the Okkervil River band "stayed in Austin where the cost of living was much cheaper. Will was there so he could be in the big meetings and meet the right people; [he] was trying to secure his future in that respect. But what it meant was, you keep this stable of musicians who you can pay less than you would have to pay musicians in New York or a bigger city, and you can get these opportunities, but you don't have to necessarily have to pay [us] as much. That was when the deal went a little bit sour for all of us, and there was a pretty big turnover."

"There is never a month where I'm like, 'Okay, I can cruise now,'" says Janet Weiss. "It is definitely not for the faint of heart, at my age." She goes on:

> That aspect of being a musician is what breaks many people. . . . In Sleater-Kinney, Carrie has three careers, Corin has two kids. I don't have any kids; I'm the one who has to be the most flexible, because they have a lot going on. So you are on two other people's schedule, and how do you fit in something in three months that is going to be satisfying and make money?

Versatility is key for Toby Dammit:

> I've tried to learn how to play lots of different kinds of music, and if someone wants me to come to Russia or wants me to go to Norway or if they want me to go to Australia or wherever, I just say yes and go and try and figure out whatever it is when I get there. That's the only way you can really survive. It's been very rare that I was ever offered any kind of a retainer, and a lot of times you have schedule conflicts—you might be working with someone on a limited project for a while, then a break comes up and they want to do some more later, but you've already started working with somebody else, and you can't. You have to tell them no. Stuff like this happens a lot, and it's hard. You create your own calendar and schedule with whoever calls first, whoever commits to a plan first. You just have to follow your gut with what you think is best for you, and/or [for] keeping money in the bank, and/or being artistically satisfied. Sometimes you can artistically satisfy yourself for two or three months, then the next month you got to go make some money and do something that maybe you don't like so much.

Joe McGinty "was offered a tour with Blondie about six years ago, and I had commitments in the city that I couldn't get out of. So I had to say no to the tour, and the guy that did that tour is still with them, but it's also like, choose your adventure. I've had plenty of great experience[s] in the past six years that I might not have had if I had been the keyboardist for Blondie all this time." Scott McCaughey's ad hoc scheduling creates a natural triage in which his leader projects "have fallen more by the wayside because they don't generally make money. I do make a living more from playing with other people." Todd Sickafoose has evolved a relationship with bandleader Ani DiFranco's booking and management from "years when I found out about Ani's schedule on short notice—and for me, short notice is like three months. That becomes a little bit unworkable. Now they have got it to about six to eight months, and that seems doable to me. . . . People can be nervous that you don't know what the word 'tentative' means. For eleven years I asked to be included on the tentative schedule for Ani's touring. They just gave me access to it in the last year, and it's been revelatory for both camps. And it turns out I do know what 'tentative' means."

Having a partner with a steady income (and, ideally, health insurance) quietly helps paper over a dry spell. Mike Sneeringer has "almost always had a significant other [who] is not involved in that lifestyle, and does expect to live in a house, or at least in an apartment, not a squat or a warehouse. [So] that has put the pressure on me to very much watch my spending."

The most common arrangements are similar to DeDomenici's in the Jeff Rosenstock band: "We get a day rate, but then if the tour does well, we get a bonus," or, as for Nigel Powell with Frank Turner and the Sleeping Souls, a "small percentage" of tour profits in exchange for an exclusive commitment within a certain window—"[so] they can plan six weeks ahead and know that we're going to be available." The Decembrists, says Jenny Conlee, are "a business, the five of us . . . because we were all there at the beginning, we are all an LLC—so I guess we get paid more than most side musicians. But the money does come in only when we tour." For Peter Hughes, "we pretty much pay ourselves when we go out." He elaborates:

> For me and for John [Darnielle], it is a little bit easier, because at this point we get royalties; things are coming in every three months from 4AD, from Merge now, and they are staggered—we

get a check every six months from each one, so every three months you get a little bit of money that is just enough to keep you afloat between tours. Then when we tour, we come home and get a big paycheck.

At this point we have been living like this for so long, I am pretty good at managing that. You get a big pile of money and we have got to make it last until whenever the next windfall comes in. We are definitely aware of it—like, if it's an off-cycle year, we have to go out at least a couple of times just to keep everybody afloat. But then we will figure out different ways to do that. That was what those duo tours were about—those were years where John and I had both become parents, so we weren't looking to do a ton of touring. Wurster was super busy with other stuff, and we weren't going to make another record for a little while. John [was finishing] his first novel. So it was like, what can we do that will be low-impact, where there is still a little bit of money coming in to tide us over to the next album cycle, when you can make real money?

The successful three-way Venn diagram of shared members between Bob Mould, Superchunk, and the Mountain Goats—not to mention Jon Wurster's comedy and John Darnielle's literary pursuits—suggests an unusually high level of communication, trust, planning, and maturity among the acts.[50] "We are constantly mapping things out," says Hughes. "Generally I am the easy one, schedule-wise. . . . At this point we are always looking nine to twelve months into the future. Like, let's block out these three or four weeks in the fall, and everybody keep that clear for Mountain Goats." Wurster says, "Scheduling got a little tougher specifically with the Mountain Goats and Bob, because both Bob and John have been in this huge creative peak in terms of wanting to do things in their songwriting output," adding:

So it's a lot of going from one band immediately to the other. In the spring, I did three weeks with the Mountain Goats and left immediately to start a tour with Bob the next day, and we went for three-and-one-half weeks and right back to a Mountain

Goats recording session, then to do a comedy thing with Tom [Scharpling]. . . . I haven't really had a personal life for the last eight years.

But in a business often run on handshake agreements and vague "understandings," misunderstandings (or worse) certainly occur. Sneeringer "would always joke with" one bandleader about joining his group, "because he had always had drummers in and out of the band. And [eventually] he said, 'Okay, why don't we jam next week?'" He continues:

> It slowly evolved into where he was asking me to join the band. . . . We had even talked about money. And after one of the rehearsals I said, "Hey, not to say 'shit or get off the pot,' but I got to know if you really want me to have this gig, because I have to tell Purling Hiss." Purling Hiss got offered the Steven Malkmus tour and it was going to be at the same time, so hey, I actually have to decide now. And he said, "If you want the gig you've got it, you will be the drummer." So I went to the next Purling Hiss practice and announced that I had to quit the band. Mike was very upset, the lead guy. And I just said, okay, this was uncomfortable, but this is me going after something I want. After all this time, I am finally going to have some success, because we could already tell the record was going to do well.
>
> And they get back from [tour] and everything is very, very different, the vibes just feel—I can't really get hold of [the band-leader]. Normally we had been talking or emailing very frequently about the logistics about the tour. We do one rehearsal with me on drums. Then we went out to dinner afterward and they basically told me, [we have someone else]. And I'm like, "Well, I already quit my touring gig"—I quit my band. It was very uncomfortable, and it stretched on for a month of not knowing whether I was getting the gig, feeling like I definitely wasn't, and ended up not getting it, being gently pushed out. I consider

those guys still my friends, but that was the first time I really felt burned.

Others seem to get an adrenaline-junkie thrill from overscheduling themselves. "Probably the [player] that I admire the most—if only for his ability to juggle schedules—is Josh Freese," says Sneeringer.

> Josh Freese has been a drummer for so many very different bands at the same time. . . . He is probably the one person I am almost confused by; like, are there five of you? How are you able to be in so many different bands? . . . I think it got to a point where he was literally on an airplane every day. But talk about taking the power of being the drummer and holding it up against being a front person—he's like, "I'm good enough to play with a million different people in a million different genres. I'm going to do it. I'm going to record; I am going to play live, and I'm just going to be a drummer." I admire that.

Indeed, says Freese, "There's been times when it gets so nuts, when I'm squeezing things in and I'm barely making it to the next thing, so stressful, I'm flying in the day of the gigs across the country—and no one likes you to do that, especially [when] you got a connecting flight." He continues:

> Knock on wood, I've never missed a gig, but there's been some close calls. There were times when I was juggling some Replacements and Devo stuff a couple years ago—let's just say it gets hectic sometimes; and when it's not completely hectic, I'm really relieved. There's times when I'm sitting around at home with my kids and walking the dog, and because I'm so used to activeness, once in a while I'll go, "I've got nothing going on today or tomorrow or the next day." Like, what's the problem with my career? I've spent so much fuckin' time triple-dipping, going on no sleep, taking red-eyes all over, back and forth—literally be in New York, come back to LA for one day

to do something, then back to New York for the gig—I should enjoy all that work that I've put in to actually have a day off, or a week off, here and there, and not freak out about it. There's times when I'll bitch and complain about the hecticness, but I kind of get off on it.

There was a time recently when I was with my drum tech at the airport at like 4:45 in the morning for a six a.m. flight somewhere—we're sitting there and walking in the airport like zombies somewhere in the Midwest. I said to him, "You know what?" He goes, "What?"

And he thought I was going to say something like "This is the worst," and I said, "I love this." And at the time I was probably forty-one or forty-two; I wasn't twenty-one doing it. I fuckin' still get off on it. I still get off on the craziness and the workaholic shit.

A pillar of the legend of Mike Watt is built on his ability to "jam econo"—that is, live frugally in the service of music-making: "You live within your means; you don't make the dream too big for the tent. . . . Can you imagine raising families? That was a decision I made not to do, because it's tough in this racket, so I made choices." He does try to pass on advice on how to tour frugally—"like regular maintenance on the van, so you won't have to fix it when it breaks"—and is prepared to make sacrifices in comfort for tours he wants to do. "I don't think all payment is in the coin. I just put myself in situations where I can [make choices] that are aesthetic. I just did a tour for Tav Falco, but it wasn't for bones [money] at all. I was compensated and stuff, but I just wanted to play with Tav Falco, a hero of mine. But to do that, you have to be in a certain kind of situation. You are living pretty econo." He elaborates:

I had a debt for a while when that sickness almost killed me in 2000. I had a tour, and the tour paid $36,000 bucks. They saved my life, so I didn't think it was money wasted. But living without big old debts, living econo, makes it easier to do those things, and I couldn't do it [if I were] a guy with three kids or something. Some of the guys—like my Secondmen, they both have families. They are longshoremen during the day, so that's how they are handling it. When it comes time for them to play, they're into it. On the other side of it, some of those [who] move to Hollywood to make it—that's so scary, I can't imagine; it's big dice rolls. . . . I want to take more risks with aesthetics, with art, than with economics. My pop was a sailor. All of us Minutemen came from lower [economic status], so you had to think econo.

Watt didn't make a full-time living as a musician until his band Firehose, in the mid-1980s. All of [the Minutemen] had other work besides working in music. I think our first paid gig was the thirty-fifth gig." He continues:

But then by '85, things were starting to change, and with Firehose, I still lived very econo. I lived in a one-room apartment that actually had only one electrical outlet, because it was built before electricity, so fuck it, we'll just put one plug in—a studio apartment, a one-room thing. With Firehose, Edward lived under a desk I built out of wood from the alley.

His bandmate in the two-bass duo Dos, Kira Roessler, "would tell you she made [different] choices," according to Watt:

She got a degree from UCLA in mechanical engineering, while she was in Black Flag, [says,] "Fuck, I'm tired of this shit," always doing Dos on the side. . . . She teaches herself ProTools and she does audio editing for sound effects, TV, movies. She's got two Emmys now and an Oscar. She has talked to me about this before: "I made my choice, I couldn't focus on music, but I need music in my life, so thank you for having Dos. We can do this; I can get my music thing out and we can do some gigs on a casual basis; I can do songwriting." But she had to—what do you say, "the bread gets buttered"—she had to do these other works.

A struggle that is rarely commented on for a freelance musician is the ways in which the financial infrastructure of the world is predicated on full-time salaried employment. Any freelancer in this system operates at a structural disadvantage: you need a work history and pay stubs and semi-permanent addresses for things like credit, leases, down payments, car and student loans. You need credit cards for the necessities of tour: rental vehicles, merch pre-orders, plane tickets. You have to file taxes quarterly (in theory), and you have a greater accounting burden: detailed Schedule C itemized deductions require organization and time commitment for preparation, you pay more to file, and you run a greater risk of audit. (Needless to say, this is all left for young musicians to figure out on their own, by painful trial and error.) On the one hand, a freelancer can write off a great deal on taxes; on the other, they do need to report a profit both to avoid their profession being classified by the IRS as a hobby and to reassure loan underwriters that they do, in fact, turn a net profit annually. Scott McCaughey "noticed when I first started having to file, and I wasn't working for somebody, and I had to file self-employment returns, I had to be a self-employed guy. What do I do then, when you get the Social Security tax thing? Oh man, that just killed me. It did seem like I was being penalized for being self-employed, when it seems like you should be rewarded for it." (For those working internationally, Joey Burns recommends a business manager to recover taxes withheld by foreign countries: "I remember back in the day thinking that at the end of the year, I would somehow try to get back the money that was taken out from income overseas, and unfortunately I learned a few years later that the money that was withheld could be applied or reduced from the top of your taxes that are paid to the government here.")

Carla Kihlstedt notes the paradoxical and contradictory messages musicians receive in the brave new digital world of the last two decades: "We used to have many fewer direct paths towards a functional livelihood, and fewer people could actually make that happen. Now, there are many more paths and many more tools and many more things you can use, both to get gigs and to get followings and to release records, and there's many more paths to getting your music out in the world, but they're all flooded, and the success of all of them is pretty tentative." The challenges are different, and not every musician is cut out to be an entrepreneur on their own behalf: "Some people are simply not set up to push themselves out into the world. . . . For all the tools that we have for social media available to us, to use it well, you have to have that piece of your personality that's totally comfortable self-promoting." As Simon Frith wrote, the music industry is a bulk business which runs on failure: it "markets far more products than it sells, and poor musicians are as necessary to the system as rich ones. . . . It is not successful musicians who are 'exploited' in this situation, but unsuccessful ones."[51]

"I try to just keep playing," said Ralph Carney. "If I don't have a lot of gigs, I'll record or I'll practice or just go take a nice walk, you know. Don't just sit and obsess that you don't have gigs. There is that thing of, 'Oh I don't have any gigs;' and [then], 'Oh, I have too many gigs'—it's the musician's lament."

6

GOING BAD

Conflicts

[Our string quartet] is an odd quadripartite marriage with six relationships, any of which, at any given time, could be cordial or neutral or strained. The audiences who listen to us cannot imagine how earnest, how petulant, how accommodating, how willful is our quest for something beyond ourselves that we imagine with our separate spirits but are compelled to embody together. Where is the harmony of spirit in all this, let alone sublimity? How are such mechanics, such stops and starts, such facile irreverence transmuted, in spite of our bickering selves, into musical gold?

VIKRAM SETH, *AN EQUAL MUSIC*[1]

The types of group disruption may be roughly divided into two classes: (a) those in which there was a real splitting of the group, and (b) those in which there were interpersonal aggressions and minor disorganizations of activity, without any permanent division of the group. . . . The second classification . . . may be subdivided into three categories . . . interpersonal aggressions, including hostility, joking hostility, blame of others, and aggressive domination of others; temporary escape from the field, including withdrawal from the problem, substitute behavior, cheating, and attempts to change problems; and general disorganization of the group activity.

JOHN FRENCH JR., "THE DISRUPTION AND COHESION OF GROUPS"[2]

Some of the pulls which on the face of it drew people together, such as mutual interdependence, the euphoria of joint perfor-mance, social interaction, also sometimes formed the focus of disagreements which weakened or eventually broke the ties. . . . Even the satisfaction of joint musical performance could produce division rather than integration: joint euphoria could turn to competitiveness or "bigheadedness" or, as one rock player put it, "one person may get carried away a bit and think it's his own band."

RUTH FINNEGAN, *THE HIDDEN MUSICIANS: MUSIC-MAKING IN AN ENGLISH TOWN*[3]

I asked musicians if, when conflicts arose, they tended to be musical or personal. Perhaps predictably, they moved to merge the two ("Is volume a musical thing or a personal thing?" asked Michael Bland). If Sarah Balliett objects to a musical choice, she says, "chances are someone in my band wrote that song or that part, and might feel personally attached to it. So a musical conflict can become personal quickly." But given that group artistic collaboration is nominally the reason you're all in the room, musicians are most likely to dig in their heels on matters of composition and arrangement—because, Katie Harkin says, "They're the—what would the movie be—*The Uncom-promisables*." (Bennett put it more formally: "Friction . . . inevitably reveals itself as grounded in the more meaningful issue of the style of the group's mutual identity construction.")[4] Courtesy is key: "Never personalize music criticism," says Peter Erskine. "'That part's not very cool,' or 'I'm not feeling that'—sometimes it hurts people's feelings," says Jenny Conlee.

More consequential conflicts can involve fractures between sup-port musicians. Since a certain division of goals is already baked into the bandleader/band dynamic, any schism within the support team can have more unpredictable effects. These schisms can be about rel-ative skill, or preparation: "If [conflict] ever is musical," says John DeDomenici, "it's just me getting on people's cases because they don't know the songs well enough . . . because it wastes my time and that pisses me off. I don't like when band rehearsals become teaching rehearsals for one guy or one gal, because I could be home hanging out with my cat, and not watching you learn your song that you should've learned already."

But, like any labor or staffing issues, musical disagreements can be proxies for other issues—including ways for subordinate workers to assert their rights and power. Eliza Hardy Jones "was in a band with a drummer who really was so stubborn—[someone would say], 'When we do this thing, maybe try this pattern there,' and the drummer would be like, 'I'm not doing that.' Just 'do not tell me what to do on my instrument. I will not play that same pattern.' . . . I think that's obtained from a personal thing where that person felt that they were heard or respected, so they could stand their ground, and they weren't going to make an exception."[5] While individual stubbornness on musical matters can have a quite powerful effect on an accommodating bandleader, there are very few stories of successful collective action. "Occasionally," wrote Drew Page of the big band era, "I've seen a group of sidemen get together and elect spokesmen to present their gripes to their leaders, but inevitably, when the time came, everybody backed out, leaving the spokesman holding the bag." In a rock world in which bands are smaller and individual members better-known and (in theory) less replaceable, one might expect more stories of this sort of thing, but the reality is quite the opposite. Reasons include the informal, less structured roles within bands—band people are not always exactly conscious of themselves as employees—and the complex and usually unspoken hierarchies within bands which discourage (if the phrase isn't comical to use in this context) class solidarity.

In the hothouse environment of a band, rarely is a grudge or a gripe only about one thing. Conflict, says Marc Capelle, may come "from musical disagreements, and somehow you figure out a way [that you're making] less money than you should be making, and they're taking more credit than they should be taking, and then it's all resentment. I don't think you can pick the corn from the shit on this one." Jim Sclavunos agrees: "It can be quite a crucible situation. You are all together in a tight space in a heated situation—be it a tour bus or van or recording studio—and you've got time limitations and budget limitations or you have got commitments to things, and people have their idiosyncrasies. But it is interesting that often these personality differences play themselves out in the rhetoric of a creative discussion: 'We can't do that because it is not the right thing for the song.' The creative argument can be levied at individuals in all sorts of ways—[or] be used as leverage for putting oneself in a better position."

Still, Sclavunos continues, you can drive yourself crazy looking for *reasons* musicians act the way they do: "A lot of musicians are very insecure, and they oscillate wildly between being completely full of themselves and [being] crestfallen and crushed, neurotic individuals. They seem to leap from one mental space to another quite quickly. If you catch somebody on the downward or upward curve, some behavior that might have been okay two hours ago might be suddenly rubbing somebody the wrong way." Bruce Kaphan tells a harrowing story of an uncooperative bandmate in an arranged musical marriage:

When I was with David Byrne's band, we met in New York to rehearse for a month before going on what turned out to be about a year's worth of world touring. And one of the guys that he got was just one of the most uncooperative and belligerent people I've ever met in my life. Imagine if you will, we were in rehearsal—and when you play a non-fixed instrument like pedal steel, it's easy enough to be out of tune all by yourself. If someone else is already out of tune, your chances of playing in tune are essentially next to nothing, because the reference is off. So there was a sample in this musician's sampler, and it was out of tune . . . and I casually asked him, "Hey, could you check the tuning on that sample? Because it feels like it's out of tune." He looked at me, folded his arms and said, "You are not my boss. You cannot tell me what to do." . . . I eventually ended up talking to David. I said, "Hey David, he won't tune that for me, but I imagine he will for you. Would you mind asking him?" So he reluctantly tuned it. Then I find out a few months later that he switched it back to out-of-tune again to see if I'd notice. . . . It's like, [you're] willing to sabotage the music—who are you, and why are you a part of this?

One musician describes a leader as "horrible . . . just like this malignant narcissistic juggernaut I would say 90 percent of the time, but that 10 percent of the time that you are actually on stage or in rehearsals and in the moment . . . and you are in the music together, [they are] one of the most passionate generous lovers you will ever have. It's whether or not you want to hang in there for that 10 percent; which, after a certain point—I prefer orgasms at least 50 percent of the time, not just 10 percent."

"Being in a band is like being married, but to way too many people," says Andrew Seward. "It's like polygamy, it doesn't work. We had fights on stage—Laura [Jane Grace] and myself, I remember I totally fuckin' punched her in Providence one time. We were both just being passive-aggressive shitheads to each other, like 'Oh, you're not talking to me?' 'No.' 'Fuck you.' You get to the end of your rope and sometimes you have to just get it out, and somebody punches somebody—*fuck you, fuck you*—and then you're best friends. That's being in a band, and it's absolutely stupid. It's the most non-adult thing in the world."

QUITTING AND GETTING FIRED

So what does one do, when a band relationship, whether on a personal or financial level, becomes intolerable? Just like any other job (if more publicly)—depending on your level of savvy, diplomacy, and courage—you can quit, or be fired. In the best cases, the departure happens smoothly (at least as narrated by the leaver): "My mother is a social worker and my father is a salesman, so it is not in my social upbringing to bring conflict into people's faces," says Stuart Bogie. "I have quit projects, probably with too much emotional drama—but always amiably, with a lot of love." "I left [Hole] very effortlessly," says Melissa Auf der Maur. "I really felt like my chapter was done. I left on very good terms with everybody. . . . But the benefit I had is that I really was an outsider. Patty and Eric were much more invested. They were tortured by not having enough control over, like, 'Let's make five records, not one in five years.' They wanted to make more music. I was just so removed—I let it be an experience that I was not in control of, whereas I could imagine if I was a founding member, I would have been losing my mind." When Steely Dan let Peter Erskine go, it "was like a relief—good, now I don't have to decide, I can go back to my jazz thing. But it's never any fun not being invited back to a party."

The power to quit is, reasonably enough, associated with retention of dignity and agency.[6] "I quit American Music Club both because I felt like I was being kept down and I felt that the music was being sacrificed," says Bruce Kaphan, "and you put those two things together at the same time, and I'm distant as quickly as possible." Brian Viglione has chosen "rather than say 'You are doing it wrong' to somebody else, I just say, 'This is the wrong environment for me, and I just need to move on to something else and find the right place and the right people to work with.'" Eliza Hardy Jones took a more proactive stance: "I did 'If this doesn't change, I'm going to quit,' and that thing didn't change, and I'm like, 'I'm going to quit now.' Then I got a call from the manager who was like, 'I understand, but will you do that?' and I said sure. I didn't want to fuck anybody over; I didn't want to leave anybody hanging, even though I gave plenty of notice. They should have been prepared to replace me if they knew they weren't going to change. But I tried really hard not to screw anybody over, and I'm super good friends with those guys, and I'm very happy to not be on the road with the band, but I also feel like in the end no bridges were burned."

The act and emotion of quitting can be more acute, especially for younger musicians: John DeDomenici remembers, "I would quit Jeff [Rosenstock]'s band every other week, probably, because we were just fighting all the time as kids." Bands that form when members are young (perhaps especially as young men) seed issues around control and compensation by simple ignorance, or stoicism. "In a band that can't communicate," says Matt Sharp, "quitting or firing isn't really an option . . . so those things just happen . . . you find yourself in a place and you don't know how you got there, but it certainly wasn't through constructive communication. Obviously with any relationship, getting into it is always easier than it is getting out." Some prefer the ugly mess: "I say we take off and nuke the entire site from orbit;

it's the only way to be sure," says Meredith Yayanos. "I got half-ass fired [once], but only half-assed because that fucker was like a wet paper bag full of pissed-on toilet paper, he was just so soggy; he was so fuckin' soft and so passive-aggressive, he couldn't even bring himself to fire me. He basically poked me with a sharp stick until I exploded and left."

The dissolution of any relationship may be, too, clouded by regret. Michael McDermott left the Bouncing Souls in 2013, after almost fifteen years with the band, to take an offer from Rome Ramirez:

I would have probably never quit the Bouncing Souls, but there was a promise of so much work, and so much promise of [Rome] going on to do other things. . . . Quitting sucks, and I'll regret quitting the Bouncing Souls for as long as I live. I'm okay with it; I mean, I don't want to die, but it definitely has been [a] heartache, and it's been hard because I'm still great friends with them. It was also one of those things where just because you realize your mistake, that doesn't mean that you can just snap your fingers and change time. We couldn't do that, because we got one of our good friends, George Rebelo from Hot Water Music, to play, and you can't just be like, "Hey George, Michael quit but he wants to come back now"—there's moral aspects of it as well.

Quitting bands totally sucks, because it's a friendship. It's a love. It's almost a greater love affair, sometimes than any woman you've ever had, because you sometimes can connect on such a higher level, on such a different level maybe than you could with your wife or your girlfriend. . . . My breakup with the Bouncing Souls was harder than my divorce from my ex-wife, I'll say that. That's because my love for them, and what we did—I think it was easier to say goodbye to her than it was to say goodbye to the Bouncing Souls. So there's some honesty for you.

Many musicians cultivate a single representative story of dismissal, from a chronological distance (Peter Hess: "I got fired once, early on, from Ernie Krivda's Fat Tuesday Big Band. I worked with Ernie for about three years in Cleveland. We played every Tuesday at a place called Mr. Small's in Cleveland, and it paid seventeen dollars and a beer. . . . He fired me for quote-unquote 'bitching'"), as anecdotes—traumatic, humorous, and teachable—of youthful lessons learned about being punctual, sober, reliable, and humble. "It went horrible," remembers Rick Steff. "It was Dexy's Midnight Runners; I was twenty, twenty-one, and it was [an] all-star British lineup of players, and we were in Switzerland recording at Montreux. I was too full of ego and probably too full of liquids . . . and was cockier than I needed to be, and pointed out things to the artist that I thought were incumbent upon me to tell him about his songwriting, [that] they sounded like other songs to me. So I was very unceremoniously fired and had to leave the country, because I had been working [illegally] in the UK, just trying to hang on until something happened. That was a necessary thing for me, just to learn a lot about humility and about what is best left unsaid sometimes, working with artists' temperament and the creative process. . . . I have since talked to Kevin Rowland and made my apologies, and we have made our peace. But that was really an eye-opener."

"Louise Mandrell fired me, [which] was totally understandable," says Bruce Bouton. "I was mean and I'd just got started and I was crazy. The guitar player and I got into a bunch of tequila in a Texas club and we were drinking blue margaritas—this was early on in my career. Ricky [Skaggs] and I have sort of run the gamut—I remember when he said he was letting me go, I said, 'We're firing each other.'" Bouton adds:

> I haven't been fired off a session, but I have been in situations where I didn't get called back, and in retrospect I know why. You gotta take care of business. You gotta be prepared. You gotta be decent to hang around with. There were times in my life where I probably drank more than I should. . . . I never showed up at a session drunk or stoned or anything like that, but there were times when I showed up on a session with a little hangover. Which is not cool. You don't have the attention. And I learned the hard way. Or I'd show up on gigs when I was out with Ricky;

we all drank and partied hard—it was that time. It was never an issue of drinking on stage, that was forbidden anyway—Ricky banned that, which was great because I realized I didn't have to have a beer when I was playing, and I didn't have to maybe smoke a little weed, like I did in the clubs on the third set. But if you went out afterwards and had too many beers, then the next day you feel like shit and you gotta perform. You gotta just keep it between the lines if you want to have a long career.

For Oren Bloedow, the youthful excess to be modulated was around his awareness of his role in various groups: "I had a meeting when I was with Lounge Lizards—I was quite young, and I was really having a lot of trouble with a lot of things that were going on. I got together with John [Lurie] to quit; we met, and I expressed a lot of dissatisfaction. At the end of the meeting, I said, 'OK, I'm not going to quit.' But then he fired me a day or so later." He goes on:

There's been a lot of replacing and being replaced in my career. I think it tends to be more about team playing and stuff like that. For instance, when I was in Meshell [Ndegeocello]'s band, there was one moment on tour where—she would normally be set up in the center—I came to the gig and they were setting her up on the side, and they were putting me in the center. I was like, "Oh no, this is terrible. What are you doing?" They said, "Well, you were complaining last night in Portland about being on top of the bass sub." It was one of these stages where the bass sub, if you were standing right on top of it, it was just like being in a washer-dryer, and you couldn't hear anything, and your whole body is vibrating, and it was just really hard to work.

I was like, "OK, I'm sorry. I shouldn't have complained. You need to be in the center; people are coming here for you, and I need to be watching you the whole time." That was a "teach you a lesson" moment: if you're going to bitch about being on top of the sub, then—I'm making this finger gesture—to accommodate you, we'll put you front and center for the show.

That's the kind of thing that's been mostly a problem for

me—being able to tolerate discomfort or any issues, in the interest of what Ernest Becker calls "letting meaningful action happen." . . . It's different working on Elysian Fields—if I was standing on a sub and it was a problem, it wouldn't be inappropriate for me to mention it; that really is a band. But in Meshell's band, I actually should have just lumped.

Simple scheduling can force a decision, from either party. When conflicts arose between Scott Brackett's work with Okkervil River and Murder by Death, he decided "I'd been doing [Okkervil] for long enough, so I decided to jump ship and make Murder by Death my full-time [gig]." Toby Dammit was "on the road in France with a wonderful woman named Keren Ann. She drew some lines in the sand for everybody and demanded answers, and I wasn't able to provide her an answer, and she said, 'If you can't give an answer today, you're going home.' I said, 'Well, I'm really sorry.' . . . A lot of it can come down to people demanding you commit to things without giving you any sort of financial stability to rely on. I never quit anything while we were actively working, but afterwards, yes, you're not available anymore." When Janet Weiss had scheduling issues with Stephen Malkmus and the Jicks, it provided an exit ramp for a stylistic mismatch: "I [had] started Wild Flag; we started that band together; and [the Jicks] didn't want to share. We had made a record and they wanted to put it out at a certain time [when] the Wild Flag record was coming out, and they didn't want to have to be flexible about that. But we also weren't the best fit, and they have a person now who fits a lot better, and that's important. I don't think it was disagreements; it was just a basic personality thing—I am a *let's-play-more; let's play-faster; let's-get-it-as-crazy-as-we-can-get-it [person]*, and I don't think they liked it like that. It's like when you break up with someone: they are a great person, but there is someone else that's gonna be more compatible."

Many bandleaders find roundabout ways to avoid firing individual players (the most common being simple ghosting), or, as per Doug Gillard, "a lot of times the dismissal will be in the form of 'I'm going to dissolve the entire band now.'"

Joe McGinty: There's been some situations where I wouldn't say I was fired, but replaced because I was unavailable for some gigs, and then somebody else filled in for the gig that I couldn't do, and kept doing the gig. Which is why they sometimes say be careful when you sub your gig out, because that person may take over.

Marc Capelle: Not being fired, but not being re-hired is the big sting. How often do you get the return calls; that is the real deal. And if you miss a cycle, are you on a later one.

Nels Cline: The cliché is, you know you're not in the band when you see an ad for the band playing, and you haven't been called.

Ralph Carney: Bands change directions, or they don't have horns, so you can't take it personally. Tom Waits is one of those people I worked [with] for years, and he just changed it up. It's like, "What did I do wrong?" They were like, "Nope, it wasn't you." That was a tough one, because I played with him [for] fourteen years, and suddenly he was just, "I'm transitioning to a different . . ."[7]

This can be the most difficult way to (in the press-release cliché) "part ways." First, because it's not always clear what's happened: "I guess I'm kind of fired from [Elizabeth] Mitchell," said Jean Cook.

Because she stopped asking me to do shows, and she had another violin player playing with her in the show. I have no idea. It was very mysterious. . . . They just stopped working with me, which made sense when they were in Woodstock, but when they came to New York and played a show at Carnegie Hall and didn't call me—okay, all right. I talked to other people who work with them as well, and I was like, 'I guess I'm fired.'"

In other cases, the feeling results from a confusion about the essential nature of the relationship: "You could consider what happened in St. Vincent as firing," says Daniel Hart.

I don't think Annie [Clark] would describe it that way, but in 2011, when she was doing her third record, she decided to go in a fairly different direction stylistically from what she had done before, so she [replaced] the entire band. It was really rough. For both of us, actually, because Annie and I go way back. . . .

We'd been playing shows and playing in bands together since she was in high school and I was in college. At that time, I definitely felt like I was the main musical collaborator. She felt like she needed to do something different, so that really tore me apart for a couple years. Not only because I loved playing in the band, and it was the main musical thing that I was doing at the time, but also because of the friendship. The way in which that decision was come to—which was without talking to anybody who had been in the band—it felt kind of shitty. Annie and I are back on really good terms and back to being friends, and I think she would agree with that assessment of it, [and] felt like it was shitty as well, and felt pretty awful about the way in which it was all done, and felt like she had done it wrong. At the time it crushed me, and the next six months was really tough for me work-wise. I found out a little bit too late that I wasn't doing St. Vincent anymore, so I had set aside time for tours on that record that I had to try to fill with touring with other bands, and there just wasn't enough lead time to get that together. So for six months I was out of work. [Eventually] it was like the best thing that could have happened, but at the time it sure didn't make me feel that way.

This kind of story is often cued by a retreat into the passive voice,[8] and closes with reassurance about subsequent reconciliation, but the raw feelings remain evident. Says Thor Harris:

A guy that I was friends with for many, many years, he got a record deal, and I think he got swept up in a lot of the sycophantic attention that he was getting, and that he kind of didn't want his old friends around. He wanted to make this leap to the next level, or something. And he fired me from that band. We're actually friends again, but it was painful.

In a way, I got fired from Shearwater. I think Jonathan [Meiburg] wanted players to be more anonymous, less of those signature kind of players; that he wanted that band to be more just about him, and have the other tracks [be] fairly predictable and real quantized and perfectly executed without a lot of soul or a lot of style, so that more of the focus was just on his voice. So he started to push—like, he wanted to bring in other drummers to do the basic tracking, and then have me play all these weird instruments on top. But I just stopped liking the music very much, which was heartbreaking, so I quit that band. That wasn't exactly like being fired, but to me, it was just as heartbreaking as being fired.

Just as often, the firing story is a no-fault case of simple misunderstanding or musical mismatch: DJ Bonebrake was rehearsing a session for the French pop star Little Bob Story. "We were rehearsing really quietly; I was playing really softly, just learning the structure. [Story] said to the producer that night, 'That DJ, he doesn't play hard enough. I need a drummer like my drummer in France, who plays like a heavy metal drummer.' . . . It was ironic—I was one of the hardest hitting drummers in LA at the time." "I think as a bass player, people are not entirely sure what you do," says George Rush, "so when shit sort of feels wrong, and it doesn't feel like things are happening or things are clicking, they look around the bandstand and say, 'I don't really know what that guy does, so I'm just going to get rid of him and we'll play with somebody else that plays the same instrument and see if it's [different].'"

All the reassurance and severance doesn't mean it doesn't sting. Michael Bland was fired by Madonna in 2002, which "was not a matter of proficiency; [it] was more of a matter [of] 'we're going a different direction.' She really liked me at the audition, but I think that aesthetically and musically she was just at a crossroads where she was headed further off into electronics. I guess I have to credit her for realizing I wouldn't and couldn't be happy just sitting back there playing a bunch of triggers. . . . No big deal really; they gave me a severance package, and I spent Madonna's money for the summer. That was great. But there was a level of embarrassment—I stayed in the house for probably a month. I didn't really come out too much during that summer at all. You don't want to talk about 'What are you doing here?' You don't want to have people telling that story over and over. People might think that you got on the gig and did something you weren't supposed to do, or said something you weren't supposed to say. I take my reputation seriously."

Sometimes all you can do is throw up your hands and file away a good story—here's Josh Freese:

> I spent a whole day in the studio with this guy [who] was known as a loose cannon, kind of [a] weird dude, and I knew that going into it. I spent the day recording with him—it's all good. End of the night, I'm leaving the studio and he started drinking at like seven or eight o'clock that night; now it's midnight, one in the morning. He says to his engineer, "Put up that thing that we played on acoustic the other night; remember, the acoustic jam?" So the guy puts up this thing and it's him jamming on the guitar. There's no click, and he's all over the place, and it's hard to make sense of it. And I have been in that position hundreds of times, where somebody goes, "Hey man, there's no click, but can you play to this thing?" And you listen to it and go "Okay, they speed up a teeny bit in that first chorus and then it settles back." You run it a couple of times, and you can make it work.
>
> Anyway, this guy's all over the place and I'm playing to it. At the end of the night, he's drunk—it just didn't sound that good. It wasn't working, and I left. So that was like the final taste in his mouth after we spent a day of doing a bunch of great shit. It was like giving a chef some stale bread and some rotten cheese, going "Make me a sandwich." You agree to it, but you can't do anything with it. No one's going to make that taste good. So I left [thinking], "That was really weird; that sucked."
>
> The next morning the record label guy calls me, like "Hey, you don't have to come back today." And I'm like, "Okay." I go, "Was it that thing last night?" "Well, he was thinking he might want to"—this, that, and the other—"try something different." I'm like, "Fuck, I knew it." I was offended; I was bummed, because I thought it went really well, then the guy got drunk and threw me this weird curveball at the end of the night, and I couldn't deliver.

My favorite part was, he actually asked me if I could recommend somebody—something to the effect of "Who would we call to come and like fix some drum tracks?" Or come swoop in at the last second to do this shit? I'm like, "To be honest, usually me! I'm the guy you call to do that. But I don't know, fuck, I'm not gonna help you out."

The topic of quitting music altogether seems to trigger a deeper, more existential anxiety, one which gets to the heart of the difference between the perception of music (and art in general) as a calling and the reality of it as work. To be in a band at some level of popularity above the entry-level can already look like having bought a winning lottery ticket; to leave such a band offends others' unfulfilled ambitions.[9]

For middle-aged musicians, especially, the idea of quitting music completely hovers somewhere between a fear and an unrealizable fantasy. "There's always the option to quit—but what's next?" asks Sarah Balliett. "Would it be better, or more fulfilling? I know a few people who have quit music entirely; I know there are some regrets." "It's something I think about," says Doug Gillard. "I'm thinking about finding a way to work toward it." One can feel like they have achieved all they need to in a career, and switch careers. But there is a perception in music that there is an aspect of failure implied, if you stop doing it. "It seems that if you play music you have to be a lifer in everyone else's eyes," says Gillard. "You are not allowed to quit." He continues:

"You can't give up on your dream," that kind of thing. It has been romanticized so much—creativity, music, writing, arts. You know, "Well, Joe over here says he is going to play until the day he dies. Look at Bob Smith, who is famous and a legendary artist; look at them, they are still doing it." I admire the person who hangs up his guitar or hangs up his bass or keyboard and says, "I just don't want to do this anymore. I'm going to do this." Why not? If someone wants to do that, why not let them?

7

PEERS AND AMBITIONS

The realization of the limits of one's talent and ambition represents a moment of considerable pathos; the lack of that realization perhaps even more so. As far back as the eighteenth century, Diderot's satire *Rameau's Nephew* depicted a talented and disciplined (real-life) musician who—overshadowed by his famous (also real-life) uncle, to the point where he is referred to not by his name but as "the nephew of Rameau"—"must endure," in the words of Lionel Trilling, "the peculiar bitterness of modern man, the knowledge that he is not a genius."[1]

The animating irony in John Seabrook's *New Yorker* profile of the singer and "top-line" writer Ester Dean is the distance between her ambitions as a solo artist and her team of collaborators' skepticism and interest in keeping her profitable behind-the-scenes role intact—sentiments which they express to Seabrook while indulging Dean:

> Dean's becoming an artist is the very last thing many people in the music industry want, because, as Dean put it to me, "to them, I'm a check. So their attitude is 'Why you want to take away my check?' "
>
> I asked Hermansen what would happen if a well-known artist wanted to record [Dean's song] "How You Love It." "If it's a super-smash, and a Beyoncé or a Rihanna wants to do it, we're

going to want to do it with them," he replied. "Because artists like that don't come along every day. So Ester is going to have to make a decision." He paused. "But Ester is smart."

But what about her own album?

Eriksen said, "A lot of writers want to be artists. Most of them can sing, and a lot of them can sing really well. But, to be an artist, that's another story. To be able to perform, to be the person everyone looks at when you walk into the room, with all the publicity and touring, and then to be able to get that sound on the record—that's not easy. You can be a great singer, but when you hear the record it's missing something."[2]

A particularly poignant musician memoir is that of former Belle and Sebastian bassist Stuart David, called *In the All-Night Cafe*. In it, David recounts the "formative year" of the band, and his dawning awareness that his talents and ambitions as a songwriter were in the inevitable process of being eclipsed by that of his bandmate Stuart Murdoch. Envy is a difficult and rarely welcome emotion to express (David, who now considers himself primarily a writer, can't resist a subtle dig at Murdoch's prose style). But David's self-knowledge adds a humility and subtlety to the circumscribed aspiration that is one of the foundational experiences of adulthood:

For a moment I felt envious of Stuart. I'd always thought I would be working with my own band in studios like this by now, recording my own songs—but it hadn't happened. Stuart had believed it would happen for him too, and now here was one of his friends confirming that it had. There was no doubting that everything had come together for Stuart at that moment; he'd hit his songwriting stride, he'd found some of the people he wanted to play on his songs, and he had the interest of the industry—enough interest to let him put his vision into action. Somehow, I was no longer writing songs, no longer had a band, and was quite aware watching Stuart arranging and mixing his songs with conviction that I didn't have the singularity of vision to pull that off for myself there and then. It was a long way from

the future I'd dreamt for myself as a teenager . . . but I realized
I was happy.[3]

The most loyal consiglieres find in their partnership with a headline artist a creative marriage, with all the comforts, compliments,
and compromises that entails. When Mike Campbell finally recorded
a solo album in 2006, Tom Petty thought it sounded too much like
the Heartbreakers—but not good enough. He called Campbell to
quash it: end of solo career. More contemporary partnerships—James
Bowman with Laura Jane Grace; John DeDomenici with Jeff Rosenstock—date back to both partners' early teens: effectively their entire
musical lives.

Nonetheless, that ambivalent place where ego and ambition
intersect—for those band people who feel the itch of both—remains
one of the hardest to talk about.[4] In the jazz world, it was common,
even expected, that ambitious sidemen would eventually graduate
to be leaders in their own right. Some bands, like Art Blakey's long-
running Jazz Messengers, became known as proving grounds for
future stars. The collective voice of a rock band, though, has proven
much more vulnerable, since it is usually the product of a long process
of group cohesion and creative development, often involving musicians whose individual idiolects may be simultaneously limited and
distinctive, and whose departure can be more damaging than their
technical skills might otherwise suggest (setting aside additional factors like charisma and public narrative). "It's the same chemistry you
see in sports," says Benny Horowitz. "You put four guys in the same
room making music together for ten years, and you put thousands of
shows under their belt all together—there is something that happens
communally [that] only happens with time and practice."

In rock and pop, too, since potential success is more unpredictable, and less reliant on technical skill for its own sake, ambitious
band people may feel more empowered to see if they've got that inde-
finable "what it takes." The financial imperative of songwriting credits encourages anyone who thinks they can write songs to try.[5] And,
simply put, some people will always want to put their own work forward. After all, they can look to a plethora of examples of non-singing

support musicians who went on to individual acclaim or to form successful bands: Glenn Frey and Don Henley, who left Linda Rondstadt's band to form the Eagles; members of Clover, who backed Elvis Costello and later formed Huey Lewis and the News; the ubiquitous Dave Grohl and Foo Fighters; and Josh Tillman, who reinvented himself from Fleet Foxes drummer into the character Father John Misty.

All of which is to say that the confrontation between a successful band person's "day job" as a support musician, and their ambitions for creative work under their own banner, is one of the most fraught of the "fraught places." It is also one of the most emotionally complicated: one takes pride in one's work and recognition as a support musician and recognizes its centrality to one's career, while nonetheless wanting an independent platform, while not wanting to be seen as crassly opportunistic, while not wishing to be compared (favorably or unfavorably) to one's "primary" group—and so on.

When bassist Joe Lally's band Fugazi shut down operations, he "still had a lot of music that I wanted to get out of me. I knew that I had a bunch of ideas [and] had to understand how to do them without the people I usually did that with." He had to be responsible for aspects of songwriting that, in a collaborative collective, hadn't been part of his remit: "If you're playing a riff, how should the next riff follow? If you have an idea vocally first, how do you find a bass line that goes underneath that? I just didn't know how to do any of that because I was always part of a unit of people writing, so I had never really seen songs from start to finish. There are Fugazi songs where I wrote the verse and the chorus, but I didn't sing on them necessarily—I sang three songs in the entire life of the band. I really felt like I was missing a lot of tools . . . because being in Fugazi there was no bandleader, and of course that was my entire experience in songwriting." Then there was the issue of expectations predicated on the legacy of the band: "To some degree, I felt I had to deliver something great. But at the same time that can stop you from doing anything, because it will never feel like it's good enough."

For Peter Hughes, the "luxury of being a sideman" in the Mountain Goats is that "ultimately, if people don't like the Mountain Goats record, I'll be bummed—well, I think it's good!—but unless they are specifically singling out, 'Hey man, that bass part is bullshit,' [which] will never happen, because I just don't think people are listening that hard. Maybe I'm wrong, but I don't have to sweat it. And with the stuff that I do, it is so different from the Mountain Goats that I don't really have an expectation of Mountain Goats fans being into it. If they are, that is surprising; and I think, oh, that is awesome, thank you; and if they are not, I'm like, okay, fine. If that were my full-time thing, then I would be bummed if people didn't like it, because that would mean it's going to be hard for me to keep doing [it]. Whereas with the Mountain Goats, you get all the benefits of people liking it, and very little of the negative feedback."

Alternately, a musician might be so bruised from an experience as the face or creative force of a band that they retreat to the relative psychological security of being a support musician. After Jason Narducy's band Verbow ended in 2002, he "basically didn't write songs for ten years. The second Verbow [album] was just so painful. It was so hard to make; it got pummeled by critics, and even I didn't really like it. We had some huge tour, Counting Crows or something, playing sheds, and I looked at the songs on the album, and I'm like, 'Well, I'm comfortable playing about four of these.'" Narducy continues:

> And it all comes down to me: I'm the one who wrote the songs, and that was tough to swallow. It made me take a step back and not really want to head into that process again. I had just done three album cycles in a row where you write, record, and tour, write, record, and tour, write, record, and tour; and the third one was the worst. You think you are getting better at something, and it was by far the worst reaction.
>
> Three years later Bob [Mould] asked me to [play with him] and I was like, "Yes, please, I miss rock."

Mike Yannich, who was the drummer and primary songwriter for the New Jersey pop-punk group The Ergs, had a similar experience: "It was when the internet started being a thing where there are a lot of people voicing their opinions, and it was not necessarily all positive. That fucked my head a little bit—once I realized people were

listening, I wanted to take a break from putting my songs out there."
Joining other people's bands was a long-term way to stay in the game,
while not having to shoulder that kind of attention: "I'm just going to
play other people's songs for the time being, and at least I get to tour."

When we spoke in 2015, Yannich (widely known as "Mikey Erg")
was, after a decade as a support musician, preparing to return to
releasing his own songs under his own name. He didn't worry about
losing the musical freedom of not being a front person ("I've always
not cared about that. . . . I love the idea of people buying a Mikey
Erg record, thinking it's going to be something totally different than
what it is, and then being surprised"). "I did enough of playing" on
other people's projects, he said. "Eventually I did need to get to a point
where I wanted to write songs again." Yannich is an object lesson in
the psychological differences between creators and supporting artists:
on the one hand, he has what can appear to be an egoless compulsion
to play; on the other, he wouldn't have been so affected by other people's opinions if he didn't have the drive to put his work forward—for
feelings to be bruised, they have to be there in the first place.

> When the Ergs started out, if [songs] got positive reactions,
> feeling a bit of validation or something, that part felt good—but
> if there was something negative it felt bad, like "Maybe I don't
> know how to fucking do this then." It was definitely a mental
> thing where I felt accepted or rejected because of what people
> would say about the songs. I eventually just needed to not feel
> that.
>
> I feel like I've gotten over that. I've gotten older, and have
> read enough books about musicians and know enough about
> music criticism to realize that you have to put that all out of
> your mind. I know that I'm better at it than I was when I was
> twenty-four. But it will be interesting to put myself out there
> again and see what happens.

"I never had a whole lot of self-confidence in terms of pushing
through to play my own music all the time," says Nels Cline. "I'm not
sure I want to hear my music all the time!"

THE INFLUENCE OF OTHERS' MUSIC

To spend a significant portion of one's career playing the music of other people can be an equivocal experience. Artists are, after all, "antennas" (Joe Ginsberg) and "sponges" (Eliza Hardy Jones). Scott Spillane bemoans the pain of "realizing that you're rewriting someone else's song after two weeks of working on it, and you're like, 'Shit, that's the same melody that so-and-so wrote.'" Jenny Scheinman says she can't keep any music she's exposed to out of her writing:

> I land in New York; I am twenty-five years old; I have no money and I know some people there, one of whom I had once taken a violin lesson from. He takes a gig in Europe and gives me his job with the Big Apple Circus. So I do that for eight months, ten shows a week. I totally learned that circus repertoire, and . . . looking back, I see that in my next couple of albums there are all these rhythms that come out of that circus business, and even some melodic ideas that just surface.

And, says Katie Harkin, "There's such a physical aspect to music that my musculature will have changed after playing [certain music] hundreds of times." In the most literal, embodied way, she says, "I've been shaped by those songs."

On the one hand are the benefits of mentorship and example, especially, says Oren Bloedow, "when it's a long apprenticeship, and it goes past that sense of intellectual wonder and lodges in the body where you're inhaling the modus operandi of somebody; you're inhaling their atmosphere. You end up replicating it the rest of your life." The experience of "being at the mercy of someone else's writing, or someone else's ideas," says Carla Kihlstedt, can be profound. "Songs teach you how to sing, and if you're only ever singing your own songs, you're only ever going to sing in one particular, or maybe a couple different, ways."

Sometimes the experience is one of technique and craft, of getting under the hood of an unfamiliar style: "Dave Sanborn needed ten or twelve charts to take on a smooth jazz cruise," says Peter Hess, "so

I transcribed some Harold Melvin & the Blue Notes stuff, and some Mills Brothers stuff, and Stevie Wonder stuff, and made really detailed accurate arrangements. Digging down deep into that stuff, it was totally extraordinary to take a peek inside and . . . to take things apart and see how they work." Josh Kantor has "the reputation of being the guy who is good at learning other people's songs quickly, [and] part of that enjoyment is getting a glimpse into the minds of these great writers. Definitely the writers that I work with regularly, I have figured out some of their tricks—and I don't use that term 'tricks' in a disparaging way. Like, this is the way that they like to transition out of the bridge, or this is the kind of change that they like to have to resolve something." Jay Gonzalez's work with the Drive-By Truckers helped him "rhythmically in particular, thinking about playing behind the beat or before the beat, whereas before it was always on top of the beat."

The influence can be that of professionalism and efficiency: "Hole was my degree in humanity," says Melissa Auf der Maur, "but the [Smashing] Pumpkins was my master's degree times ten in music. I had to learn a catalog where we'd have to play three hours a night, so I had three binders with the entire [Pumpkins] catalog written in my crazy chicken scratch—but glow-in-the-dark, 'cause I'd have to look at the pages [on stage]—because the shows were so long and the songs were so complex, and [Billy Corgan would] want to change the key, redo that version of the song in a different key, tons of weird tunings (I was often tuned down to E flat), lots of rearranging of songs, like doing acoustic-set versions of songs we had been playing in another way. My first practice, tough-guy Billy explained, 'Here's the three rules. You don't get sick, no days off, and you can't make a mistake.'" Peter Hughes points to the influence of songwriter Franklin Bruno's seriousness of purpose: "Franklin's songwriting was very formal, and still is, and my writing became a lot more disciplined because of playing with him. . . . Just being around John [Darnielle] and Franklin, who were aware of the craft of songwriting and treated it as such. Whereas I was coming from a much more nonchalant place, where I was writing songs, but I wasn't really taking it that seriously. I remember Franklin saying at one point to me—because I had this affectation that he didn't think I was aware of, [where when] I would talk about writing songs, I would say, 'I made this song up.' And one day Franklin called me out: 'Why do you say that, why don't you say you *wrote* a song? Because that is what you are doing, you are actually writing a song.' I had this weird aversion to thinking of myself as a songwriter, because that would force me to be accountable and take responsibility and actually be good, rather than just make some shit up. That was the big [eye-opener] to me, making me realize that if I'm going to do this, I should take it seriously, and I should aspire to making something good."

Other times, the adjustment is one of taste. Auf der Maur and Nate Brenner came out of their experiences with Hole and Tune-Yards, respectively, with a new appreciation for a kind of straight-forward pop music they had previously disdained. Nels Cline, a fixture in the worlds of avant-jazz, art-rock, and improvised music for decades, joined the alt-country band Wilco in 2004. Cline credits the band for his late-life discovery of "the beauty of the triad. I resisted for years playing music—and even listening to too much music—that was really triadic, and not fanciful in the harmonic department, or a drone, or something. So if I play music that's very straightforward and triadic, but that has a signature point of view or a sound, that has seeped into my own music, and I'm able to embrace—I've done two records now that strangely depend on major triads, not minor chords, or some sort of enigmatic sound, and I've never done that before. I think this came from playing with Wilco."

The challenge is to keep one's bigger-name projects from subsuming one's reputation. "You have to fight to keep your identity in that respect," says Scott Brackett. "People identify you—'Are you a song-writer? Are you a side player? Are you a front man?' or whatever. You have to remember that that is contextual, and it doesn't mean that that's what you're doing for your entire life—just, that's what you're doing for that group. You have to really give yourself the talk, to keep your confidence from getting shaken in that respect."

I call this the "parentheses problem"—if you work with a name artist, their name is perpetually attached to yours in parentheses whenever you perform or publish; or you can be dismissed as aping a style you were part of creating. These associations are not without their benefits, as Jon Rauhouse points out: "Sometimes I get hired because I have a giant resume, and people want [to] tap into that, or use that, or borrow that" to get the boldface names on their own press releases. Because of his long CV prior to joining Wilco, Cline has a realistic sense of humor about his role in the group, and in the rock ecosystem. "I'm not sure that a lot of Wilco fans are listening to my records. . . . The best thing is that they come out to my shows. . . . I probably would maybe get fifty people before Wilco, and post-Wilco I would get like a hundred. And there's a huge difference between fifty and a hundred when you're in a little jazz club." It's just a matter of managing their expectations: "What they expect is probably some expressive or even innovative guitar work. I'm not sure they're paying all that much attention to my composition, and I actually have a certain degree of suspicion of the whole idea of the guitar solo. I do it because I like playing the guitar, but I'm not a shredder, nor am I just a what we might call a 'primitive noise god.' . . . If they haven't heard my music, they're probably just expecting me to play a bunch of groovy guitar and do some looping and stuff."

As discussed elsewhere in the book, one runs the risk of being typecast as a specialist in whatever stylistic perception accrued to one's most high-profile gig. "A lot of writers or reviewers," says Doug Gillard, "tend to compare anything that you do to the outfit that you have been in, and they automatically think [of] a song on your record. . . . 'Oh yeah, it sounds like the band he was in.'" Those sets of lazy or automatic reference points can be a trap. "I would be mortified if I wrote a song and somebody said, 'Oh, that sounds like Nick Cave,'" says Jim Sclavunos. "But some people say that no matter what the fuck it sounds like. I'll have kazoos in it, and they will still say it sounds like Nick Cave. . . . I might be overly sensitive, whereas the person making the comparison might see it as a compliment. . . . I'm quite lucky that I've gotten involved with a lot of really interesting music makers, so I have a lot to draw on. But I also like to think that I'm part of the reason they have been interesting at some point. So if somebody says, 'That sounds like such-and-such's band that you were in'—well, I guess that makes sense, because I was in that band making that music at that time."

HAPPY BAND PEOPLE

As long as someone has a vision of what they want, I'm happy
to do whatever it takes. So whether I'm playing drums on a
breakfast cereal commercial or I'm playing drums for one of
the great jazz artists of all time—sure, they're very different, but
they both require a high level of craftsmanship and attention.
And for me these varied experiences inform one another, so
I don't see them as being limiting. I don't see them as being
exclusionary. I see it all as just part of being a musician.

PETER ERSKINE

It is easy to present a cliché of a bitter band person. The truth is, band
people—like any workers—have complaints about their bosses and
co-workers, wish they made a little more money, feel uncomfortable
asking for it, see co-workers get promotions they wanted: all the petty
gripes of a working life. For the most part, though, they do feel fulfilled in their work; those with ambitions to front their own projects
typically have the opportunity to do so, and those without have the
pleasures of a craftsperson. "I got to play in the big leagues," wrote
Billy Bauer;[6] Jimmi Mayes called himself "a sideman to the stars and
a witness to music history."[7]

Many musicians identify in themselves a lack of the confidence,
ambition, or self-assurance to comfortably annex center stage, and
even luxuriate in that lack: "My job is so easy," says Jenny Conlee.
"I get to go up there and just play." "It's a relief," says Jay Gonzalez.
"[In] a conversation, I feel more comfortable if someone [else] is driving the conversation." Joe Lally appreciated the relative anonymity: "I
didn't do a million interviews and my face wasn't the most prominent
face in the band. I could always walk around in big crowds at shows
and . . . be able to move around among them without it being a big
issue."

"It's like working in the engine room of a ship," says Nigel Powell.
"You don't have to serve anybody drinks. . . . I think it was Phil Collins
who describes being a drummer as being the goalkeeper of the band.
It's not particularly glamorous, and at least 80 percent of the time

people don't even notice that you're there; and you're not the star, but it's vital that you are there. Otherwise the game is really not going to go your way."

For Jon Wurster, "Both John [Darnielle] and Bob [Mould] have suggested me having a mike back at the drums, but . . . it's not my show. People are coming to see Bob Mould, and they may like what we do as a band, but it's Bob Mould's name on the ticket. People are coming to see the Mountain Goats to hear John's words and his songs, and I don't want to get in the way of that. I'd be tempted to say something funny, and that's not what those bands are about."

Others add the rejuvenating benefits of musical promiscuity: "I love playing on other bands' records," says Sarah Balliett. "The best part is stepping into new styles, new tones. Sometimes . . . I realize the rut I had been in without even knowing it." Eliza Hardy Jones points out that on her own project, she's writing to her own strengths and skills: "[so] being asked to do something that [she] wouldn't normally do, pushing against [her] own limitation" keeps her from falling into the common trap of "just doing the easy thing."

"I only ever wanted to make songs happen—it didn't matter in what capacity," says Kelly Hogan. "It's just a blast to be part of a good song. . . . Which [sometimes] means singing two or three words just once, a minute and forty-five seconds into the song. So when people ask me, 'What's the hardest part of singing back-up?' I can honestly tell them, '*Not* singing.'"

ACKNOWLEDGMENTS

I initially pitched this book as what I believed would be a quick, not-too-difficult follow-up to *The Humorless Ladies of Border Control*. The joke was on me as the years stretched out, with regard to the truism that interviewing and research are the fun part, and that too much material can be a curse. I want to thank Casey Kittrell and the University of Texas Press for their trust and patience, and my family—Maria, Lesia, and Artem—for enduring my hair-tearing. Special thanks are also due to Maria Sonevytsky for her formidable intellectual inspiration, challenge, and example.

The book would not have been possible without the monotonous but necessary transcription work done by Jim Christie and, especially, Genevieve Crane.

There are, of course, a long list of musicians to whom I wanted to speak, and for one reason or another couldn't make contact: Kid Congo Powers, Bryce and Aaron Dessner, Pete Thomas, Benmont Tench, Mike Mills, Mike Campbell, Steve Nieve, Garth Hudson. Almost immediately, I began compiling an expanding list of the countless others I'd have loved to include: Mike Huguenor, Steve Selvidge, Matt Sweeney, Frank Piegaro, Cat Popper, Greg Saunier, Chuck Leavell, Atom Willard, Colin Stetson, Brad Logan, Richard Reed Perry, Joe Reinhart, Josh Kaufman, Greg Leisz, Claudia Gonson, Mark Spencer, Betsy Wright—volume two awaits.

Also worth mentioning are the people held in respect by their peers, the names which came up at the ends of interviews, usually attached to some version of the phrase "you know who you should totally talk to": Trevor Dunn, Rebecca Cole, Joanna Bolme, Jim Spate, Will Kimbrough, Danny Barnes, Kullen Fuchs, Greg Fox, Doug Max

Crawford, Gail Ann Dorsey, Matt Chamberlain, Dave Phillips, Greg Suran, Jon Boquist, John Stirratt, Rob Pope, Eric Paparazzi, Paul Niehaus, Carl Broemel, Matt Rowland, Richie Kirkpatrick, Anthony La Marca, Ryan Sawyer, Marc Ribot, Jon Theodore, Kevin March—someone out there has you in their pantheon of great band people.

As always, I want to acknowledge the childcare apparatus that allows me, like all working parents, to write, perform and teach, and without whom none of this would be possible: the Berkeley (CA) and Red Hook (NY) public school systems, the Bard Nursery School, Woolly Mammoth Preschool, Stella Marienthal-Legendre, Teryn Kuzma, and Clara Brownstein.

NOTES

INTRODUCTION

1. Robert Faulkner identifies "social comparison" as a primary root of negative self-perception in the artistic community, which is "populated by great [figures] to whom one compare's one's achievements and against whom one is likely to fail" (53).

2. Neville, *20 Feet from Stardom*.

3. "It is the members of the middle class who are culturally authorized to be creative and to make a career of it . . . [and] who were more willing to professionalize," wrote ethnomusicologist Timothy D. Taylor of a contemporary southern California indie rock scene ("Social Class and the Negotiation of Selling Out," 66).

4. For a contrary take on how class can shape musical ideology, see Taylor, "Social Class and the Negotiation of Selling Out."

5. Miège, *The Capitalization of Cultural Production*, 93.

6. Helm and Davis, *This Wheel's on Fire*, 103.

7. Becker and Carper, "The Elements of Identification," 342.

8. Becker, *Art Worlds*, x.

9. A handful of common referents emerged over the course of my interviews: U2 and R.E.M. have become iconic of "the bands who split everything equally"; Herbie Flowers's bass line on "Walk on the Wild Side" stands in for every instrumental hook that doesn't translate into songwriting credit; and Tom Petty and his band are cited over and over again as archetypes of various bandleader/band people relationships: Benmont Tench, the initial leader who is quietly sidelined; Stan Lynch, the outspoken sideman who can't accept his place in the pecking order; and, especially, the egoless lieutenant Mike Campbell—who inspires a particular fascination.

10. Nels Cline points out that there are other incentives in play for jazz and improvised groups: "In Europe, most [jazz] promoters look down on the idea of coming back again and again with the same unit—they want to see variation, so you'll find most of the people here in New York are not necessarily going to convene the same band for years running. They're going to switch things up so they can keep getting gigs in Europe."

11. I have included a few representatives of these more professionalized worlds—Bruce Bouton, Peter Erskine, Joe Ginsberg—who have to some extent straddled the divide.

12. Sisario, "Gender Diversity in the Music Industry?"; Smith et al., "Inclusion in the Recording Studio?"

13. Toynbee, "Fingers to the Bone or Spaced Out on Creativity?," 43.

14. A writer mourning the departure of Amy Klein from the band Titus Andronicus called this the "curse of the fan favorite." Of course, this can be as much a matter of group chemistry and shared experience as individual irreplaceability, as per H. Stith Bennett: "As time investment in a group grows, the importance of each individual increases considerably . . . [sometimes] the fact that one person out of five quit was sufficient to disintegrate the group, since 'it just wouldn't be the same thing after all we'd been through together'" (108).

1. TRAINING AND EARLY GOALS

1. Leight, *Side Man.*

2. Frederickson and Rooney, "The Free-Lance Musician as a Type of Non-Person," 236.

3. Frederickson and Rooney, "The Free-Lance Musician as a Type of Non-Person," 230.

4. Frederickson and Rooney, "The Free-Lance Musician as a Type of Non-Person," 236.

5. Lewis, "Take Out My Guitar and Play," 32.

6. Lewis, "Take Out My Guitar and Play," 32.

7. Bennett, *On Becoming a Rock Musician*, 20, 27.

8. "I think I still have my leather jacket left over from that period," he added.

9. MacLeod, *Club Date Musicians*, 142.

10. As a young musician in New York, I came to refer to "the Oberlin mafia"—grads of the Oberlin music programs who would move to New York en masse and start getting each other gigs.

11. Self-styled "sideman extraordinaire" Gary Church wrote, of his job in a Dixieland band at Disney World, that "there are two kinds of musicians that work at Disney. One kind is the type that have . . . pretty much done it all. They've fought the music business all their lives and finally got a good, secure steady job and they're damned happy to have it. The others are younger guys that somehow got the best job they'll ever have right off the bat, and they didn't realize it" (48).

12. Berliner, *Thinking in Jazz*, 22.

13. Berliner, *Thinking in Jazz*, 37

14. Berliner, *Thinking in Jazz*, 57–59.

15. Bennett, *On Becoming a Rock Musician*, 21.

2. "PLAYS WELL WITH OTHERS": THE SOCIAL LIVES OF BANDS

1. Beck, "Introduction" and "Practice," *Cultural Work*, 7–8.

2. Status-ranking of musicians is an old game. In his sixth-century *Fundamentals of Music*, Boethius divides musicians into three categories: performer, composer, and critic. He places performers at the bottom, since they are merely reproducing notes on a page; composers next, since, while they may create art, they may do so by pure inspiration, without conscious intent. Only the

philosopher of music, he says, has the objectivity and the necessary breadth of essential knowledge to truly judge the value of a performance. See Boethius, *Fundamentals of Music*, 50–51.

3. This sensitivity to caste extends into other realms. Drummer Jimmi Mayes remembered that "it used to drive Otis [Williams, of the Temptations] crazy that a sideman—a nobody like me—could be getting some [romantic] attention from Patti [LaBelle]. He used to talk to me about it sometimes. He just couldn't figure it out" (34).

4. Helm and Davis, *This Wheel's on Fire*, 103.

5. Notably, though, later in our talk, Watt himself—speaking later in his career and in the context of bands in which he worked unambiguously either as a bandleader or what he called a "sidemouse"—underscored the traditional power structures of a band as absolutely critical: "If you are going to do collaboration, that means you put in some, they put in some, and together that's the whole. If I'm going to be the shot caller, then you take directions. You have to play those roles. What I think is important is that you play more than one role. There's something called 'sideman-itis,' you know. These guys after a while get bitter and resentful; they never get to express themselves. They are always having to process other people's directions. Then there are the cats who are never sidemen themselves, so it's hard for them to have empathy. They just 'make it be so,' and this kind of shit. I see three distinct [roles]: you call the shots; you take the shots; you collaborate. That's the way I have found it."

6. Springsteen, *Born to Run*, 231.

7. White and Lippitt, "Leader Behavior and Member Reaction in Three 'Social Climates,'" 597–604.

8. Scheidlinger, "Freudian Concepts of Group Relations," 59–60.

9. Berliner, *Thinking in Jazz*, 417.

10. Weinstein, "Creativity and Band Dynamics," 199.

11. Schuller, Musings, 257.

12. Bennett, *On Becoming a Rock Musician*, 39.

13. Hyden, "Drive-By Truckers Carry On."

14. For the qualifications of a good bandleader, see chapter 3.

15. Weinstein, "Creativity and Band Dynamics," 189.

16. Berliner, *Thinking in Jazz*, 438.

17. Weinstein, "Creativity and Band Dynamics," 188.

18. "The presence or absence of interaction before a show was also related to band cohesiveness," is Groce and Dowell's deadpan comment ("A Comparison of Group Structures and Processes," 28–29).

19. Church, *The Autobiography of a Nobody*, 77.

20. A band, ironically, whose demise was instigated by a literal divorce.

21. Festinger, Schachter, and Back, "The Operation of Group Standards," 222.

22. Cohen, *Rock Culture in Liverpool*, 36.

23. Cartwright and Zander, "Group Cohesiveness: Introduction," *Group Dynamics: Research and Theory*, 73–74.

24. Groce and Dowell, "A Comparison of Group Structures and Processes," 25.

25. Cohen, *Rock Culture in Liverpool*, 43.

26. Cohen, *Rock Culture in Liverpool*, 45.

27. Groce and Dowell, "A Comparison of Group Structures and Processes," 24.

28. Stahl, *Unfree Masters*, 25.

29. Helm and Davis, *This Wheels's on Fire*, 141.

30. Jagger refutes this widely circulated anecdote.

31. The Ellington example is instructive in several ways: the attentiveness of their naturally evolved leader to the specialties of each band member enhanced their recognizability as individual voices, but they ran the risk of their artistry's being subsumed by his charisma and public image—especially his non-performing compositional right-hand man Billy Strayhorn.

32. Stahl, *Unfree Masters*, 34–35.

33. Cartwright and Zander, "Leadership: Introduction," 543, and "The Structural Properties of Groups: Introduction," 423.

34. Tanner, *Sideman*, 21.

35. Communication, wrote Cartwright and Zander, "in a hierarchy may serve as a sort of substitution for actual locomotion to a higher status position" ("The Structural Properties of Groups," 425).

36. "It *is* a band," says Joe Ginsberg, "but Wilco is still Jeff Tweedy—I see Wilco and I see the *band*, but I'm thinking about Jeff Tweedy. It just is what it is."

37. Cartwright and Zander. "The Structural Properties of Groups," 418.

38. Finnegan, *The Hidden Musicians*, 260.

39. Stebbins, "Class, Status, and Power among Jazz and Commercial Musicians," 200.

40. "The bigger they got, the more curious people became about Tom Petty," wrote Zanes. "Some new walls were erected between the leader and his band. 'He got exactly what he wanted,' says Stan Lynch. 'Too bad . . . Like, 'You want this? Now it's all on you . . . you begged for this, actually took it from others to have all this'" (151). While Campbell established himself as a loyal right hand, drummer Stan Lynch chafed under his new boss: "We gotta be united against the boss. We're a band, we gotta watch this guy" (227). Lynch eventually left the band.

41. Zanes, *Petty*, 171.

42. Stogdill, "Leadership, Membership and Organization," 42, 46.

43. Lally also preferred not to be put on the spot: "If interviewing or being filmed and questioned isn't the most comfortable thing for you, it's not that you don't feel that you're allowed to be talking for the band, it's just that if you don't feel comfortable on camera, you don't really look for the opportunity to talk about the band on camera."

44. Powell left the band in late 2020.

45. Becker, *Art Worlds*, 301.

46. Stogdill, "Leadership, Membership and Organization," 41.

47. Faulkner, "Orchestra Interaction," 147.

48. Faulkner, "Orchestra Interaction," 156.

49. Berliner, *Thinking in Jazz*, 440.

50. Church, *The Autobiography of a Nobody*, 15.

51. Church, *The Autobiography of a Nobody*, 71.

52. Page, *Drew's Blues*, 150.

53. "Orchestra performers as organizational members," wrote Robert Faulkner, "experience work problems with conductors to the degree that directives are vaguely defined, grossly incompatible with performers' standards, unconvincing as musical interpretations, and technically unsound as guides for the successful execution of the music" ("Orchestra Interaction," 156).

54. "Like professionals in other organizations, these performers resist illegitimate intrusions into their sphere of competence and feel maligned under imputed incompetence," wrote Robert Faulkner ("Orchestra Interaction," 156).

55. MacLeod, *Club Date Musicians*, 144.

56. Berliner, *Thinking in Jazz*, 416.

57. Shaw, *The Trouble with Cinderella*, 173.

58. Not always—"I do [the interviews]," says Lori Barbero of Babes in Toyland. "[Singer] Kat [Bjelland] doesn't really do interviews hardly at all. Sometimes I wish that she would do interviews, but I don't think she's done an interview in I don't know how long. She'd always be like, 'You say it, you tell 'em.'"

59. David, *In the All-Night Cafe*, 134.

60. "Every band needs a sex symbol," wrote Jacob Schlichter, "and every sex symbol needs a weird-looking guy to stand next to. Wearing the crown of accessibility is a common fate of drummers" (68).

61. Hurwitz, Zander, and Hymovitch wrote, "Individuals with relatively little power to influence others behave toward those with relatively more power in an essentially ego defensive manner" (483).

62. Weiss left Sleater-Kinney in 2019.

63. Schlichter, *So You Wanna Be a Rock & Roll Star*, 165–167.

64. Becker, *Art Worlds*, x–xi.

65. Frederickson and Rooney, "The Free-Lance Musician as a Type of Non-Person," 225, 228.

66. Stebbins, "A Theory of the Jazz Community," 328.

67. Adorno and Horkheimer, "The Culture Industry," 96.

68. Adorno and Horkheimer, "The Culture Industry," 120.

69. These are by no means unrelated—a form of "professionalization . . . in a more Bourdieusian sense," wrote Tim Taylor, is "how do people learn the culture of a particular field, and how do they act once they are in it?" (Taylor, "Social Class and the Negotiation of Selling Out," 70).

70. William Bruce Cameron wrote, "A jazzman virtually never asks or tells a fellow jazzman how he sounds or how he should behave, unless the two are unusually intimate. Subtle hints only may be dropped; if a man does not pick them up, he is tolerated if he is good and avoided if he is not" (181).

71. Durocher and Marinelli, "The Sideman Channel." https://www.youtube.com/channel/UCsDOsSHwXjmT4fok-WUc9NQ.

72. For Kantor, the social aspect is, in many ways, the main attraction: "A lot of the stuff that I'm playing—this is not intended to be a disparaging remark in any way—it's just not complex music. . . . The social element is important for me

because I have the day job, so I can say, how do I maximize the enjoyment of this, and the social part is that. Because my main music gig is the baseball games, and that's very solitary."

73. MacLeod, *Club Date Musicians*, 20.

74. Becker, *Art Worlds*, 86.

75. Peter Hess points out that it's not a given "whether someone who *wants* to be likable is ever going to *be* likable."

3. THE WORK OF BAND PEOPLE

1. Stahl, *Unfree Masters*, 65.

2. Weinstein, "Creativity and Band Dynamics," 188.

3. Weinstein, "Creativity and Band Dynamics," 194–195.

4. Jones, "The Music Industry as Workplace," 156.

5. Banks, *The Politics of Cultural Work*, 8.

6. Stahl, *Unfree Masters*, 1.

7. Faulkner, *Hollywood Studio Musicians*, 5.

8. Rare is the band in a position to provide a health insurance plan for its members.

9. Stahl, *Unfree Masters*, 14.

10. Frith, *Sound Effects*, 79.

11. Taylor, "Maintenance and Destruction of an East Side Los Angeles Indie Rock Scene," 2.

12. To quote Andrew Beck: "What marks out popular music making is the sheer size of its 'tank' of labor waiting to be recruited. . . . This characteristic of the musical labor market has a number of causes: low cost entry into production, continuing traditions of collective practice, a series of 'proto-markets' in the form of small-scale gigs and clubs, a bohemian ethos by dint of which long periods of unemployment yield an accretion of status" (37). Similarly, Frederickson and Rooney: "The supply of musicians far exceeds the market's demand, and consequently a monopoly of the services does not exist. This situation gives rise to easy replaceability of performers. . . . Just as truck farmers pick up the first laborers who show up at the street corner, the music contractor also has a large pool of people he can call. But unlike the laborer, the free-lance musician practices a highly developed skill which is devalued as a result of the large number of competitors" (223).

13. Becker, *Art Worlds*, 351.

14. Becker, *Art Worlds*, 1.

15. Becker, *Art Worlds*, 3, 7.

16. Weinstein, "Creativity and Band Dynamics," 191.

17. Small, *Music of the Common Tongue*, 315–316, 333–334.

18. Finnegan, *The Hidden Musicians*, 167.

19. Finnegan, *The Hidden Musicians*, 167.

20. Finnegan, *The Hidden Musicians*, 236–237.

21. Finnegan, *The Hidden Musicians*, 267–268.

22. Becker, *Art Worlds*, 87.

23. Fisk and Nichols, *Composers On Music*, 318.

24. "The vague ways in which performers express disfavor make it difficult for performers to fathom their differences," wrote Paul Berliner (425).

25. Though "it would just save a lot of time if it was just there on a page."

26. "I'm making that up," he added. "That wasn't her exact description."

27. Matt Kinsey takes an even more literal approach: "You try not to be too obvious with it, [but] sometimes if there's a bird [in the lyric], I will make a bird sound or something, and it works."

28. A brief look at Carney's discography will reveal an artist infamous for this kind of approach.

29. Toynbee, "Fingers to the Bone or Spaced Out on Creativity?," 48.

30. The studio can be an invaluable aid to this kind of self-knowledge, says Bruce Kaphan: "One of my best friends is a psychologist; and in the course of his work, he's done a lot of what he calls video therapy, which is where he'll get into a group situation, videotapes people interacting with each other, and plays it back for them. And the feedback that we get as human beings seeing ourselves from that third-person point of view, being able to more objectively observe who we are in terms of how we interact in the world—that's the beauty of the studio."

31. Durocher and Marinelli, "The Sideman Channel."

32. "Keith Moon was fabulous in the Who, but he wasn't really that adaptable," says Jon Wurster. "There is a great Noel Gallagher quote where he says, 'Keith Moon was great in the Who, but he would have been shit anywhere else.'"

33. I myself identify with this category.

34. Zanes, *Petty*, 260.

35. Zanes, *Petty*, 241.

36. Adorno and Horkheimer. "The Culture Industry," 132.

37. Becker, *Outsiders*, 87.

38. Bruce Kaphan seconds that for producers: "There are some producers who you recognize the production before you recognize the artist, and I feel like that's putting the cart before the horse."

39. Berliner, *Thinking in Jazz*, 418–419.

40. Paul Berliner quoted Calvin Hill: "Earlier in my career. . . . I played a certain way according to whoever I was playing with. . . . If I played with, say, Joe Schmo on the piano, then I was playing more like Fred Schmo on the bass than Calvin Hill" (419).

41. Benny Horowitz has "suffered from the other end of the spectrum, which is being with a producer . . . stripping you back and playing so much for the song that you forgot to have any fun, and forgot to make it sound very cool, and forgot to fight for stuff that you think should be in there."

42. There's always a counter-argument: "I'm not real big on keeping a beat," says Bill Stevenson. "I'm big on playing a phrase. Phrases are like circles, you know, beats are like straight lines or squares."

43. Ralph Carney will "also say, 'For the money that you're paying me for this, I'm not going to do more than two [revisions]; I'm not going to keep changing it and changing it.'"

44. Finnegan, *The Hidden Musicians*, 267.

45. For Benny Horowitz, "performing has gone from 'Let me drink a bunch of fucking caffeine and shred this and sweat my ass off and leave it all out there' to, 'I want to play perfectly over this incredibly complex PA system to many thousands of people for two hours. And what do I need to do to do that? Do I need to stretch, do I need to not drink a beer, not smoke a joint anymore, not do this and that?' So it has gone from a Mountain Dew and a blunt and forty minutes of furiously pounding my drums; to a green salad and a tea and twenty minutes of stretching and then going out and putting my in-ears in and trying to be perfect."

46. I knew an engineer who called the box of auxiliary percussion "the money box," because once an inexperienced band pulled it out, billable hours could pass while various band members tried to get a usable tambourine take.

47. Rick Steff, on the other hand, tries in the studio "to be a lot more selective about [my parts]; try to make it as minimal as I can if that is what it requires."

48. Said Wurster, "There's a song, the Husker Du song called 'Makes No Sense At All,' that I always try to do a couple of iconic fills in there. I try to do those the best I can."

49. Said Gonzalez, "He toured with them a little bit, but he was older. He is an awesome dude, but definitely the kind of guy who would apparently just wander off and they would frantically be looking for him. Then I think he might have fallen down some stairs and hurt himself. He still kind of has the partying disposition of the late '60s, but not so much the body to maintain it. But a sweet dude, and then they couldn't do it anymore."

50. Faulkner, *Hollywood Studio Musicians*, 44.

51. Mayes and Speek, *The Amazing Jimmi Mayes*, ix.

52. "Sometimes you are a wet nurse; sometimes you are a shrink; sometimes you are the biggest pain in the ass there is," said Rick Steff.

53. Mayes and Speek, *The Amazing Jimmi Mayes*, 19.

54. "Without a piano," wrote Levon Helm in *This Wheel's on Fire*, "Bo [Diddley] tuned his guitar by ear. . . . [Bandleader] Sam [Taylor] searched for the key they were in. When he found it, he'd adjust the mouthpiece of his saxophone to sharp or flat to allow for Bo's 'by ear' tuning. Then he signaled the band, holding up two fingers and one across in the shape of an A, then gave a thumbs-up to tell them it was on the sharp side. (One night I overheard one of the horn players tell his buddy, 'You never know what key lurks in the heart of Bo Diddley')" (60).

55. Still, he says, "I try not to take on too many roles. . . . The more other things I do besides just play my instrument, the more I feel like I want to voice other opinions that I necessarily might not have the right to."

56. Berliner, *Thinking in Jazz*, 436.

57. Frith, *Sound Effects*, 77.

58. Page, *Drew's Blues*, 217.

59. Scott Brackett has moved, in his career, from indie rock to "improvisation based on prompts that we use as limitations or direction for improvising, so we never play the same composition—and that is a direct result of having to go out and play the same tight 45 [minute set] every night."

60. Not to say that Cline isn't familiar with the feeling: "One [Mike] Watt tour . . . If I was honest, I was developing a certain degree of dread for the same sequence. I was thinking, like, 'God, I sure would love to change this up tonight, just to keep it interesting or something.' But I didn't say anything. When Watt gets an idea, he sticks to it."

61. He adds that "Sometimes it's fun to fuck up on stage."

62. Baldwin, "Sonny's Blues," 46.

63. Fisk and Nichols, *Composers on Music*, 431.

64. A Virgin Records A&R man took Bruce Kaphan "to one side and put his arm around me, and said, 'Ah, pedal steel. The kiss of death.'"

65. Musicians do tend to turn the question back on themselves. "I'm completely infuriated and nauseated, and I've just had it with my limitations as a musician all the time," said Oren Bloedow. "It's never the instrument, it's always me." "If I do get tired and frustrated," said Shahzad Ismaily, "I get tired and frustrated with myself on that tool, never the tools themselves."

66. Rick Steff suggests "learn[ing] to voice chords the way a guitar player does."

67. Michael McDermott said he regularly fields the suggestion, "'You play drums, that must be cool to take out your aggression—' and it's like, 'No, no, I never do that.' . . . I would never take the frustration out on my instrument, because I just love it."

68. Although Glenn Kotche said he has used his drums as a primary tool while writing for string quartet: "When I write on drum set it's more about the rhythms. I get the overall architecture of the piece, what it's about, what I wanted to say, the character of it all; and the notes come [later]. The rhythms are there, but the actual pitches come after that."

69. There were a lot of Ringo jokes, I pointed out. "But Ringo was always a clown," Sclavunos responded. "They were all clowns. Ringo went for broad laughs, but if there was a press conference, they were all there. They all answered questions; questions were directed to all of them; and if there was not a directed question, they would all contribute."

4. THE FAMILY BUSINESS: MUSICIANS WITH CHILDREN

1. Becker, *Outsiders*, 114, 117.

2. Stebbins, "A Theory of the Jazz Community," 327.

3. Stebbins, "A Theory of the Jazz Community," 326.

4. MacLeod, *Club Date Musicians*, 146.

5. Frankly, said bassist Peter Hughes, sometimes, touring can feel like a relief. After years of experiencing tour as "really intense, really exhausting work," he became "Mr. Stay-At-Home-Dad. And *that* shift is exhausting. So the way that I think of tour has really changed. . . . Now I make no bones about the fact that, [when] I go on tour, that is my vacation. . . . The amount of time to yourself that you have, versus when you are home where you have zero time to yourself . . . tour[ing] is a total luxury."

5. THE ARTIST AND THE ARTISAN: MONEY AND CREDIT

1. Plutarch, *Plutarch's Lives*, 201.

2. Becker, *Art Worlds*, 16–17.

3. Becker, *Art Worlds*, 272.

4. Becker, *Art Worlds*, 80.

5. Becker, *Art Worlds*, 82.

6. Cameron, "Sociological Notes on the Jam Session," 179.

7. Faulkner, *Hollywood Studio Musicians*, 10, 69.

8. MacLeod *Club Date Musicians*, 161.

9. Durocher and Marinelli, "The Sideman Channel."

10. Shaw, *The Trouble With Cinderella*, 326.

11. Gill and Odegard, *A Simple Twist of Fate*, 65.

12. Toynbee, *Making Popular Music*, 35.

13. Becker, *Art Worlds*, 354.

14. Becker, *Art Worlds*, 14.

15. Quoted in Miège, *The Capitalization of Cultural Production*, 94.

16. Frith, *Sound Effects*, 272.

17. Zanes, *Petty*, 107.

18. Zanes, *Petty*, 133, 151.

19. "That is not the case when it comes time to write and record," she adds. "Someone is usually doing more of that work," and that's what songwriting credits are for.

20. Still, wrote Gary Church, "I've found that as a musician you stand a lot better chance of making a living if you work for someone who needs money as badly as you do" (45).

21. Taylor, "Maintenance and Destruction," 7.

22. See Taylor's "Circulation, Value, Exchange, and Music" on the exchange of "intangible things [which] are shot through with conceptions of value" (266).

23. Becker, *Art Worlds*, 16.

24. George Rush "did a theater piece this past fall. . . . The money wasn't great, but it was consistent work for six weeks. I found out about midway through the run [that] one of the musicians—even though it wasn't a union gig—had arranged in one of these obscure union rules to get himself another chunk of money [for] cartage. I was absolutely furious with myself for not having had the stomach or the fortitude or the foresight to say yeah, I'm going to be trucking a few instruments around, I should get a little more money."

25. Miège, *The Capitalization of Cultural Production*, 88.

26. Helm and Davis, *This Wheel's on Fire*, 209.

27. While Helm blamed Robertson's dominance of songwriting credits for the decline in the group's productivity—"I think that's why there were no more classic Band songs after that, because people weren't willing to put in that time developing the music and not get something from it" (229)—other sources, including Band producer John Simon and Robertson, indicate more chemical reasons for both the credits and creative decline. If the majority of a band is too wasted to pay attention to business, someone is inevitably going to step up to sign the paperwork.

28. Sara Cohen described a familiar dynamic in a Liverpool group in which "when only one or two members of a band received [publishing] royalties friction often arose. The singer/songwriter of two local bands, for example, each paid fellow band members a weekly wage out of the advance from their record company and kept all royalties themselves, despite the fact that both extracted ideas and expertise from fellow members which they used and developed in their own compositions. Such an arrangement often discouraged the others from investing creative input into the band's material or prompted them to leave the band. Members of another well-known local band complained bitterly when the band's songwriter received all the royalties, arguing that they were entitled to a share because it was the image they presented that sold the band's material (64). . . . The attitude of [the bands] towards composition and rehearsal highlighted a contradiction between the strong ideals of democracy and egalitarianism they held and the individualist tendencies that existed alongside them" (143).

29. Weinstein, "Creativity and Band Dynamics," 193.

30. Weinstein, "Creativity and Band Dynamics," 195.

31. Frith, *Sound Effects*, 76.

32. Schlichter, *So You Wanna Be a Rock & Roll Star*, 38.

33. "Arrangement is my secret passion," says Janet Weiss. "Quasi, Sleater-Kinney, Wild Flag, those are bands that I definitely do a lot of arranging in, and no one knows that. The band members know. It's something I take a lot of pride in."

34. "Walk on the Wild Side: The Story behind the Classic Bass Intro Featuring Herbie Flowers," an extract from BBC1's *The One Show*, broadcast June 9, 2010, https://www.youtube.com/watch?v=XBXUP5GYJs.

35. Miège, *The Capitalization of Cultural Production*.

36. Becker, *Art Worlds*.

37. Stahl, *Unfree Masters*.

38. Toynbee, "Fingers to the Bone or Spaced Out on Creativity?," xiv, 30.

39. Becker, *Art Worlds*, 35, 361. Becker went on to single out another potential hazard: supporting specialists can "develop specialized aesthetic, financial, and career interests which differ substantially from the artist's." He gave the example of orchestra musicians who "may sabotage a new work which can make them sound bad because of its difficulty, their career interests lying at cross-purposes to the composer's" (25).

40. Miège, *The Capitalization of Cultural Production*, 45.

41. In fact, "top creators"—the pop aristocracy—might resist a change to a non-royalty (even salaried) system that would spread risk around, since it's in their interest to retain a percentage model.

42. Stahl, *Unfree Masters*, 24–25.

43. Stahl, *Unfree Masters*, 24.

44. Ray closed the discussion by offering me some unsolicited advice: "Basically people really don't want to hear about this shit."

45. Sara Cohen included an anecdote about one band's percussionist "who was only given the status of 'band member' when he began to play keyboards and contribute more to the composition of the music" (65).

46. On many streaming services, album credits are absent or quite hard to find.
47. Miège, *The Capitalization of Cultural Production*, 74.
48. Merriam and Mack, "The Jazz Community," 214.
49. Stahl, *Unfree Masters*, 11.
50. In 2023, Wurster left Superchunk.
51. Frith, *Sound Effects*, 84.

6. GOING BAD: CONFLICTS

1. Seth, *An Equal Music*, 14.
2. French, "The Disruption and Cohesion of Groups," 125.
3. Finnegan, *The Hidden Musicians*, 270.
4. Bennett, *On Becoming a Rock Musician*, 54.
5. Drummers occupy a paradoxical position in terms of inter-band power: on the one hand, they are (because of their physical position on stage) rarely the faces of the bands; and because of the harmolodic orientation of copyright law, rarely enjoy legal ownership of songs. On the other, they have nearly unrivalled on-stage power, to start and stop songs and set tempos. This combination of actual power and symbolic powerlessness makes them ideal scapegoats if something goes wrong. Mike Sneeringer echoes a common analogy when he says, "The drummer [is like a] goalie, where you can be blamed for a lot of shit—kids don't understand, the ball has to get past six other kids before the goalie missed it. It is just like, 'You let it go in.'"
6. Interestingly, several musicians also made a point to say "and I've never auditioned" for a gig ("I feel glad because I don't even know what that is," claimed Glenn Kotche)—another small way of claiming a measure of power.
7. This dynamic can run both ways: "Usually if I don't like the band after I've got through playing with them," said DeDomenici, "I'll just say I'm busy. I don't like to close the door on a musical thing, because there could always be a reason that you would want to go back. It's pretty much how my jobs are too—I don't ever quit any of them; I just stop saying I'm available. But I always could be available, because you never know when you want to go back to something!"
8. "After about five years I was no longer able to fake my enthusiasm [for The Losers Lounge band]," said George Rush. "But not being mature enough or smart enough to leave on my own, I was invited to leave, and it was suggested that if I wanted to be a double bass player, I should be a double bass player."
9. When the announcement that I had left the Hold Steady became public in 2010, the music-news writeups gave me the peculiar sense of reading my own obituaries—that as far as the music world was concerned, I may as well have been dead.

7. PEERS AND AMBITIONS

1. Trilling, *Sincerity and Authenticity*, 29.
2. Seabrook, "The Song Machine."
3. David, *In the All-Night Café*, 152.

4. Fred Wesley's memoir *Hit Me, Fred* contains that combination of fragile ego, deference, and self-pity that defines a certain kind of support musician—both thankful for the attention they get for certain prominent gigs, defensive about the breadth of the rest of their catalog, and nursing bitter grudges over thwarted dreams of independent recognition. To be fair, Wesley worked with a series of notoriously demanding (if not abusive) bandleaders, from Ike Turner to James Brown.

5. The timing of these moves can be difficult, and represents a considerable gamble: Faulkner noted "the fear of staying 'too long' in the bands, the potential erosion of success in terms of this shared conception of career timing, and the growing lack of status rewards" (Faulkner, *Hollywood Studio Musicians*, 82).

6. Bauer, *Sideman*, 142.

7. Mayes and Speek, *The Amazing Jimmi Mayes*, 4.

LIST OF
INTERVIEWS

Interviews were edited for concision and clarity.

Melissa Auf der Maur—bass
Ara Babajian—drums
Sarah Balliett—cello
Lori Barbero—drums
Todd Beene—pedal steel
Michael Bland—drums
Oren Bloedow—guitar
Stuart Bogie—woodwinds
DJ Bonebrake—drums
Bruce Bouton—pedal steel
Scott Brackett—trumpet, keyboards
Nate Brenner—bass
Joey Burns—guitar
Marc Capelle—keyboards
Ralph Carney—woodwinds
Brian Chase—drums
Nels Cline—guitar
Jenny Conlee—keyboards
Jean Cook—violin
Toby Dammit—drums, keyboards
John DeDomenici—bass
East Bay Ray—guitar
Peter Erskine—drums
Josh Freese—drums
Doug Gillard—guitar
Joe Ginsberg—bass
Jay Gonzalez—keyboards
Caitlin Gray—bass

Katie Harkin—guitar, keyboards
Thor Harris—drums
Daniel Hart—multi-instrumentalist
Peter Hess—woodwinds
Kelly Hogan—vocals
Benny Horowitz—drums
Peter Hughes—bass
Shahzad Ismaily—
    multi-instrumentalist
Eliza Hardy Jones—keyboards, vocals
Josh Kantor—keyboards
Bruce Kaphan—pedal steel, piano
Carla Kihlstedt—violin, vocals
Matt Kinsey—guitar
Glenn Kotche—drums
Joe Lally—bass
Gerry Leonard—guitar
Scott McCaughey—guitar
Michael McDermott—drums
Joe McGinty—keyboards
Jason Narducy—guitar, bass
Nigel Powell—drums
Jon Rauhouse—guitar, pedal steel,
    banjo
George Rush—bass, tuba
Jenny Scheinman—violin, vocals
Jim Sclavunos—multi-instrumentalist
Andrew Seward—bass

Matt Sharp—bass
Todd Sickafoose—bass
Mike Sneeringer—drums
Scott Spillane—horns
Rick Steff—keyboards
Bill Stevenson—drums
Brian Viglione—drums
Paul Wallfisch—keyboards

Mike Watt—bass
Janet Weiss—drums
Jim White—drums
Doug Wieselman—woodwinds
Jon Wurster—drums
Mike Yannich—drums
Meredith Yayanos—violin, vocals,
   theremin

BIBLIOGRAPHY

Adorno, Theodor, and Max Horkheimer. "The Culture Industry: Enlightenment as Mass Deception." In *Dialectic of Enlightenment*, pp. 94–136. New York: Continuum, 1993.

"Amy Andronicus and the Curse of the Fan Favorite." https://www.nbcnewyork .com/local/amy-andronicus-and-the-curse-of-the-fan-favorite/1912200/.

Baldwin, James. "Sonny's Blues." In *The Jazz Fiction Anthology*, edited by Sascha Feinstein and David Rife, 17–48. Bloomington: Indiana University Press, 2009.

Banks, Mark. *The Politics of Cultural Work*. New York: Palgrave Macmillan, 2007.

Bauer, William. *Sideman: The Autobiography of Billy Bauer*. Albertson, NY: William H. Bauer Inc., 1997.

Beck, Andrew, ed. "Introduction." *Cultural Work: Understanding the Cultural Industries*, pp. 1–12. New York: Routledge, 2003.

Becker, Howard S. *Art Worlds*. Berkeley: University of California Press, 1982.

Becker, Howard S. *Outsiders: Studies in the Sociology of Deviance*. New York: The Free Press, 1963.

Becker, Howard S. "The Professional Dance Musician and His Audience." *American Journal of Sociology* 57, no. 2 (1951): 136–144. http://www.jstor.org /stable/2772074.

Becker, Howard S., and Blanche Geer. "A Note on the Theory of Latent Social Roles." *Administrative Science Quarterly* 5, no. 2 (September 1960): 304–313.

Becker, Howard S., and James Carper. "The Elements of Identification with an Occupation." *American Sociological Review* 21, no. 3 (June 1956).

Bennett, H. Stith. *On Becoming a Rock Musician*. Amherst, MA: University of Massachusetts Press, 1980.

Berliner, Paul F. *Thinking in Jazz: The Infinite Art of Improvisation*. Chicago: University of Chicago Press, 1994.

Body, Sean. *Wish the World Away: Mark Eitzel and the American Music Club*. London: SAF Publishing, 1999.

Boethius, Anicius Manlius Severinus. *Fundamentals of Music*. Translated by Calvin M. Bower and edited by Claude V. Palisca. New Haven, CT: Yale University Press, 1989.

Cameron, William Bruce. "Sociological Notes on the Jam Session." *Social Forces* 33, no. 2 (1954): 177–182. doi:10.2307/2573543.

Cartwright, Dorwin, and Alvin Zander. "Group Cohesiveness: Introduction."

In *Group Dynamics: Research and Theory*, edited by Dorwin Cartwright and Alvin Zander, 3–91. White Plains, NY, and Evanston, IL: Row, Peterson and Company.

Cartwright, Dorwin, and Alvin Zander. "Group Pressures and Group Standards: Introduction." In *Group Dynamics: Research and Theory*, edited by Dorwin Cartwright and Alvin Zander, 137–150. White Plains, NY, and Evanston, IL: Row, Peterson and Company.

Cartwright, Dorwin, and Alvin Zander. "Leadership: Introduction." In *Group Dynamics: Research and Theory*, edited by Dorwin Cartwright and Alvin Zander, 535–550. White Plains, NY, and Evanston, IL: Row, Peterson and Company.

Cartwright, Dorwin, and Alvin Zander. "The Structural Properties of Groups: Introduction." In *Group Dynamics: Research and Theory*, edited by Dorwin Cartwright and Alvin Zander, 415–427. White Plains, NY, and Evanston, IL: Row, Peterson and Company.

Church, Gary. *The Autobiography of a Nobody: The Life and Times of a Sideman*. Self-published, 2010.

Coffman, James. "Everybody Knows This Is Nowhere: Role Conflict and the Rock Musician." *Popular Music and Society* 1, no. 1 (1971): 20–32.

Cohen, Sara. *Rock Culture in Liverpool: Popular Music in the Making*. Oxford: Clarendon Press, 1991.

David, Stuart. *In the All-Night Café: A Memoir of Belle and Sebastian's Formative Year*. Chicago: Chicago Review Press Incorporated, 2015.

Duke, Osborn. *Sideman: A Novel*. New York: Criterion, 1956.

Durocher, Dave, and George Marinelli. "The Sideman Channel." https://www.youtube.com/channel/UCsDOsSHwXjmT4fok-WUc9NQ.

Ellington, Duke. *Music Is My Mistress*. New York: Da Capo Press, 1973.

Faulkner, Robert R. *Hollywood Studio Musicians: Their Work and Careers in the Recording Industry*. Chicago: Aldine Atherton, 1971.

Faulkner, Robert R. "Orchestra Interaction: Some Features of Communication and Authority in an Artistic Organization." *The Sociological Quarterly* 14, no. 2 (Spring 1973): 147–157.

Fearnley, James. *Here Comes Everybody: The Story of the Pogues*. Chicago: Chicago Review Press, 2014.

Festinger, Leon, Stanley Schachter, and Kurt Back. "The Operation of Group Standards." In *Group Dynamics: Research and Theory*, edited by Dorwin Cartwright and Alvin Zander, 204–222. White Plains, NY, and Evanston, IL: Row, Peterson and Company.

Finnegan, Ruth. *The Hidden Musicians: Music-Making in an English Town*. Middletown, CT: Wesleyan University Press, 2007.

Fisk, Josiah, and Jeff Nichols, ed. *Composers on Music: Eight Centuries of Writings*, 2nd ed. Boston: Northeastern University Press, 1997.

Frederickson, Jon, and James F. Rooney. "The Free-Lance Musician as a Type of Non-Person: An Extension of the Concept of Non-Personhood." *The Sociological Quarterly* 29, no. 2 (Summer 1988): 221–239.

French, John R. P., Jr. "The Disruption and Cohesion of Groups." *Group*

Dynamics: Research and Theory, edited by Dorwin Cartwright and Alvin Zander, 121–134. White Plains, NY, and Evanston, IL: Row, Peterson and Company.

Frith, Simon. *Sound Effects: Youth, Leisure, and the Politics of Rock 'n' Roll*. New York: Pantheon Books, 1981.

Gill, Andy, and Kevin Odegard. *A Simple Twist of Fate: Bob Dylan and the Making of "Blood on the Tracks."* New York: Da Capo Press, 2004.

Gopnik, Adam. "Long Play: The Charmed Lives of Paul McCartney." *New Yorker*, April 25, 2016.

Groce, Stephen B., and John A. Dowell. "A Comparison of Group Structures and Processes in Two Local Level Rock 'n' Roll Bands." *Popular Music and Society* 12, no. 2 (1988): 21–35.

Guralnick, Peter. *Lost Highways: Journeys and Arrivals of American Musicians*. Boston: Little, Brown, 2013.

Hajdu, David. *Lush Life*. New York: Farrar, Straus, Giroux, 1996.

Helm, Levon, with Stephen Davis. *This Wheel's on Fire: Levon Helm and the Story of the Band*. Chicago: A Cappella Books, 2000.

Hogan, Kelly. "From the Desk of the Flat Five: Thoughts on the Documentary *20 Feet from Stardom*." *Magnet Magazine*. https://magnetmagazine.com /2017/02/16/from-the-desk-of-the-flat-five-thoughts-on-the-documentary -20-feet-from-stardom/.

Hurwitz, Jacob I., Alvin F. Zander, and Bernard Hymovitch. "Some Effects of Power on the Relations among Group Members." *Group Dynamics: Research and Theory*, edited by Dorwin Cartwright and Alvin Zander, 483–492. White Plains, NY, and Evanston, IL: Row, Peterson and Company.

Hyden, Steven. "Drive-By Truckers Carry On." *Grantland*, March 4, 2014. https:// grantland.com/features/drive-by-truckers-carry-on/.

Jones, Mike. "The Music Industry as Workplace: An Approach to Analysis." In *Cultural Work: Understanding the Cultural Industries*, edited by Andrew Beck, pp. 147–156. New York: Routledge, 2003.

Leight, Warren. *Side Man*. New York: Dramatists Play Service, Inc., 2000.

Lewis, George H. "Take Out My Guitar and Play: Recruitment of Popular Music Performers." *Popular Music and Society* 7, no. 1 (1979): 32–36.

MacLeod, Bruce A. *Club Date Musicians: Playing the New York Party Circuit*. Urbana and Chicago: University of Illinois Press, 1993.

Malone, Kasper "Stranger." In *My Best To You . . . : Eighty Years as a Sideman*. Bloomington, IN: Trafford Publishing, 2011.

Mayes, Jimmi, with V. C. Speek. *The Amazing Jimmi Mayes: Sideman to the Stars*. Jackson: University Press of Mississippi, 2014.

Merriam, Alan P., and Raymond W. Mack. "The Jazz Community." *Social Forces* 38, no. 3 (1960): 211–222.

Miège, Bernard. *The Capitalization of Cultural Production*. Bagnolet, France: International General, 1989.

Mills, Theodore M. "Power Relations in Three-Person Groups." In *Group Dynamics: Research and Theory*, edited by Dorwin Cartwright and Alvin Zander, 428–443. White Plains, NY, and Evanston, IL: Row, Peterson and Company.

Negus, Keith. *Producing Pop: Culture and Conflict in the Popular Music Industry.* New York: Oxford University Press, 1992.

Neville, Morgan, dir. *20 Feet from Stardom.* Anchor Bay, 2014.

Page, Drew. *Drew's Blues: A Sideman's Life with the Big Bands.* Baton Rouge: Louisiana State University Press, 1980.

Pinheiro, Ricardo F. "The Jam Session and Jazz Studies." *International Review of the Aesthetics and Sociology of Music* 45, no. 2 (December 2014): 335–344.

Plutarch. *Plutarch's Lives, Vol. 1: The Dryden Translation,* edited by Arthur Hugh Clough. New York: Random House, 2001.

Scheidlinger, Saul. "Freudian Concepts of Group Relations." *Group Dynamics: Research and Theory,* edited by Dorwin Cartwright and Alvin Zander, 52–61. White Plains, NY, and Evanston, IL: Row, Peterson and Company.

Schlichter, Jacob. *So You Wanna Be a Rock & Roll Star: How I Machine Gunned a Roomful of Record Executives and Other True Tales from a Drummer's Life.* New York: Broadway Books, 2004.

Schuller, Gunther. *Musings: The Musical Worlds of Gunther Schuller.* London: Oxford University Press, 1989.

Schütz, Alfred. "Making Music Together: A Study in Social Relationship." *Social Research* 18, no. 1 (March 1951): 76–97.

Seabrook, John. "The Song Machine." *New Yorker,* March 26, 2012.

Seth, Vikram. *An Equal Music.* New York: Vintage, 1999.

Shaw, Artie. *The Trouble with Cinderella.* New York: Farrar, Straus and Young, 1952.

Sisario, Ben. "Gender Diversity in the Music Industry? The Numbers Are Grim." *New York Times,* January 25, 2018.

Small, Christopher. *Music of the Common Tongue: Survival and Celebration in Afro-American Music.* New York: Riverrun, 1987.

Smith, Stacy L., Katherine Pieper, Karla Hernandez, and Sam Wheeler. "Inclusion in the Recording Studio? Gender & Race/Ethnicity of Artists, Songwriters & Producers across 1,100 Popular Songs from 2012 to 2022." USC Annenberg Inclusion Iniative, January 2023. https://assets.uscannenberg.org/docs/aii-inclusion-recording-studio-jan2023.pdf.

Smith, W. O. *Sideman: The Long Gig of W. O. Smith; A Memoir.* Nashville: Rutledge Hill Press, 1991.

Springsteen, Bruce. *Born to Run.* New York: Simon & Schuster, 2016.

Stahl, Matt. *Unfree Masters: Recording Artists and the Politics of Work.* Durham, NC: Duke University Press, 2013.

Stebbins, Robert A. "Class, Status, and Power among Jazz and Commercial Musicians." *The Sociological Quarterly* 7, no. 2 (Spring 1966): 197–213.

Stebbins, Robert A. "A Theory of the Jazz Community." *The Sociological Quarterly* 9, no. 3 (Summer 1968): 318–331.

Stogdill, Ralph M. "Leadership, Membership and Organization." *Group Dynamics: Research and Theory,* edited by Dorwin Cartwright and Alvin Zander, 39–51. White Plains, NY, and Evanston, IL: Row, Peterson and Company.

Stone, Gregory P., and William H. Form. "Instabilities in Status: The Problem of

Hierarchy in the Community Study of Status Arrangements." *American Sociological Review* 18, no. 2 (April 1953): 149–162.

Tanner, Paul. *Sideman: Stories about The Band.* Los Angeles: Cosmo Space, 2000.

Taylor, Timothy D. "Circulation, Value, Exchange, and Music." *Ethnomusicology* 64, no. 2 (Summer 2020): 254–273.

Taylor, Timothy D. "Maintenance and Destruction of an East Side Los Angeles Indie Rock Scene." *The Oxford Handbook of Economic Ethnomusicology*, edited by Anna Morcom and Timothy D. Taylor. New York: Oxford University Press, 2020. doi: 10.1093/oxfordhb/9780190859633.013.27.

Taylor, Timothy D. *Making Value: Music, Capital, and the Social.* Durham, NC: Duke University Press, 2024.

Taylor, Timothy D. "Social Class and the Negotiation of Selling Out in a Southern California Indie Rock Scene." *The Bloomsbury Handbook of Popular Music and Social Class*, edited by Ian Peddie, 59–75. London: Bloomsbury, 2020.

Taylor, Timothy D. *Working Musicians: Labor and Creativity in Film and Television Production.* Durham, NC: Duke University Press, 2024.

Toynbee, Jason. "Fingers to the Bone or Spaced Out on Creativity? Labor Process and Ideology in the Production of Pop." In *Cultural Work: Understanding the Cultural Industries*, edited by Andrew Beck, 39–55. New York: Routledge, 2003.

Toynbee, Jason. *Making Popular Music: Musicians, Creativity, and Institutions.* New York: Oxford University Press, 2000.

Trilling, Lionel. *Sincerity and Authenticity.* Cambridge, MA: Harvard University Press, 1971.

Vulliamy, Graham, and Edward Lee, eds. *Pop Music in School.* 2nd ed. Cambridge: Cambridge University Press, 1980.

"Walk On the Wild Side: The Story behind the Classic Bass Intro Featuring Herbie Flowers." An extract from the BBC1's *The One Show*, broadcast June 9, 2010. https://www.youtube.com/watch?v=XBXUP5GqYJs.

Weinstein, Deena. "Creativity and Band Dynamics." In *This Is Pop: In Search of the Elusive at Experience Music Project*, edited by Eric Weisbard, 187–199. Cambridge, MA: Harvard University Press, 2004.

Wesley, Fred, Jr. *Hit Me, Fred: Recollections of a Sideman.* Durham, NC: Duke University Press, 2002.

White, Ralph, and Ronald Lippitt. "Leader Behavior and Member Reaction in Three 'Social Climates.'" *Group Dynamics: Research and Theory*, edited by Dorwin Cartwright and Alvin Zander, 585–611. White Plains, NY, and Evanston, IL: Row, Peterson and Company.

Wilhelm, Sidney, and Gideon Sjoberg. "The Social Characteristics of Entertainers." *Social Forces* 37, no. 1 (October 1958): 71–76.

Zanes, Warren. *Petty: The Biography.* New York: Henry Holt & Co., 2015.

INDEX

accordion, 2, 112, 113, 166. *See also* keyboards

Against Me!, 77, 124, 133, 148, 199. *See also* Grace, Laura Jane; Seward, Andrew

amateur musicians, 14, 95, 148, 270n12

ambition, 3–4, 8–10, 12, 18–19, 21, 24, 47, 53, 95, 96, 116, 184, 190, 249, 251–256, 259, 261, 277n5. *See also* ego

Antibalas, 35–36, 153, 171. *See also* Bogie, Stuart

Arcade Fire, 35, 82

arranging and arrangements, 8, 61, 100, 132, 151, 152–153, 156, 158, 167, 210, 212–214, 216–217, 219–220, 236, 252, 258, 275n33

artisans (musicians as), 1, 7, 9–12, 16, 17–18, 40, 112, 117, 163, 182, 187–194, 257–258, 261

Art Worlds (Becker), 10–11, 58, 86, 97, 188, 275n39. *See also* Becker, Howard

Auf der Maur, Melissa, 20, 47, 56, 66, 89, 91, 168, 212, 239, 258, 259

authorship, 11, 15, 33, 97, 194–195, 211, 213–214, 218. *See also* songwriting credit

autocracy. *See* hierarchy; political organization of bands

Babajian, Ara, 20–21, 71, 74, 87, 129, 179, 181, 184–185, 188, 197. *See also* Leftover Crack; Slackers, the

Babes in Toyland, 66, 160, 269n58. *See also* Barbero, Lori

backup singer(s), 3–4, 15, 41

Balliett, Sarah, 21, 63, 74, 121, 126, 127, 128, 129, 133, 149, 155, 176, 199, 213, 236, 249, 262. *See also* Murder by Death

Band, the, 10, 31–32, 152, 172, 207, 274n27. *See also* Helm, Levon; Robertson, Robbie

bandleaders, 25, 31, 33, 40–42, 47, 49–53, 56, 58–80, 81, 150, 191, 239, 265n9, 272n54; bad traits of, 64–67, 216, 228; as center of attention, 29–30, 50, 52–53, 73–80, 268n36, 268n40; clarity on the part of, 59–60, 65, 103; communication and miscommunications with, 103, 110, 228, 237, 244; and cultivating group identity, 50, 61–62; and delegating/demonstrating trust, 60–61, 98, 102–103, 112, 126–127; and diplomacy, 53, 98–99, 102–104; as disciplinarian, 68–69; good traits of, 59–64; humility of (or lack thereof), 62–63, 65–66; and money, 196, 197; passivity of, 65; and sensitivity to logistics, 63–64, 222, 224; as spokesperson, 67, 70–80, 268n43, 269n58; and taking responsibility, 66–67, 68; tyranny of, 64, 277n4

band membership (as status or source of identity), 3, 14–16, 18, 20, 42–43, 45–58, 70, 73–81, 85, 100–102, 124,

employees, musicians as, 1, 13, 30, 32, 53–58, 65–66, 95, 202, 237. *See also* "hired guns," musicians as

Erg, Mikey. *See* Yannich, Mike

Erskine, Peter, 25, 65, 104, 118, 128, 138, 139–140, 155, 173–174, 181, 184, 196, 236, 240, 265n11

extra-musical skills, 97, 148–153, 221–233, 272n55. *See also* "good hang"

Fallon, Brian, 79, 215

family (band as), 12, 30, 38, 42–46, 93; band as marriage, 44–45; band as polyamory, 38, 44

family (musicians with): musicians and parenthood, 96, 179–185; musicians whose parents are musicians, 26, 82; parental expectations and advice, 4, 6; spouses and partners, 179–181, 226, 241

Faulkner, Robert, 59, 60, 94, 148, 189–190, 265n1, 269n53, 277n5

Fela! (musical), 109, 156, 171

Finnegan, Ruth, 99, 100, 130, 176

firings from bands, 40–41, 241–249, 276n8. *See also* conflict; quitting

Flowers, Herbie, 210, 265n9

Freese, Josh, 25, 40–41, 44, 65, 84, 114, 115, 119, 121, 130–131, 144–145, 203, 206–207, 218–219, 229–230, 249–250

Frith, Simon, 95, 295, 208, 233

frontperson. *See* bandleaders

frustration: career, 3, 8–9; with material, 153–155; with one's instrument, 162–168, 170–171, 173–177; with self, 273n65, 273n67. *See also* boredom

Fugazi, 34, 53, 85, 160, 254

Gano, Gordon, 30, 147

Gaslight Anthem, 79, 215

gender politics. *See* sexism

Gillard, Doug, 7, 59, 78, 127, 148, 157, 167, 197, 217, 244, 249, 260

Ginsberg, Joe, 23, 51, 63, 68, 121, 193, 216, 257, 265n11, 268n36

Gira, Michael, 74, 117, 124. *See also* Swans

Gonzalez, Jay, 23–24, 51, 56, 68, 87, 145, 146, 160–161, 171–172, 196, 258, 261, 272. *See also* Drive-By Truckers

"good hang," 16, 19, 33, 150, 269n72; disinclination to prioritize being a, 87–89, 270n75; relative importance of being a, 80–89, 97

Grace, Laura Jane, 77, 133, 239. *See also* Against Me!

Gray, Caitlin, 63, 90–91, 134, 148, 149, 157, 196

group dynamics. *See* hierarchy

guitar, 4, 8, 31, 32, 61, 84, 99, 116, 118, 119–120, 124, 146, 160, 162–163, 167, 169–172, 177, 190, 194, 248, 249, 260, 272n54, 273n66

Haggard, Merle, 44, 61

Harkin, Katie, 88, 114, 142, 143, 146, 165, 191, 196, 236, 257

Harris, Thor, 78, 83, 117, 123, 124–125, 126, 133, 136, 150, 165, 192, 220–221, 246–247

Hart, Daniel, 35, 87, 139, 164, 196, 245–246

health insurance, 54, 222, 226, 270n8

Heartbreakers, Tom Petty and the, 51, 118, 198, 253, 265n9, 268n40

Helm, Levon, 10, 31–32, 47, 207, 272, 284n27. *See also* Band, the

Hess, Peter, 11, 23, 42, 63, 71–72, 108–109, 110, 116–117, 125, 128–129, 134, 155, 164, 185, 188, 202, 212, 222–223, 241–242, 257–258, 270n75

hierarchy, 11–12, 31–38, 41, 46–58, 169–170, 216, 265n9, 266n2, 267n3, 267n5, 276n5, 268n35; and competition/dominance, 29–30, 269n61; creative (*see* creative collaboration); employee vs. band member, 54–58; financial, 198, 207–211, 214–215,

Potter, Grace, 62, 72–73, 157, 198, 223
Powell, Nigel, 55, 77–78, 110, 128, 136,
 201, 210, 212, 226, 261–262, 268n44
practicing, 129–132. *See also* rehearsal
preparation, 131–132, 135, 148–149,
 152, 236–237
Prince, 180, 224
producers, 9, 25, 56, 106, 108–109, 112,
 136, 138, 190, 205, 247, 271n30,
 271n41. *See also* recording

quitting: bands, 47, 71, 228–229, 239–
 241, 243–244, 247, 266n14, 276n7,
 276n9; music, 14, 21, 231, 249. *See
 also* conflict; firings from bands

Radiohead, 34, 215
Rauhouse, Jon, 62, 71, 74, 96, 151, 167,
 205, 260
recording, 1, 5–6, 8, 108–109, 111, 113,
 172, 174, 184, 191, 203, 206, 221,
 224; home, 206, 132; ideologies of,
 126, 127, 130, 135–142, 271n38,
 272n47; as site of conflict, 51–52,
 55–56, 82, 90, 123–124, 237, 242,
 248–249; versus live performance,
 130, 132–142. *See also* producers
rehearsal, 129–132, 236–237. *See also*
 practicing
R.E.M., 34–35, 96, 160, 265n9
reputation, 14, 65, 77, 82, 86, 87, 97,
 148, 151, 189, 202, 204, 211, 248,
 258, 259. *See also* "good hang"
Ribot, Marc, 1, 62, 163
Robertson, Robbie, 47, 172, 207,
 274n27. *See also* Band, the
Rosenstock, Jeff, 57, 72, 118–119, 152,
 156, 200, 226, 240. *See also* DeDomenici, John
royalties, 7, 199, 207–209, 221, 226–227,
 275n28. *See also* "mail money";
 songwriting credit
Rush, George, 25, 57, 61, 65, 84, 122,
 204, 247, 274n24, 276n8

saxophone, 82, 109–110, 113, 126, 130,
 141, 162, 164–165, 171, 177, 272n54.
 See also woodwinds
scheduling, 43, 182, 184, 221–230, 244,
 246
Scheinman, Jenny, 23, 34, 40, 92, 154,
 162, 164, 182, 183, 185, 193, 257
Schlichter, Jacob, 77, 209, 269n60
Sclavunos, Jim, 23, 39, 50, 52–53, 67,
 84–85, 107–108, 117, 125, 174–175,
 197, 218, 237–238, 260
"secret weapons," 12, 78, 100, 126,
 253, 266n14. *See also* "hired guns,"
 musicians as; session musicians;
 sidemen; support musicians
Semisonic. *See* Jacob Schlichter
"serving the song," 118–123, 125,
 127–128
session musicians, 5, 12–14, 16, 18, 23,
 25, 54–55, 103, 120, 145, 174, 189–
 190, 192, 194, 196, 203, 205–206,
 210, 212, 216–217, 242, 247, 271n43.
 See also "hired guns," musicians as;
 "secret weapons"; sidemen; support
 musicians
Seward, Andrew, 34, 44, 77, 81, 124,
 199, 239
sexism, 13, 89–92
Sharp, Matt, 26, 69–70, 104–105, 240
Shearwater, 126, 192, 246–247
Sheff, Will, 54, 64, 214, 224. *See also*
 Okkervil River
Sickafoose, Todd, 61, 102, 126–127, 132,
 155, 167, 226
sidemen, 3, 10–13, 17–18, 25, 49, 50,
 64–65, 67, 68, 76, 82, 84, 112, 114,
 150, 237, 253–254, 259, 261, 265n9,
 266n11, 267n3, 267n5. *See also*
 "hired guns," musicians as; "secret
 weapons"; session musicians; support musicians
Slackers, the, 75
Sleater-Kinney, 77, 143, 215, 225,
 269n62, 275n33
Sleepytime Gorilla Museum, 32, 91, 212